EXPERIENCING THE BEATLES

The Listener's Companion
Gregg Akkerman, Series Editor

Titles in **The Listener's Companion** provide readers with a deeper understanding of key musical genres and the work of major artists and composers. Aimed at nonspecialists, each volume explains in clear and accessible language how to listen to works from particular artists, composers, and genres. Looking at both the context in which the music first appeared and has since been heard, authors explore with readers the environments in which key musical works were written and performed.

EXPERIENCING THE BEATLES

A Listener's Companion

Brooke Halpin

ROWMAN & LITTLEFIELD
Lanham • Boulder • New York • London

Published by Rowman & Littlefield
A wholly owned subsidiary of The Rowman & Littlefield Publishing Group,
Inc.
4501 Forbes Boulevard, Suite 200, Lanham, Maryland 20706
www.rowman.com

Unit A, Whitacre Mews, 26-34 Stannary Street, London SE11 4AB

British Library Cataloguing in Publication Information Available

Library of Congress Cataloging-in-Publication Data

Names: Halpin, Brooke.
Title: Experiencing the Beatles : a listener's companion / Brooke Halpin.
Description: Lanham : Rowman & Littlefield, [2018] | Series: Listener's companion | Includes
    bibliographical references and index.
Identifiers: LCCN 2017006659 (print) | LCCN 2017009194 (ebook) | ISBN 9781442271432
    (cloth : alk. paper) | ISBN 9781442271449 (electronic)
Subjects: LCSH: Beatles. | Rock music—England—1961–1970—History and criticism.
Classification: LCC ML421.B4 H325 2018 (print) | LCC ML421.B4 (ebook) | DDC
    782.42166092/2—dc23 LC record available at https://lccn.loc.gov/2017006659

Printed in the United States of America

CONTENTS

SERIES EDITOR'S FOREWORD

The goal of the Listener's Companion series is to give readers a deeper understanding of pivotal musical genres and the creative work of their iconic composers and performers. This is accomplished in an inclusive manner that does not necessitate extensive music training or elitist shoulder rubbing. Authors of the series place the reader in specific listening experiences in which the music is examined in its historical context with regards to both compositional and societal parameters. By positioning the reader in the real or supposed environment of the music's creation, the author provides for a deeper enjoyment and appreciation of the art form. Series authors, often drawing on their own expertise as both performers and scholars, deliver to readers a broad understanding of major musical genres and the achievements of artists within those genres as lived listening experiences.

The Beatles was one of the first topics considered when the Listener's Companion series was originated. Beethoven, the blues, and the Beatles: those "three Bs" would cover great swaths of the most important musical territory of the last two hundred years and were at the top of the list for the series. But topics get jostled, book proposals stall, authors come and go, and even the Beatles had to wait their turn until the right time and place. Fortunately, *Experiencing the Beatles* by Brooke Halpin now stands ready to walk the reader through the expansive and highly creative recorded catalog from, as Ringo Star puts it, "a great little rock band." That little band formed when the rock genre was still a candidate for "temporary fad" and hardly seemed likely to alter music history. How obvious it all seems now. *Of course* the Beatles were going to be the most famous band ever. *Of course* their music would influence decades of the world's greatest musicians and composers. This sense of manifest destiny for the Beatles makes discussing their music exceedingly challenging. Placing the reader into an environment where the magnitude of the Beatles was not so apparent is a delicate matter. Take "Yesterday" as just one example. Here is a song that now lives in the pantheon of rock legend. Its poetic potency and gravitas in the Beatles' oeuvre is now viewed as undisputed. But in the context of the time, it was an out-of-place acoustic song with a nice melody but no discernable chorus. For all practical purposes, it was a Paul McCartney solo feature rather than a Beatles ensemble piece. The point being that the music of the Beatles needs *context* to be understood and enjoyed to the fullest extent. This is where Brooke Halpin is able to make his palpable contribution. As the host of his weekly radio show, *Come Together with the Beatles*, Halpin regularly delves into the people, places, and events surrounding the Beatles catalog, giving him an astute appreciation for the music. By speaking to hundreds of people who "were there" when the music was being conceived, recorded, and first enjoyed, Halpin has just the kind of insight that is so right for the Listener's Companion series. Reading Halpin's words will give you the benefit of his lifetime of study and surely motivate you to revisit your Beatles recordings with a heightened comprehension of not only your old favorites but a few of the lesser-known gems as well.

Gregg Akkerman

ACKNOWLEDGMENTS

It would be impossible to write this book without there having been John Lennon, Paul McCartney, George Harrison, and Ringo Starr playing in a band called the Beatles; Franco Sciannameo and Gregg Akkerman for introducing me to Rowman & Littlefield; Natalie Mandziuk, who worked with me on editing this book; and to Beatles fans throughout the world who keep the Beatles and their music alive.

INTRODUCTION

The Beatles. Then. Now. Forever. No other band has sustained their popularity the way the Beatles have, decade after decade. With each decade, new fans are attracted to the Beatles. Their massive, worldwide audience is composed of multiple generations—grandparents, parents, and their children who love the Beatles. The band's popularity today is greater than what it was when the Beatles were together in the 1960s. Why? Because the Beatles were a unique combination of four distinct, multitalented musicians. John. Paul. George. Ringo. If it had been John Lennon, Eric Clapton, Jack Bruce, and Charlie Watts, I'm sure they would have sounded very good, but they would not, could not be the Beatles. The Beatles were in the right place at the right time, when rock and roll wasn't rolling that much and songs in the United States about cars and surfing were losing their luster.

Like most teenagers in the late 1950s and early 1960s, the Beatles listened to the hits of the day by Lonnie Donegan, Cliff Richard, the Everly Brothers, Buddy Holly, Chuck Berry, Elvis Presley, and many others. They learned how to play the hit songs by those recording artists and played wherever they could to get in front of an audience. The audience was important; it gave the Beatles the attention and recognition that fueled their rock-and-roll ambitions. They developed a new sound as a result of working endless hours at clubs in Hamburg, Germany, where they honed their musical skills. And when they sang, their singing voices sounded different from other bands; you could hear their Liverpudlian accents. Once Brian Epstein became their manager, the

Beatles' appearance changed from looking like tough guys in leather outfits to wearing matching collarless suit jackets. Brian was a persistent manager who refused to take no for an answer and was not discouraged when every record label in London turned down the Beatles—except for one. It was George Martin at EMI's Parlophone label who, upon hearing the Beatles for the first time, detected something special about these four lads from Liverpool. The Beatles were charming, witty, hard-working musicians who were driven by the same dream—to make it to the big time with hit records. Together, John, Paul, George, Ringo, Brian Epstein, and George Martin were the hugely successful winning combination that made the Beatles eternal superstars.

In this book, you will find out how the final formation of the Beatles happened, what their influences were, and how they conquered America. You will experience their staggering U.S. concert tour schedules, their unparalleled recording history, and their varied movies, and you will discover why the Beatles ultimately had to break up. The focus of this book is primarily on the English language singles and albums that were released in the United States from 1964 to 1970. I do reference a few solo Beatles recordings as the subject matter relates to the history in certain chapters. I do not write about the *Hey Jude* album because it contains only previously released singles, nor do I write about compilation albums that were released after the Beatles split up. Additionally, I do not cover the predominately spoken word album, *The Beatles Story*. Time-capsule vignettes will enable you to time travel and get a feel for what it was like to experience the Beatles when they were together. At the end of each chapter, you will find "Suggested Listening," a list of songs that represent a sampling of what the chapter has explored. If you want to experience the remarkable evolutionary arc of Beatles songs and how they mixed musical genres and created new ones, it's best to listen to *all* of their songs.

How does one experience the amazing magnitude of the Beatles' songs? By listening to their music and lyrics, many times over. Because there is so much going on musically and lyrically, it's impossible to thoroughly understand their songs after hearing them only once. Multiple listenings will help you comprehend their wide range of songs. With this book, I will take you on the Beatles' evolving musical journey with songs that more than likely will resonate with you for the rest of your life.

TIMELINE

July 7, 1940	Ringo Starr (Richard Starkey) is born in Liverpool, England
October 9, 1940	John Winston Lennon is born in Liverpool, England
June 18, 1942	James Paul McCartney is born in Liverpool, England
February 25, 1943	George Harrison is born in Liverpool, England
January 24, 1962	Brian Epstein signs the Beatles to a management contract
June 6, 1962	First recording session with George Martin; Pete Best on drums
August 16, 1962	Ringo Starr replaces Pete Best as the Beatles' drummer
January 10, 1964	Vee-Jay Records releases the album *Introducing the Beatles*
January 20, 1964	Capitol Records releases the album *Meet the Beatles!*
February 7, 1964	The Beatles travel to the United States for the first time
February 9, 1964	The Beatles perform on *The Ed Sullivan Show*

February 11, 1964	The Beatles perform their first U.S. concert in Washington, DC
April 10, 1964	Capitol Records releases *The Beatles' Second Album*
June 26, 1964	United Artists Records releases the album *A Hard Day's Night*
July 20, 1964	Capitol Records releases the album *Something New*
August 11, 1964	United Artists releases the movie *A Hard Day's Night*
August 19, 1964	The Beatles begin their first U.S. tour
December 15, 1964	Capitol Records releases the album *Beatles '65*
June 14, 1965	Capitol Records releases the album *Beatles VI*
August 13, 1965	Capitol Records releases the album *Help!*
August 15, 1965	The Beatles begin their second U.S. tour at Shea Stadium
August 25, 1965	United Artists releases the movie *Help!*
December 3, 1965	Capitol Records releases the album *Rubber Soul*
June 20, 1966	Capitol Records releases the album *Yesterday and Today*
August 5, 1966	Capitol Records releases the album *Revolver*
August 12, 1966	The Beatles embark on their final U.S. tour
August 29, 1966	The Beatles' last concert, Candlestick Park, San Francisco
June 1, 1967	Capitol Records releases the album *Sgt. Pepper's Lonely Hearts Club Band*
August 27, 1967	Brian Epstein dies
November 27, 1967	Capitol Records releases the album *Magical Mystery Tour*
December 26, 1967	Apple Corps. releases the movie *Magical Mystery Tour*

November 13, 1968	Apple Films releases the movie *Yellow Submarine*
November 22, 1968	Apple Records releases the album *The Beatles* (a.k.a. the *White Album*)
January 13, 1969	Apple Records releases the album *Yellow Submarine*
September 26, 1969	Apple Records releases the album *Abbey Road*
April 10, 1970	The Beatles officially announce their breakup
May 13, 1970	Apple Films releases the movie *Let It Be*
May 18, 1970	Apple Records releases the album *Let It Be*

I

BEATLES ROOTS

Covering American Songs

Liverpool is the city where the River Mersey meets the Irish Sea. Because it is a seaport and the gateway to the Atlantic Ocean, it was a target and repeatedly pounded with bombs from Nazi warplanes during World War II. As a result, more than ten thousand homes were destroyed. It was during an air attack on October 9, 1940, that John Winston Lennon was born. James Paul McCartney was born on June 18, 1942; George Harrison was born on February 25, 1943; Ringo Starr (birth name, Richard Starkey) was born on July 7, 1940. All four Beatles were born during World War II, at a time when Liverpool was crumbling. John, Paul, George, and Ringo didn't know that they would rise from the rubble, form a band, and become worldwide superstars.

Liverpool was a bustling seaport in the late 1950s and 1960s. Ships sailed to and from America. Some of the crew members returned to Liverpool with records that were popular in the United States. Songs by the Everly Brothers, Ray Charles, Chuck Berry, Carl Perkins, Buddy Holly, Little Richard, Elvis Presley, and many more made their way into the emerging rock-and-roll scene taking shape in Liverpool. John, Paul, George, and Ringo heard "Peggy Sue," "That's All Right (Mama)," "Sweet Little Sixteen," "Roll Over Beethoven," "Honey Don't," "Lucille," and countless other songs that were hits in America. Not only were the Beatles influenced by the music they were hearing, they also imitated the way the recording artists looked, with their hair slicked back, Elvis style. When the Beatles performed in the late 1950s and early 1960s, they played mostly songs by American recording artists. The Beatles' budding music career was rooted in American rock and roll and rhythm and blues.

Before becoming popular throughout England, the Beatles played cover songs at several clubs in Hamburg, Germany. Like Liverpool, Hamburg was severely damaged by bombing raids during World War II. When the Beatles arrived for the first time in 1960, Hamburg had rebuilt itself and was an economically thriving city. It was in Hamburg where the Beatles sharpened their musical skills and developed their sound by playing six to eight hours a night for rowdy audiences who shouted at the Beatles to "make show!" They played at the Indra, the Kaiserkeller, the Top Ten Club, and the Star Club, which were located in the Reeperbahn red-light district. This was the naughty section of Hamburg, where one could easily find strippers, prostitutes, and trans-vestites. This tawdry environment led to big eye-opening experiences for the Beatles. Being young, healthy males, it was impossible for the Beatles not to partake in activities beyond playing their musical instruments.

The Beatles' job in the Hamburg clubs was not only to play music; they had to entertain the audiences, and entertain they did, especially John. For example, he sang and played guitar on stage in his underwear with a toilet seat around his neck. The Beatles did everything they could to keep the audience in the clubs. The longer the audience stayed in the clubs, the more they drank, and that was the club owners' primary objective. Generally, the audiences were demanding and could be violent. Hamburg, being a seaport on the Elbe River, was a crime-ridden city, with lots of sailors and roughnecks who frequented the clubs. The audiences were known to be rough and rowdy, at times throwing beer bottles at the Beatles and shouting at them to play songs that they wanted to hear. While the Beatles were adding cover songs to their play list to fill up the long hours they had to perform, they would make every attempt to satisfy the audience's requests. In doing so, they learned more cover songs, which contributed toward building their repertoire. Some of the cover songs the Beatles performed in Hamburg include "Hippy, Hippy Shake," "Sweet Little Sixteen," "What'd I Say," "Bésame Mucho," "To Know Her Is to Love Her," "Little Quinnie," "I'm Talking

About You," and dozens of other songs, some of which would later be recorded and released by the Beatles.

From August 1960 to May 1962 when the Beatles played in Hamburg, Pete Best was the Beatles' drummer. Rory Storm and the Hurricanes, another band from Liverpool, were also playing in Hamburg at the same time. The drummer with the Hurricanes was a fun-loving lad named Richard Starkey, also known as Ringo Starr. In October 1960, the Hurricanes and the Beatles played at the same club, the Kaiserkeller. The two bands took turns playing, which allowed them the opportunity to hear each other. At a recording session in Hamburg, John, Paul, and George backed up Lou Williams from the Hurricanes. Because the Beatles' drummer wasn't available, Ringo played drums at the recording session. That was the first time John, Paul, George, and Ringo recorded together, and it was certainly a twist of fate for Pete Best and Ringo Starr. And to further connect Ringo with John, Paul, and George, when the Beatles returned to Liverpool and had engagements at the Cavern Club and the Kingsway Club, Ringo performed live with the Beatles for the first time. John, Paul, and George already had their eyes and ears set on Ringo and preferred his drumming over Pete's, and it was a surprise and a big blow to Pete when he was replaced by Ringo. On August 16, 1962, Brian Epstein, the Beatles' manager, fired Pete Best. A year before, on November 9, 1961, Brian was so impressed when he heard the Beatles for the first time at the Cavern Club that a few months later, on January 24, 1962, the Beatles signed a management contract with Brian. When Ringo performed with the Beatles for the first time at the Cavern Club in Liverpool, it caused quite a stir. Pete was popular with many fans, who shouted at the Beatles during their performance that they would never accept Ringo. After a temporary rebellion, Ringo soon won the hearts of the local Liverpool fans. The final winning piece to the Beatles' formation and eventual success was in place.

When the Beatles played cover songs, even though the songs resembled the originals, they sounded different. There was an edgy, raw quality to the Beatles' music, defined by the sound of their dominant guitars. The Beatles sang with their native Liverpudlian accents, which gave the songs a distinctive sound. When John, Paul, and George harmonized together, it was a unique blend of singing voices that created an excitement, an urgency, and in some cases, almost a plea. The Beatles had personalized American rock-and-roll and rhythm-and-blues songs and had distinctively made them their own.

Six cover songs performed by the Beatles are on the album *Introducing the Beatles*, released on the Vee-Jay Record label in January 1964. Look at the album cover and you will see four smiling, clean-cut young men dressed in matching tailor-made suits and vests, wearing button-down collared shirts, knit ties, and cufflinks. A far cry from their slick-haired, leather-clad days in Hamburg, the Beatles didn't look like long-haired rock and rollers. On the back cover of *Introducing the Beatles*, at the bottom, it states, "America's Greatest Recording Artists Are on Vee-Jay Records." It's strange to see that printed on the back of a Beatles album. After all, England's Beatles were certainly not American. Part of the appeal for the American record-buying audience was the fact that the Beatles were English.

The first cover song on the album, "Anna (Go to Him)," written and recorded by Arthur Alexander, is a song about losing love to another man. The original Alexander recording features a dominant drum pattern over the piano and guitar parts. Arthur's lead vocal is articulate and out front, but he doesn't cut loose, and his singing sounds controlled. The background voices are very much in the background, adorned with orchestral strings. In keeping with the original recording, Ringo plays the same rhythmic drum pattern; however, instead of piano, George plays the recurring melodic riff on guitar. The sound of the Beatles' guitars was the fundamental ingredient in establishing their instrumental sound. Unlike Arthur, John delivers a convincing, heartfelt emotional lead vocal, with a sad, descending "oh, oh, oh, oh, oh, oh" coming out of the bridge. Paul and George's supporting background "Anna" vocals are smooth and haunting. To give the Beatles' recording more of an edge and to stay focused on the guitars, bass, and drums, they didn't add any strings to the song. Unlike the original fade-out, the Beatles end the song definitively, with John declaring, "Go to him." So the difference between the two versions is significant. "Anna (Go to Him)" speaks of heartbreak and the perils of young love. Teenagers connected with these songs, perhaps having had emotional experiences of losing a girlfriend or boyfriend to another person. Not only were the Beatles connecting with fans with songs about love, romance, and unfulfilled fantasies, they were also connecting with them through songs about the loss or absence of love.

"Chains" was written by Gerry Goffin and Carole King. The original recording was sung by three females called the Cookies. On their recording, brass accents were added along with handclaps. George delivers the lead vocal on the Beatles' "Chains," and John plays an introductory harmonica part. John and Paul sing the harmony parts. Unlike the Cookies' more rhythm-and-blues recording, John's harmonica part and George's guitar strumming makes the Beatles' version of "Chains" folksy. Singing about possessive love and invisible chains bound to a lover unwillingly, all the Beatles wanted to do was to be set free from all of those chains.

Another cover song, "Boys," written by Luther Dixon and Wes Farrell, was originally recorded by the Shirelles, a popular female singing group in the early 1960s. A rhythm-and-blues-styled recording with a Ray Charles influence, it features a rhythm section led by the piano along with bright electric guitar accents. Given the exciting subject matter of kissing, the vocals sound laid back. But with the Beatles' version, that all changed. Instead of females singing "Boys," the Beatles delivered the song from their male perspective. In the spotlight, Ringo sings lead vocal and plays a very snappy drum part. Instead of a sax solo, as in the Shirelles' recording, George plays an electrifying guitar solo. Paul plays a pulsating bass part throughout the song and a boogie-woogie-styled bass line during the chorus and guitar solo. John, Paul, and George support Ringo with harmonized background vocals, singing "bop shoo wa" and "yeah, yeah, boys." Paul's boogie-woogie bass line during the chorus provides an exciting musical counterpoint to the vocals and adds more dynamics to the song. The difference between the two recordings is remarkable and a great example of how the Beatles made a cover very much their own.

A rhythm-and-blues recording by the Shirelles covered by the Beatles is "Baby It's You," written by Burt Bacharach, Mack David, and Barney Williams (Luther Dixon). The prominent instruments on the original are the piano; a bouncy, accented electric guitar; and tambourine. An organ solo takes place in the middle of the song. On the Beatles' version, John sings an intimate and convincing lead vocal. Instead of an organ solo, George Martin, the Beatles' record producer, plays an ethereal celesta solo, doubled by George Harrison's lead guitar, played on the low strings. Paul and George sing the introductory and background *sha, la, la, la, las*. It doesn't matter what others are saying about you, John doesn't want anyone other than *you*.

On *Introducing the Beatles*, the Beatles also covered "A Taste of Honey," a song about dreaming and kissing and coming back for more. Originally an instrumental for a Broadway play and film of the same name, the music was composed by Bobby Scott and Ric Marlow, and afterward lyrics were written by Marlow. The Beatles' version is quite similar to the cover version recorded by Lenny Welch, with George playing arpeggio guitar figures (a sequential series of notes) and Ringo playing the drums with brushes. However, Welch's recording has female background singers and an accompanying organ part, and the ending fades out on a minor chord. The big difference with the Beatles' cover is the ending; the Beatles end their version with a major chord. After hearing a minor chord played during the song, harmonically it's quite startling to one's ears. Paul sings a smooth lead vocal, with John and George singing background vocals so prominently they're not really background voices at all.

The last song on the *Introducing the Beatles* album is "Twist and Shout," written by Phil Medley and Bert Berns. Originally recorded by the Top Notes and made famous by the Isley Brothers, the Beatles' version was based on the Isley Brothers' recording. Making it their own, the Beatles recorded it at a quicker tempo and instead of brass accents and a brass ensemble interlude, it's all guitars and commanding vocals. "Twist and Shout," with John's growling vocals, is a powerful way to end the album. He was suffering from a cold at the recording session, and yet John was able to deliver one of his best lead vocals ever. The vocal *ah* harmony building at the middle of the song, topping off with Paul's high-pitched scream, adds to the excitement. And the Beatles repeat the harmony *ahs* toward the end of the song, immediately followed by an uplifting, ascending climax. The Beatles' recording of "Twist and Shout" was so powerful and popular that it was released as a single on the Tollie record label and reached the number one spot on the U.S. *Cashbox* singles chart for April 1964. The Beatles started their performance with this song during their 1964 North American summer concert tour. It was the perfect opening number to excite the audience. When John asked the girls to twist closer to him, their bodies, rocked with Beatlemania, twisted and shouted for the Beatles.

Many people (including me) thought some of the songs that the Beatles covered were originals. After playing "Twist and Shout" with my band the Pandemoniums for two and a half years, we had the good fortune to back up the Isley Brothers. When we met with them before the concert to go over the play list, Ron Isley said that one of the songs they were going to perform was "Twist and Shout." "Oh, we certainly know that one, 'Twist and Shout' by the Beatles," I said. "The Beatles?" asked Ron. "Yeah, that's their song," I said knowingly. "Really? Actually, we recorded it before the Beatles did and it was our hit single in nineteen sixty-two," replied Ron. It was an embarrassing moment, but it illustrated how strong the Beatles had made their imprint on "Twist and Shout" and other songs that they covered.

In addition to "A Taste of Honey" on *Introducing the Beatles*, there's another Broadway show song on the 1964 *Meet the Beatles!* album. "Till There Was You," written by Meredith Willson, is from the musical *The Music Man*. On the original single, Anita Bryant sings a dynamic version with an orchestral accompaniment. Peggy Lee also recorded the song, giving it a soft, mellow sound. The Beatles' musical interpretation and arrangement of the song is truly their own, and it demonstrated their versatility with a wide range of musical styles. It appealed to an older audience that liked Broadway musicals and introduced a more sophisticated, harmonically complex song to the younger teenage fan base. Played on acoustic guitars by John and George with Ringo playing bongos, it cast the Beatles in a softer, non–rock-and-roll light. Paul's lead vocal style is "legit," sounding cleaner, purer, and nothing like his rock-and-roll voice. George's lead guitar intertwines perfectly with Paul's vocals.

More than half of the songs on *The Beatles' Second Album* are cover songs. Released a few months after *Meet the Beatles!*, *The Beatles' Second Album* is their definitive rock-and-roll album. Even though the title lacked creativity, the Beatles' covers were more than exciting. The back cover states, "Never before has show business seen or heard anything like them." And it was true. Straightaway, George's driving lead guitar starts off the album with Chuck Berry's "Roll Over Beethoven." One of the many cover songs that the Beatles had played for years, the recording of "Roll Over Beethoven" captured the live energy from their club performances. Paul's bass lines lock perfectly with Ringo's drumming, and George sings with a rocking Liverpudlian accent. On Chuck

Berry's recording, his guitar is out front when he plays the introductory opening riff guitar solo, but while Chuck sings, his guitar blends with the rhythm section. George's Chuck Berry–styled guitar playing on the Beatles' version is louder than Chuck's throughout the entire song. At the end of the Beatles' version, the band abruptly stops, followed by an isolated guitar chord.

John and George sing lead vocals on "You Really Got a Hold on Me," written by Smokey Robinson and originally recorded by the Miracles. Overall, the Beatles' version is similar to that of the Miracles, but the Beatles did put their personal stamp on their recording. They strengthen the original opening piano riff by George Harrison doubling it on the low strings of his guitar, with George Martin playing the piano part. Unlike the Miracles' version, a brass section was not included, and the Beatles came up with a definitive drum pattern and guitar riff for an ending instead of the Miracles' fade-out. John's vocals are bluesy, and his falsetto leaps are brilliantly executed.

Think back to what it was like to listen to the Beatles on the radio in 1964. . . . Ever since radio stations began playing Beatles songs, your black Zenith transistor radio has become your prized possession. You carry it with you throughout the house, and at night you bring it to bed with you. The local radio station, WDRC, has received advanced promotional copies of The Beatles' Second Album *before it was available for purchase at the record stores. The rich sound of George's low-string guitar riff comes through the small two-inch speaker, followed by the DJ's recorded voice superimposed on the song, saying, "Big WDRC, exclusively." It's "You Really Got a Hold on Me," a song from the Beatles' new album, and the DJ's booming voice makes it sound all the more exciting. You have to leave the radio turned on, and you can't go to sleep because the Beatles really have a hold on you.*

Another song in which George sings lead vocal, "Devil in Her Heart," originally titled "Devil in His Heart," was written by Richard Drapkin and recorded by the female rhythm-and-blues singing group the Donays. This is an interesting choice for the Beatles to cover considering that the original song was about the devil in *his* heart and the song wasn't a hit single. Expanding on the original, Ringo overdubbed maracas to his drum track. The big difference is the male voices of George, John, and Paul singing the song instead of female voices, as on the original. While the Donays' version ends with a fade-out, the Beatles end the song with a definitive guitar-chord flourish.

John sings the lead vocal on "Money (That's What I Want)," written by Janie Bradford and Berry Gordy Jr. and recorded by Barrett Strong. Unlike Barrett's recording, which has a tambourine playing throughout the song, female background vocals, and a fade-out ending, the Beatles' version starts with a piano riff played by George Martin. Ringo then sets up the song's pounding rhythm, playing drum patterns on his snare and tom-toms, accenting the second and fourth beats. Instead of a tambourine, as on the original recording, all four Beatles added handclaps to reinforce the rhythm of the song. "Money (That's What I Want)" intensifies and builds to a vibrant climax, with John declaring, "That's what I want." Compared with Barrett's singing, John's lead vocals are guttural, powerful, and intense.

The Beatles were impressed with the way Little Richard sang, and Paul especially took pride in his ability to sing like him. In 1962, the Beatles and Little Richard shared the stage at the Star Club in Hamburg, where Little Richard sang "Long Tall Sally," written by Robert Blackwell, Enotris Johnson, and Richard Penniman (Little Richard). The Beatles had never heard anyone sing with such howling intensity, and Richard's signature high *wooo*s. It's no surprise then that the Beatles added "Long Tall Sally" to their repertoire. Another fine example of what the Beatles sounded like when performing live, their recording of "Long Tall Sally" captures the intense energy of the Beatles. Paul's upper-register lead vocal is hard to beat. Given the fact that George played nearly all of the lead guitar solos in 1964, it's a bit of a departure for the song's first lead guitar solo to be played by John. George plays the second solo, accenting an ascending rhythmic build. Adding to the intensity of the recording, George Martin plays a persistent, pounding piano part.

John sings the sixth cover on *The Beatles' Second Album*, "Please Mr. Postman," written by Brian Holland, Freddie Gorman, William Garrett, Georgia Dobbins, and Robert Bateman. The original version, recorded by the female singing trio the Marvelettes, was a number one hit in the United States in 1961. The Beatles sped up the tempo and began with Paul and George singing "wait," followed by John's lead vocal and Ringo's snare and bass drum pattern. John's vocals are filled with an emotional intensity, which is all the more prominent in the

vocal/drum breaks toward the end of the song. Paul and George support John with perfect vocal harmonies.

Coming off the heels of their financially successful and critically
acclaimed first feature film, *A Hard Day's Night*, and the accompanying
album, Capitol Records rushed the release of the *Something New* album. Capitol knew there was an insatiable, massive Beatles-buying audience, and they took advantage of it and pleased millions of Beatles
fans. There are two cover songs on *Something New*: "Slow Down" and
"Matchbox." On "Slow Down," written and recorded by Larry Williams
in 1958, John delivers a screaming lead vocal, especially during the last
verse. Instead of the sax solo, as on the original record, George plays a
lead guitar solo, which he starts on the low strings and then fingers his
way up to the top strings. Ringo pounds out perfectly tailored drum fills
during the breaks, and George Martin plays fast, rollicking rock-and-
roll piano.

Having a variety of singing voices was one of the key factors that
gave the Beatles a versatile sound. Ringo takes the lead vocal spot on
the rockabilly song "Matchbox," written and originally recorded by Carl
Perkins. On the *Something New* album version, George is credited as
playing lead guitar; however, on the *Live at the BBC* recording, before
the lead guitar solo, Ringo says, "Alright, John." Ringo's vocals sound
entirely different than Carl Perkins's southern singing voice. Once
again, George Martin plays a rocking piano part that gets louder during
the last verse. The chord structure of both "Matchbox" and "Slow
Down" is the same, namely a standard three-chord progression, which
has been and is still used in hundreds of rock-and-roll songs.

The *Beatles '65* album contains four cover songs, the first one being,
"Rock and Roll Music," written and recorded by Chuck Berry. It's
entirely appropriate that the Beatles would cover this song given their
love for early rock-and-roll songs. The Beatles sped up the tempo and
made their guitars more prominent. The song starts with a quick,
punching lead guitar, and John passionately sings his heart out. We
believe him when he declares, "It's gotta be rock-and-roll music." Considering the fact that George Martin is a classical musician, his piano
playing on "Rock and Roll Music" is very rock and roll. His descending
piano riff perfectly complements John's vocal when he sings, "If you
wanna dance with me."

"Mr. Moonlight," written by Roy Lee Johnson and originally recorded by Dr. Feelgood and the Interns, was another song that the Beatles had played for years during their live performances. John belts out the opening vocal line as if he's howling at the moon, followed by Paul and George joining his lead vocal with harmonies. What makes the Beatles' recording different from Dr. Feelgood's is John's vocal phrasing and his rhythmic placement with the melody. And unlike a guitar solo played on the original recording, Paul plays a deep, low-toned organ solo, adding to the nocturnal mood.

Even though it was John who had sung "Honey Don't" during their live shows, Ringo sings on the Beatles' recording of the rockabilly-styled "Honey Don't," another song written and recorded by Carl Perkins. George plays a bouncy, twangy lead guitar throughout the song, interplaying with John's big rhythm-guitar strumming. Paul's bass line mirrors George's guitar part during the choruses. To give the listeners a variety of singing voices, the Beatles wanted to have Ringo sing one song per album; thus "Honey Don't" was given to Ringo. This song is strongly identified with Ringo, who continues to perform it live today.

A true testament to how much the Beatles, especially George Harrison, loved songs written by Carl Perkins, the *Beatles '65* album concludes with another one of his songs: "Everybody's Trying to Be My Baby." George's lead vocals are processed with a plentiful amount of reverb and delay effects. The Beatles added more musical breaks during the verses and emphasized syncopation during George's second lead guitar solo. Unlike Perkins's recording, the Beatles end the song once but continue playing a second ending. This was one of the songs that the Beatles played during their live performances from 1963 to 1965. No doubt, during that time period—and beyond—everybody *was* trying to be George's and the other Beatles' baby!

The Beatles recorded four more cover songs on the *Beatles VI* album, released about six months after *Beatles '65*. Harking back to their Hamburg days, they recorded "Kansas City/Hey, Hey, Hey, Hey," written by Jerry Leiber and Mike Stoller. Modeled on Little Richard's recording, Paul delivers a commanding vocal performance. The "hey, hey, hey, hey," part of the song is a perfect call and response between Paul's lead vocal and John and George answering in unison and then in harmony on "bye, bye." Instead of a sax solo, as played on Richard's recording, John plays a Chuck Berry–influenced lead guitar solo.

George Martin plays the piano. "Bad Boy," written and recorded by Larry Williams, is a basic three-chord rock-and-roll song. On Williams's original recording, along with the standard rhythm section (piano, guitar, bass, and drums), a baritone and tenor sax were added to the band. The Beatles sped up the tempo on their recording and replaced the sax solo with George's lead guitar. Similar to the original recording, George plays a recurring lead guitar riff during the verses, and Paul plays an overdubbed electric piano part.

John and Paul were big Buddy Holly fans, and yet the Beatles covered only one of his songs: "Words of Love." Unlike their more unique cover songs on which the Beatles stamped their distinctive sound, the Beatles' version of "Words of Love" is nearly identical to the way Holly recorded it. John and Paul's vocal harmonies, sung in their lower to middle register, blend together perfectly. George's bright lead guitar and Ringo's clicking percussion round out this classic cover. Since Holly's single version was not a hit, the Beatles brought this song into the spotlight and turned millions of listeners on to "Words of Love."

On *Beatles VI*, the Beatles covered another song written and recorded by Larry Williams: "Dizzy Miss Lizzy." Williams's original recording has the same backing band as he had on "Bad Boy." On the Beatles' recording, George starts the song with his piercing lead guitar riff. John delivers an exciting, screaming lead vocal, similar to his vocal performance on "Bad Boy." George plays the recurring lead guitar riff throughout the song and a double-tracked lead guitar solo. Paul plays a pulsating electric piano part, much like he did on "Bad Boy." The Beatles end the song with a major sixth guitar chord, a final chord that George was quite fond of using. He played it on other Beatles recordings. For example, the final chord in "Matchbox" is a major sixth chord. The Beatles' cover made "Dizzy Miss Lizzy" famous, heard by millions of fans throughout the world.

It was very fitting for the Beatles to cover "Act Naturally," written by Johnny Russell and recorded by Buck Owens and the Buckaroos. By the time the song was released as the B-side single to "Yesterday," the Beatles had appeared in two feature-length films, and it was true; their acting *was* natural. All they had to do was be themselves. And even more appropriately, the affable Ringo sings the lead vocal. After all, the movie *Help!* was centered around Ringo's character, and he was featured in a solo scene in *A Hard Day's Night*. The Beatles created a lead guitar introduction and an ending to the song, played by George, which doesn't exist on the Buck Owens recording. Paul harmonizes with Ringo during the bridge of the song and on the last verse. George plays a country-styled guitar part, which gives the recording its country and western twang. To give the song a click-clack beat, Ringo's hi-hat taps along with John's rhythm guitar. As the lyrics in the song stated, Ringo hoped that we would go see him in the movies, and his wish was certainly granted.

The choice of cover songs that the Beatles recorded illustrates the early evolution of their sound. All four Beatles closely identified with these songs. They had played many of them for several years and knew how to play the songs convincingly. The Beatles understood the lyrics, and they perceived themselves as rock and rollers who could deliver the songs with excitement. Since the artists who recorded these songs were successful, the Beatles believed that they would also be successful by following the path of these hit makers. They idolized Elvis Presley, who in the eyes of the Beatles was the king. Be like Elvis, sing like Elvis, look like Elvis, and maybe one day the Beatles would be kings.

The majority of the cover songs the Beatles performed were confirmed hits, playing songs that their audience would not only recognize but want to hear. It was a pretty sure-shot way for the Beatles to satisfy their audience and simultaneously start to build a fan base.

Let me bring you back to the days when the Beatles played at the Cavern Club in Liverpool. . . . The buzz had been building for days. Talk about the Beatles performing at the Cavern seemed to be on everyone's lips. You had to go see this new band. Before you leave your house, you check your hair in the bathroom mirror. Yes, that's good, with your hair slicked back in a pompadour style, you look like a Teddy Boy. Once inside the Cavern, you see dozens of girls sitting close to the stage. The Beatles, dressed in all-leather outfits, are onstage, snacking on food and drinking. The Cavern is packed full. It feels as though you are in a dank cave. Then it happens. Paul steps up to the microphone and the Beatles rip into "That's All Right (Mama)." A raw sensation takes over your body as the sound of the Beatles bounces off the Cavern walls. John sings "I Got a Woman." The girls near the stage swoon as the Beatles croon and sweep them off their feet. The Beatles exude a primal energy, and you surely feel it. The Beatles are addictive.

Completely uncharacteristic of rock-and-roll and rhythm-and-blues songs, "Till There Was You" is clearly the odd one in the bunch. Why did the Beatles cover this song? Because it illustrated an entirely different talent that the Beatles had; they were not limited to playing only rock-and-roll songs. Paul's father was a musician who played in a jazz band, and dance hall music, big band, and a variety of other musical styles were played in the McCartney household. So Paul was the Beatle who could most easily identify with the style of "Till There Was You." It's no wonder then that Paul sings lead vocals on the recording. When deciding to include it on *Meet the Beatles!* and perform it on *The Ed Sullivan Show*, the decision-making process included the band's record producer, George Martin, and their manager, Brian Epstein. Although it went against John's rock-and-roll image, "Till There Was You" did give the Beatles sonic diversity. It also broadened their appeal when the Beatles were introduced to American audiences for the first time.

Part of the Beatles' claim to fame was their unique renditions of these rock-and-roll and rhythm-and-blues songs. The Beatles were inspired by and loved these American songs, made them their own, and sent the songs back to America, Beatles' style.

I, along with thousands of aspiring musicians who had bands at the time when the Beatles released these records, learned how to play nearly all of the songs that the Beatles had covered. My band members and I would sit around the hi-fi and listen to these Beatles covers, figure out the musical parts of the songs, scribble down the lyrics, and then excitedly rehearse them with the goal of sounding like the Beatles. We felt as though we were part of the Beatles when they were the biggest, most successful band in the world. The excitement we shared was unparalleled. These rock-and-roll and rhythm-and-blues songs were relatively easy to learn, but it was singing them like the Beatles that was more challenging. So to make the songs sound more like the Beatles, I sang them with a Liverpudlian accent. And it worked like a charm. As much as my band loved to play these songs, the local audiences loved to hear them all the more. Even though they were originally American songs, the Beatles had popularized them, so I and millions of others considered them to be Beatles songs. These American rock-and-roll and rhythm-and-blues songs provided the Beatles with the very foundation from which they wrote their original songs.

While it was exciting for the Beatles to play and record the songs that they loved by American recording artists, they wanted something more. The Beatles wanted to perform and record their own songs. So they began writing original songs. Naturally, the sound and style of their early songs were influenced by the American rock and rollers and rhythm-and-blues artists that the Beatles covered and emulated. And while the Beatles' recorded cover songs are important in the development of their sound, their original songs catapulted them to superstardom. The Beatles reached a level of success that far exceeded their wildest dreams.

Suggested Listening: "Boys"; "Twist and Shout"; "Till There Was You"; "You Really Got a Hold on Me"; "Honey Don't"; "Words of Love"

2

IN THEIR OWN WRITE
Rock-and-Roll Originals

The vast majority of original songs written and recorded by the Beatles are rock and roll. Therefore, this chapter and the following one are big. Some of these rockers are also featured in chapter 5, "Live Beatles: *The Ed Sullivan Show* and Live Concert Songs." As stated in the introduction, the Beatles songs I write about in this book are based on U.S. releases. With the exception of songs written by George Harrison and a few by Ringo Starr, nearly all of these songs are credited to John Lennon and Paul McCartney as writers. For the most part, it should be noted that the Beatle singing lead vocal is the primary writer of that song, except for some of the original songs that Ringo and George sing, which are written by John and Paul. To help you grasp and take in the enormity of the songs, I have segmented the rock-and-roll originals chapters into years, starting with 1961.

1961

While the Beatles were in Hamburg, they were a backing band for Tony Sheridan, a singer and guitarist from Norwich, England, who performed at the Kaiserkeller. Reciprocating the gesture, Sheridan often joined the Beatles onstage and played guitar with them during their shows. Bert Kaempfert, a record producer from Polydor, was impressed with Sheridan's and the Beatles' live performances. Kaempfert brought Sheridan and the Beatles into the recording studio, where they recorded "My Bonnie" and "The Saints," with Sheridan singing lead vocal. During the recording sessions, without Sheridan, the Beatles recorded a cover version of "Ain't She Sweet," written by Milton Ager and Jack Yellen, with Lennon singing lead vocal. The Beatles also recorded an original instrumental titled "Cry for a Shadow," which is the only Harrison-Lennon composition. Once the Beatles had become a huge success in America, in March 1964, MGM Records released "Cry for a Shadow" as an A-side single. The drummer on that record is Pete Best. The distinctive sound of John's bright electric Rickenbacker guitar starts "Cry for a Shadow" on which he plays a series of three chords. Then the three other Beatles come in. George plays a note-bending lead guitar part throughout the song while Paul and Pete provide a bass and drum foundation. The bass part and matching bass drum play a *da, da-dum* rhythm, which is the same rhythm that is used in "A World Without Love," a number one hit song written by Paul McCartney and recorded by Peter and Gordon in 1964. John didn't care much for "A World Without Love" and thought that after the opening lyrics, "Please lock me away," the song was finished. Paul's bass lines at the end of the sections known as the bridge in "Cry for a Shadow" are an early indication of his gifted melodic bass playing.

1962–1963

During 1962 and 1963, the Beatles recorded and released singles and albums in the United Kingdom. "Please Please Me," "From Me to You," and "She Loves You" were released in the United States, but remarkably they didn't chart well and were hardly played on radio stations. In America in early 1964, the Beatles were ready to explode, and they would forever change the face of rock and pop music.

1964

The Beatles had a massive creative output in 1964. Six albums were released in America: *Introducing the Beatles, Meet the Beatles!, The*

Beatles' Second Album, *A Hard Day's Night*, *Something New*, and *Beatles '65*. That same year their first feature-length film, *A Hard Day's Night*, was released. The songs from *A Hard Day's Night* are covered in chapter 7, "Acting Naturally: Movie Songs."

In January 1964, the Beatles were in England, feeling accomplished after achieving a number of successes. After years of hard work and thousands of performances, they had risen to the top as England's most popular band. Everywhere they performed, fans became overwhelmed with excitement and screamed uncontrollably. The fans had caught a new bug, and it was spreading wildly throughout England. The bug was called Beatlemania. In the United Kingdom, their second single record, "Please Please Me," became a number one hit in 1963. Even though they were basking in their homeland fame, the Beatles were anticipating what might happen when they would travel to America for the first time. Other English recording artists didn't do well and were considered a flop when they came to the United States and performed for American teenagers, who favored American bands and recording artists like the Beach Boys, Roy Orbison, and the Four Seasons. Despite the fact that English recording artists such as Cliff Richard and the Shadows were not a big success in the United States, preparations were being made for the Beatles to come to America. Knowing that "I Want to Hold Your Hand" was rapidly climbing up the U.S. record charts and Capitol Records was going to release the *Meet the Beatles!* album, Vee-Jay Records released *Introducing the Beatles* on January 10, 1964, ten days before the Capitol release. Vee-Jay could have released *Introducing the Beatles* in 1963 but chose not to because the singles "Please Please Me" and "From Me to You" were not successful when released in the United States in 1963.

Brian Epstein, the Beatles' manager, had secured a national televised performance by the Beatles on the hugely popular *The Ed Sullivan Show*. The stage was set. Just prior to coming America, the Beatles performed in Paris at the Olympia Theatre.

It was destined to happen. In Paris, the Beatles received a telegram from Capitol Records informing them that their single "I Want to Hold Your Hand" had reached the number one spot on the U.S. hit parade. With that major accomplishment, the Beatles were ecstatic and celebrated the momentous occasion with their manager. With a number one–selling record in America, their hopes that they would be welcomed and accepted seemed more possible.

Radio stations throughout the United States were playing "I Want to Hold Your Hand," and a growing number of American teens were becoming infatuated with the Beatles. Why was "I Want to Hold Your Hand" so popular? Because it was a positive, exciting, energetic song about love. Many Americans had been depressed after the assassination of President John F. Kennedy, so the timing of the Beatles' uplifting song couldn't have been any better. With "I Want to Hold Your Hand," the Beatles didn't waste any time getting the listener excited. The first verse begins with "Oh yeah, I'll tell you something." (There's that positive word *yeah*, which the Beatles used in "She Loves You" and as "oh yeah" in "I'll Get You.") The Beatles think you will understand what they are singing about, and the verse ends with a high-pitched "hand," immediately followed by the chorus. The bridge at first gets a little softer and personal, with lyrics that "touch you," then builds to a climax with feelings that the Beatles can no longer hide. Adding variety to the vocal arrangement, on the second bridge Paul harmonizes with John. The song ends with a driving rhythmic finish while John and Paul sustain the word *hand*.

The first step in having a physical connection with someone is with your hands. With "I Want to Hold Your Hand," the Beatles tell you directly that they want to connect with you on multiple levels. First, they want to physically touch you. Second, they do so by touching you with their music and lyrics. Teenage girls strongly identified with this song and fantasized about the Beatles holding *their* hands. It was a powerful song that ignited Beatlemania in the lives of teenagers throughout the world.

"I Saw Her Standing There" is a heart-throbbing song about young romance and the excitement of meeting a seventeen-year-old girl who looks way above average. The up-tempo, driving beat supports Paul's vocals, and John sings a lower harmony part on the chorus. During the bridge of the song, Paul and John harmonize and make a reference to "I Want to Hold Your Hand" when they sing "held her hand." Paul emphasizes the word *mine*, by hitting his highest vocal note in the song. Something as subtle as using the same word *hand* created lyric continuity with their early songs. Paul belts out a scream that introduces George's lead guitar solo. Paul's dynamic bass playing drives the song;

however, it's not an original bass line. The bass line that Paul plays in "I Saw Her Standing There" is note for note from Chuck Berry's song "Talkin' About You." It's interesting to note that "I Saw Her Standing There" appeared on *Introducing the Beatles* and *Meet the Beatles!* On *Meet the Beatles!*, you can hear Paul's complete count off, "One, two, three, four!" On *Introducing the Beatles*, you only hear Paul say "Four!" "I Saw Her Standing There" was the B-side to "I Want to Hold Your Hand" on the Capitol Records release. "I Saw Her Standing There" was also a Top 20 hit, peaking at number fourteen on the *Billboard* chart, making this record the first Beatles double-sided hit single. And all eight Beatle hands overdubbed a clap track on both songs.

In 1964, record hops gave teenagers a chance to meet and dance to the hit songs of the day. Some record hops were hosted by local radio DJs, which made the events more exciting. These DJs were important to local teenagers, who listened to them on their respective radio station. After all, the DJs were the ones who played the Beatles' records.

Let me take you to a record hop, where teens gathered and radio DJs played records. . . . It's March 1964, and you and your friends go to a record hop. You're excited at the prospect of meeting a cute girl and, better yet, dancing with her. Before you leave your house, you comb your hair repeatedly, in the style of the Beatles, swooping down on your forehead. To make sure your mop top stays in place, you keep your trusty comb in your jacket pocket. Inside the church hall, girls are gathered on one side of the hall, boys on the other side. The DJ plays "I Saw Her Standing There." Then you see "her" standing there and your heart goes boom! The positive energy of the song gives you the courage to approach her. She smiles at you. You ask her if she likes the Beatles and she says she loves them. You tell her that you love them, too. Your bodies start moving to the driving beat of the song. Now you're dancing with her.

"I Saw Her Standing There" encompassed what millions of teenagers fantasized about. The Beatles were the ones who paved the way for young teenagers to meet, play their records, dance to their songs, and experience the over-the-top excitement of young, infatuated love.

John wrote "Please Please Me." Originally, it was slower than the released version, and there were no vocal harmony parts. George Martin suggested that the tempo should be sped up. The Beatles reworked the arrangement. They played it faster, added vocal harmonies, and

John played a recurring harmonica riff. After the final recording, George Martin announced to the Beatles, "Here's your first number one." John and Paul's harmonizing vocals in "Please Please Me" demonstrate how well their voices work together. Paul sings a repetitive high note in the verses while John's melody moves up and down below Paul's vocal, creating a moving two-part harmony. The melody in the chorus of "Please Please Me" leaps and falls dramatically. George plays a guitar riff, which is doubled by Paul an octave lower on the bass, between the verses and choruses. During the bridge section, on the lyrics "my heart," Ringo punctuates the words with a variety of drum rhythms. The song ends with driving guitar chords interspersed with Ringo's fast drum fills. John pleads with listeners to "come on, please, please me." That's what John and the Beatles wanted, to be pleased. Much to their delight, that's what they got from their fans in the U.K. and eventually throughout the entire world.

With "Thank You Girl," female fans fantasized that the Beatles were singing to them. When John and Paul wrote the song, that's exactly what they wanted to do—thank all of their female fans. John and Paul sing about thanking the girls for being good to them and for loving the Beatles. "Thank You Girl" begins with John's harmonica riff supported by guitars, followed by the full band. The song features John and Paul's harmonizing vocals. The ending *oh*s are bathed in reverb as Ringo plays snappy drum fills on his snare and tom-toms.

On *Introducing the Beatles*, John and Paul both sing lead vocals on "There's a Place." This song is about a place in your mind where you can go where there's no sadness or sorrow. "There's a Place" begins with John playing the harmonica, followed by John and Paul's isolated vocal harmonies singing the opening word *there*. This introduction creates suspense before the music kicks in. In the bridge, on the lyrics "don't you know that it's so," John and Paul harmonize in octaves, which gives the vocals a layered depth. With this song, the Beatles had created a place where you can escape to, away from school, your parents, and the rest of the world. A place where you can feel inspired, excited, and accepted. A place with the Beatles.

Come on, come on, come on! Dance with me! One of the Beatles' obscure songs, "Little Child" rocks with excitement at the prospect of dancing with that little child. John and Paul wrote the "filler" song quickly, needing one more song to complete their U.K. album *With the*

Beatles. In the United States, "Little Child" is on the *Meet the Beatles!* album. The lyrics "I'm so sad and lonely" were taken from "Whistle My Love," a song in the 1952 Walt Disney movie *The Story of Robin Hood and His Merrie Men*. "Little Child" was written for Ringo, but he didn't want to sing it. So John sings the lead vocal and fills the song with his wailing blues harmonica playing. "Little Child" is the only song in the Beatles' catalog in which John plays harmonica for the entire song. Along with the harmonica, Paul's piano playing adds enthusiastic energy to the song. It's the wild energy in the song that compels you to get up and dance. But it has to be a short dance. "Little Child" is a quick one-minute, forty-eight seconds long. The "come on" lyrics from "Please Please Me" are loud and clear in "Little Child."

As you can hear when listening to "Please Please Me," "Thank You Girl," "There's a Place," and "Little Child," the harmonica was an out-front instrument in the Beatles' 1963–1964 sound.

A stark contrast to the *Introducing the Beatles* album cover, the *Meet the Beatles!* album cover looks more sophisticated. It features a photograph of the Beatles with half-lit, black-and-white faces, tinted blue, taken by London photographer Robert Freeman. On the back cover is a smaller photo of the Beatles wearing stove-pipe trousers, Cuban heeled boots, and collarless Pierre Cardin suit jackets. This one singular photo sent shock waves through those who saw it for the first time. These Beatles looked completely original. Yes, their faces on the front cover are half lit; however, the songs on the album shine brightly.

A departure from John's and Paul's positive love songs on *Meet the Beatles!*, George's "Don't Bother Me" reveals a man who can't be bothered with anyone other than the girl who left him. George wrote the song when he was sick in bed and didn't want to be bothered. He sings the lead vocal and plays a lead guitar solo based on the melody in the verses. During the bridge, George sings that he'll never be the same without her and that she'll always be the only one for him. The claves played by Paul and the bongos played by Ringo give the song a Latin feel. "Don't Bother Me" is the first song that George wrote on his own and is positioned as the first song on side two of *Meet the Beatles!*

The opposite of not wanting to be bothered, Paul wrote "Hold Me Tight," which is also on the *Meet the Beatles!* album. It feels so right to hold your girlfriend, to have your girlfriend hold you tight. "Hold Me Tight" is another example of the desire to be close and intimate with your girlfriend or boyfriend. The Beatles fuel that desire and top it off at the end of the song by saying, "It's you." There are a lot of vocals on this song. Paul sings the lead vocals and John and George sing harmony, answering Paul in the chorus. However, listen carefully to the high harmony above Paul's lead vocals in the chorus on the word *you*. John and George don't sing that high, so Paul must have overdubbed the high harmony. There's also lots of clapping on "Hold Me Tight" on all four downbeats. George and John propel the song forward with constant chug-a-chug guitar parts.

All the girls who adored Ringo melted away when he sang the rocking "I Wanna Be Your Man." Ringo kept repeating the title throughout the song. In addition to playing a Bo Diddley beat on his drums, Ringo plays maracas and tambourine. John ignites the song by playing the opening tremolo guitar part. During the chorus, George plays a descending guitar riff after Ringo sings the title. John and Paul join Ringo on the chorus with harmony. George Martin plays organ on the recording. Adding excitement to the song, John and Paul scream during George's lead guitar solo. Written by John and Paul, "I Wanna Be Your Man" was recorded by the Rolling Stones before the Beatles recorded it. The Rolling Stones were looking for a new song to record, and John and Paul gave it to them. "I Wanna Be Your Man" became the Rolling Stones' second Top 20 hit single.

In contrast to the happy "I Wanna Be Your Man," John shows the sadder side of his emotions with "Not a Second Time." There will be no more crying for John. He will not tolerate getting hurt a second time. John wrote the pleading, "No, no, no, not a second time." With strong demonstrative lyrics, John sings the lead vocals with a convincing serious tone. It sounds like he means what he sings. John's tired of hearing the same old line and wondering why. The lyric content of "Not a Second Time" can be interpreted as a precursor to John's more threatening "You Can't Do That," which was recorded a few months later. Ringo plays a bouncy drum break before and after the piano solo played by producer George Martin.

"She Loves You" immediately grabs your attention with the chorus that starts the song. It's impossible not to love or at least not like this powerful song. Who wouldn't be thrilled to know that she loves you. John and Paul sing the song and hit their highest notes on the word *you*, making the song personal. George's perfectly placed guitar fills between the vocals, and Paul's pronounced bass part with Ringo's punchy drumming make the song all the more dynamic. To further drive the positive message of her loving you, the Beatles end this powerhouse song by singing the confirming "yeah, yeah, yeah." All of this is accomplished in a little more than two minutes. It's amazing that when "She Loves You" was initially released in the United States in September 1963, it didn't climb the record charts, mainly because of a lack of advertising or marketing dollars to promote it. Once Beatlemania had rocked America in early 1964, the Beatles' record-buying audience was insatiable. "She Loves You" was number two for five consecutive weeks and number one for two weeks on the U.S. charts. The reason why it was held in the number two position was because "I Want to Hold Your Hand" was number one. Two Beatles songs were competing with each other for the number one spot.

"Any Time at All" is written by John, who sings the lead vocals. But because John couldn't reach the high notes in the chorus, Paul sings the second "anytime at all." Paul wrote the middle instrumental section, which features a climbing piano part. George plays a rising lead guitar part on his electric twelve-string, paralleling Paul's piano playing. John and Paul were going to write lyrics for this instrumental section, but they ran out of time. The song's lyrics are personal. John asks you to look into his eyes. He will try to make the sun shine for you. He has a shoulder for you to cry on, anytime at all. All you gotta do is call, and John will be there.

On *The Beatles' Second Album* with the song "You Can't Do That," John doesn't mince his words. He's going to let you down and leave you if you don't shape up. The lyrics are actually threatening and deal with possessive love. George introduces the song with a riff played on his electric twelve-string Rickenbacker, followed by the rest of the band. Sung in John's lower-pitched voice, you can hear his intensity as he belts out the lyrics and ends each verse saying that you can't do that. A song about jealousy, it's John who plays the guitar solo. During the solo, Paul and George sing in harmony, emphatically declaring that you can't do that. As if sounding an alarm, Ringo bangs a cowbell throughout the song. "You Can't Do That" reveals the direct, outspoken side of John.

Similar to the beginning of "You Can't Do That," "I Call Your Name," starts with a guitar riff played by George on his twelve-string Rickenbacker. Another song on *The Beatles' Second Album*, "I Call

Your Name" is written by John, who sings the lead vocal. His guitar playing shines as he plays a rhythm in between Ringo's constant downbeats. John can't sleep without her so he calls her name, but she's not there. During the guitar solo, the rhythm of the song changes. John plays upbeat strumming, which contrasts with the song's characteristic downbeats. George's intricate playing under John's vocal during the sections after the verses (known as the bridge) creates a melodic counterpart to the vocal melody. During the verses and chorus, Ringo overdubbed a cowbell, adding a ringing percussive sound to his drumming. The Beatles were influential, and still are, with other recording artists. On the Mamas and the Papas' 1966 debut album, *If You Can Believe Your Eyes and Ears*, they recorded a cover version of "I Call Your Name."

"I'll Cry Instead," which was released on two Beatles' albums—*A Hard Day's Night* and the U.S. album *Something New*—is a brisk-paced John song about crying and being mad. Mad because he lost his girlfriend, and even though he's crying about the loss, he's going to be vengeful; he's going to break her heart. Not just one girl's heart but all the girls' hearts. The lyrics are similar to "You Can't Do That," with threatening words. George's guitar picking dashes in and out before and after John's vocals, and Paul plays a walking bass line (descending notes) during the breaks at the end of the verses. "I'll Cry Instead" was intended to be used as one of the featured songs in the movie *A Hard Day's Night*, but the director, Richard Lester, decided not to include it. He preferred the more upbeat lyrics that are in "Can't Buy Me Love" and used that song instead.

"When I Get Home" on the *Something New* album is a pounding rock-and-roll song written and passionately sung by John. It begins with the dramatic, explosive vocal chorus, "Whoa-I," sung by John, Paul, and George, followed by "a whole lot of things to tell her." The chorus is powerful as Paul's voice hits a high note on "I" just as Ringo attacks his crash cymbal. John has no time for trivialities and no business being with somebody else; he's got a girl waiting for him at home. He says he has a lot to say when he gets home. Once he is home, John sings that he loves her more, until he walks out the door again. When he gets home, John uses his body language as he holds her and loves her, but we don't really know what he says to her.

In October 1964, the Beatles were in the recording studio putting together songs for their *Beatles '65* album, including the song "I Feel Fine." They rehearsed the song then took a break, and John leaned his Gibson acoustic guitar attached with a pickup against his amplifier. Suddenly, feedback screeched in the recording studio, and John and Paul were intrigued with the loud humming sound. The Beatles' spontaneous creativity convinced them to include that wowing sound in the song. George Martin recorded it and put it at the beginning of "I Feel Fine." Wow indeed. Hearing that for the first time in late 1964 was a new sonic experience. The long, sustained feedback was an audio innovation. The Beatles had struck a positive vibrating nerve and were the first to incorporate accidental feedback into a song. The introductory feedback roars into John's rhythmic guitar riff, which is the foundation of "I Feel Fine." That guitar riff and Ringo's drumming are modeled after the guitar and drum parts in Bobby Parker's 1961 song "Watch Your Step." George doubles John's guitar riff while Ringo beats a rolling rhythm on his tom-toms and snare drums. Paul lays down the bass line, playing on the first and third beats. Paul and George sing harmony with John on the "I Feel Fine" chorus. On the bridge, John, Paul, and George harmonize, singing "I'm so glad" and "she's so glad." George plays a brief sliding lead guitar solo on his upper strings. After the solo, Paul, George, and Ringo stop playing, and the opening of the song returns as John plays his guitar part. Ringo slaps his drums and gives the signal for George and Paul to get back in the song. Everyone wants to feel fine, and you will feel fine when listening to this song written by John.

"She's a Woman," the B-side to the "I Feel Fine" single, starts with George and John punching out staccato chords on the second and fourth beats before Paul and Ringo come in. Paul's bass part dances around the electric-guitar chords while he sings a lead vocal reminiscent of the way Little Richard sings. Paul's woman doesn't buy him presents or give boys the eye. She only gives him love and never makes him jealous. Creating a counter melody, Paul overdubbed a piano part that answers his vocal line. With his fingers racing up and down the guitar neck, George plays a dazzling lead guitar solo. Instead of maracas, Ringo added a shaker known as a *chocalho*. "She's a Woman," written mostly by Paul, is a song about a woman who understands, who seemingly is satisfied with her man, accepts him, and loves him unconditionally. "She's a Woman" and "I Feel Fine" were released on *Beatles '65* on December 15, 1964. Five of the songs on that album are folk-rock songs covered in chapter 6, "A Lighter Side: Folk-Rock and Country-Rock Songs." The remaining four songs are covers, which you can read about in chapter 1, "Beatles Roots: Covering American Songs."

1965

In 1965, the Beatles released three albums, *Beatles VI*, *Help!*, and *Rubber Soul*. The songs from *Help!* are covered in chapter 7, "Acting Naturally: Movie Songs." As you discover the Beatles' songs recorded in 1965, you will notice that their lyrics progressively changed and their overall sound evolved. The songs on *Rubber Soul* are a strong indication as to where the Beatles as writers and recording artists were headed. They began to use new instruments, and the lyrics became introspective and emotionally complex. The Beatles were never comfortable being stagnant. Their evolution was a major factor as to how and why the Beatles were able to sustain their popularity year after year, decade after decade.

"You Like Me Too Much," a song written by George, is his second song to appear on a Beatles album. The lyrics are more positive than his earlier "Don't Bother Me." "You Like Me Too Much" begins with multilayered tremolo-sounding keyboards. Paul and George Martin play a Steinway grand piano, and John plays an electric Hohner Pianet. John plays the rhythmic electric keyboard part throughout the song. Not only does George sing the lead vocals, he also harmonizes with himself on the choruses and the bridges. The instrumental in the middle of the song is a dialogue between George's lead guitar part and the piano part. The song ends with a piano variation of what was played in the introduction, but this time with the full band. You, the reader/listener, are bound to like the Beatles, and if you like them too much, no need to worry. George and the Beatles like you, and it's really true.

"What You're Doing," written by Paul, who sings the lead vocals, begins with Ringo playing a drum pattern with a booming bass drum. The first words of the verses—*look, I'm, you've, and, please,* and *you've*—are accentuated with harmony sung by John and George. Paul asks why would it be so much to know what you're doing to him.

George's bright, twelve-string electric guitar chimes the repetitive guitar part throughout the song, and the Beatles' studio piano player, George Martin, plays a tremolo piano part under George Harrison's guitar solo. Paul's vocal climbs in the bridge sections. He's waiting for you and wondering what you're going to do. His voice tops with high notes on the words *you* and *do*, and then the melody cascades on the word *me*. After the last chorus, the song returns to a variation of the beginning, with Paul adding his bass line to Ringo's drumming.

"Every Little Thing" is written by Paul. He sings the verses in unison with John, but John's lead vocals are much louder than Paul's. On the "every little thing she does" chorus, Paul harmonizes with John. Paul overdubbed a piano part, playing it in the lower register. "Every Little Thing" marks something new with the percussion track. For the first time, Ringo plays a timpani drum, typically used in symphonic orchestras and not on rock-and-roll songs. "Every Little Thing" shows how the Beatles' songwriting continued to evolve, as did their desire to expand their use of instruments beyond guitars, pianos, and drums. When I first heard the percussion sound, I wondered what it was. Then I looked at the back of the *Beatles VI* album and saw a photo of Ringo hitting a timpani drum. Ah-hah! The placement of the timpani part in the chorus of the song is an answer to the lyrics "she does." The timpani answers with a b-boom!

A softer side of John is revealed with "Yes It Is." Written by John, this song features three-part harmonies sung by John, Paul, and George. "Yes It Is" also features a new sound on a Beatles record— George uses a volume pedal on his guitar part. The volume pedal creates a swelling crescendo and decrescendo sound without hearing an attack played on the notes. The mood of the song and lyrics are melancholic, which deal with lost love. The vocals are pleading as they tenderly sing, "Please don't wear red." Red was the color that "my baby wore." John turns up the emotion on the bridge. He sings that he could be happy, but he can't forget her. John reaches his highest notes in the song with "oh yes it is." The color play with the words *red* and *blue* are clever and poetic. Yes it is, it's true, red will make him blue.

When "Yes It Is" was being played on radio stations in May 1965, my band the Pandemoniums played in a musical titled *Krazy Kruze* in Middletown, Connecticut. *Krazy Kruze* was a story about a group of people traveling on a cruise ship and making a stop in Liverpool. Of all things, we played the part of being the Beatles, performing dockside when the "kruze" docked in Liverpool. You can imagine how thrilled we were to be acting as the Beatles as we played "Ticket to Ride," "She's a Woman," and "I Feel Fine." Adding to the Beatles experience, some girls in the audience actually screamed when we played. For those girls, we were local Beatles.

"I'm Down," written by Paul, demonstrates his ability to sing a screaming rocker. Using the upper register of his singing voice, the song begins with Paul declaring, "You tell lies." Singing with so much intensity, his voice sounds like two voices singing simultaneously, creating a multiphonic sound. Paul's vocals are high pitched and guttural. The background vocals on "I'm Down," sung by John and George, are layered. When they answer Paul, a low voice sings long "down" notes, with the two higher voices singing in harmony "I'm really down," "down on the ground." George plays a lead guitar solo, starting on his low strings, fingering up to his high strings, and then back "down" to his low strings. John plays rhythm guitar and an organ on "I'm Down." Before he plays an unconventional organ solo toward the end of the song, Paul screams and says, "Hurry up, John!" In addition to drumming, Ringo plays the bongos, which are brought up in the mix during the climatic ending chorus. Paul's vocals during the ending chorus are outrageous. For Paul to be singing "I'm Down" in 1965 was most peculiar. The Beatles were worldwide superstars. They continued to break music industry records, performed at sold-out stadiums, and were a big success on the big screen with their second movie, *Help!* What could Paul and the Beatles possibly be down about? The word *down* was also used in the song "Help!," which was the A-side of the B-sided single "I'm Down."

George Harrison has a thing or two to say with his song "Think for Yourself." With accusatory lyrics about telling lies and causing more misery, "Think for Yourself" is a thought-provoking song, similar to some of John and Paul's introspective songs on *Rubber Soul*. Always looking for new sounds, straight off the bat your ears are tantalized with a fuzz bass line, which Paul overdubbed in addition to his low-frequency bass part. In the absence of a lead guitar part, the melodic fuzz bass line takes the role of a lead instrument. This fuzz bass innovation distinctly sets "Think for Yourself" apart from the other songs on *Rubber Soul*. Paul and John provide rich vocal harmonies with George's lead vocals. John plays a pulsating organ part, and George plays electric guitar primarily on the second and fourth beats. Ringo hits his snare drum on the fourth beat during the verses, then hits it on the second and fourth beats in the chorus. He also plays tambourine and maracas. George says that you have to think for yourself because he won't be there with you.

John and Paul, being particularly fond of words, decided to write a song titled "The Word." "The Word" is a message song, and the message is love. The chord structure in the song is simple, but what the Beatles do with it is a sound sensation. Starting with a piano introduction, the groove of the song is established with Ringo's drumming, Paul's bouncy piano part and darting bass line, and George's bright syncopated guitar chords. "The Word" consists of two main sections: the vocal-rich chorus and the adjoining verses. The song begins with John, Paul, and George singing harmonies in the chorus, followed by John singing the short verses. The vocal harmonies are what make "The Word" a sonic gem. During the verses, George plays a repetitive guitar riff while John's guitar and Paul's bass play a chord progression that moves upward. After George Martin plays a sustaining harmonium solo, Paul adds another high harmony on top of the voices in the chorus. The Beatles want to show you the light. They did, and the Beatles lit up the world with "The Word," and the word *love* is "so fine."

"You Won't See Me," written and sung by Paul, is a departure from his usual happy, upbeat lyrics. He was having problems with his girl-friend Jane Asher, who was ignoring him. Paul sings an arcing melody during the verses and can't go on and will lose his mind if Jane won't see him. While some of the lyrics are "filled with tears" and deal with a troubled relationship, the music is brisk and bright. Paul plays a melodious bass line and a rhythmic piano part, while George plays accented chords. John and George sing harmony on the song's title and unison and harmony on "ooh, la, la, la," starting with the second verse and the fade-out ending. Ringo plays a rat-a-tat rhythm on his closed hi-hat, as well as tambourine on the words *see me*. In the "time after time" bridge, Paul stresses the word *missing* as a plea to Jane Asher.

The lyrics in the song "Run for Your Life," written by John, blatantly address possessive love and extreme jealousy. A far cry from the love songs that John wrote in 1963 and 1964, he actually sings the following threatening lyrics: "I'd rather see you dead little girl" and "You better run for your life." John also declares that he's a wicked guy. Even though John said, after the Beatles disbanded, that "Run for Your Life" was his least-favorite Beatles song, he put a lot into this song. John sings the lead vocal and plays an acoustic twelve-string guitar and an electric slide-guitar part. John plays the slide guitar before and after George's lead guitar riffs and also interplays with George during the lead guitar solo. Paul and George harmonize with John on the chorus.

Let's say that you're a guitar player. As soon as you hear the opening guitar riff on "Day Tripper," you are turned on and inspired. Once you learn how to play it, you don't want to stop playing the ascending riff. A song about drugs and being teased, "Day Tripper" is perfectly suited for the guitar, with the first note starting on the low open E string. Written by John, with a little help from Paul, "Day Tripper" is one of the few songs in which John plays the lead guitar solo. During the guitar solo, another ascending electric-guitar part played by George, climbs its way up the scale along with *ahs*. The underlying guitar part creates a harmonic tension and explodes with a dynamic climax. Both John and Paul sing the lead vocals, including the overdubbed harmonies. The "hook" of the song is the brilliant recurring guitar riff that starts the song, played by John and George. Paul comes in playing the same riff an octave lower on his bass. Next, Ringo shakes his tambourine along with John's rhythm guitar, and then Ringo barrels in with a propelling drum-roll. Recorded during the *Rubber Soul* recording sessions in October 1965, in January 1966 "Day Tripper" hit the number five spot on the U.S. *Billboard* record chart.

1966

You always wanted to play the drums. Rhythmic drum patterns have always played in your head. Then you heard "Rain." Turned on by the song, you bought your first drum kit, or at least you bought some drum-sticks or maybe bongos. I know the feeling. During my classes in high school, I would drum Ringo's drum part to "Rain" on my desk while teachers lectured about math equations or American history. My math teacher had zero tolerance for my drumming and she would send me to the principal's office on a regular basis. While I did buy bongos, I never learned algebra.

The recording of the song "Rain," written by John, is Ringo's favorite recorded performance. "I think I just played amazing," said Ringo in Barry Miles's book, *Paul McCartney: Many Years from Now*. Ringo's drumming is stunning on the recording, and Paul's bass playing is in your face, brilliant, and functions as the lead instrument in "Rain." The Beatles were not satisfied with the way the bass parts were being recorded. George Martin and the engineers at Abbey Road did something about it with "Rain" and likewise with "Paperback Writer." They engineered a speaker to function as a microphone. As a result, the bass became the prominent instrument in "Rain." During the first chorus, Paul plays even quarter notes on the root chord G. During the second chorus, as a variation Paul plays a triple-figure bass line repeated against the even beats of the guitar chords. The Beatles' sound was evolving, and "Rain" ushered in Paul playing dominant bass lines. John sings the lead vocals, and Paul and George sing the background harmonies "when the sun shines down," "when the rain comes down," and "when it rains and shines." They also sing with John on "sun shines," "show you," and "hear me" at the end of the verses and the long, held "rain" and "shine" melody in the chorus. At the end of the song, John's backward vocals are interspersed with Paul and George singing "rain." What are the backward lyrics? They're the words John sings in the first verse, played backward. Listen to "Rain" and you'll hear Paul's amazing bass line played on his Rickenbacker bass guitar, Ringo's spectacular drumming, and John's backward vocals.

Paul owns an Epiphone Casino guitar, and he played it on "Paperback Writer," which is written primarily by Paul. The song begins with a series of overlapping vocal harmonies singing the song's title in the style of a musical round, followed by Paul playing the opening guitar riff along with Ringo's drumming. Paul's prominent bass playing introduces the first verse. After the second and fourth verses, the isolated "paperback writer" vocals are processed with echo delay. The main character is a writer who wrote a dirty story about a dirty man. The writer needs a break, will make changes to his manuscript, and claims that the willing publisher will make a million dollars overnight. John doesn't play any guitar on "Paperback Writer," but he does play the tambourine and sings harmony with George on the chorus. There being no lid on the Beatles' creativity, during the last verse John and George sing the French lullaby "Frère Jacques" as background vocals to Paul's lead vocals. Out of all four Beatles, at the time of this recording, John was the only real paperback writer, having written two books: *In His Own Write* and *A Spaniard in the Works*. Paul wrote "Paperback Writer" after being challenged by one of his aunts, who asked him if he could write a song that wasn't about love. Evidently, he could. The song was a number one hit in nearly every country soon after it was released in June 1966.

At the same time in the United States, Capitol Records released the *Yesterday and Today* album with the following songs: "Drive My Car," "I'm Only Sleeping," "Nowhere Man," "Dr. Robert," "Yesterday," "Act Naturally," "And Your Bird Can Sing," "If I Needed Someone," "We Can Work It Out," "What Goes On," and "Day Tripper." The initial release had a photo of the Beatles dressed in butcher cloaks, adorned with beheaded baby dolls and pieces of meat. The album cover caused an uproar, so Capitol rereleased the album with a photo of the Beatles looking disgruntled. If you own the "butcher" cover, you're fortunate. It's a collector's item, and the value increases with each passing year.

"And Your Bird Can Sing," written mostly by John, is a compact song running only two minutes long. It features dual harmonizing lead guitar parts played by Paul and George. The brilliant, melodic lead guitar parts don't sound like rock and roll; they sound more classically rooted, running up and down the musical scale. The guitars begin the song and play around John's lead vocals. Paul and George sing harmony in the verses, with John on the lyrics "and your bird can sing," "me," and "and your bird is green." They also harmonize with John in the last verse where the bird "can swing." During the bridges, Paul and George play sequenced guitar riffs beneath John's vocals and then rise for the lead guitar solo. All four Beatles overdubbed handclaps during the dual lead guitar solo. "And Your Bird Can Sing" ends with Paul's and George's dual guitars. In England, the word *bird* is another word for girl.

Paul had a new song idea in his head when he went to John's for a writing session. Together they polished off the song "Drive My Car," the title of which was a slang expression for having sex. The song's foundation is a guitar riff played by George and doubled by Paul on his bass. Paul and John sing the lead vocals. Their vocals are raspy and soulful, especially in the verses. George joins John and Paul and sings with them on the choruses. Paul plays the lead guitar solo, which he was doing often in 1965 and 1966. He also plays the syncopated piano part during the chorus. John doesn't play any instruments in "Drive My Car." Ringo drives the song along with an added cowbell to his drum track. Before the lead guitar solo and at the end of the song, John, Paul, and George sing, "Beep, beep, beep, beep, yeah." The song is about a wannabe movie star who says she can show you a better time and is looking for someone to drive her car.

"I'm Only Sleeping" is a dreamy song written by John. John was being straightforward when he sang, "Please don't wake me" and "Don't shake me." He loved to sleep, and when Paul would go to John's house for song-writing sessions, many times Paul would have to wake up John. The tempo and rhythm of the song is slow and lazy, and underlining its sleepy quality, Paul yawns during a break in the music. He also plays a number of transitory solo bass riffs. Paul and George sing background vocals, including "float up stream" and *oohs*. A few weeks before the Beatles recorded "I'm Only Sleeping," they recorded John's amazing "Tomorrow Never Knows," with John singing "float down stream" instead of "float up stream."

"I'm Only Sleeping" has an extraordinary, unprecedented backward lead guitar part played by George. You can hear it for the first time in the second verse beneath the lyrics "running everywhere" and "there's no need." After John sings, "Waiting for a sleepy feeling," George's solo takes center stage, winding and bending, sounding like a floating, unconscious voice. The song ends with layered backward guitars and fades out. You can find out more about "I'm Only Sleeping" in chapter 9, "Recording Studio Wizardry: Psychedelic and Electronic Songs."

Take a trip with Doctor Robert and he'll pick you up. But who is Doctor Robert? The song "Doctor Robert," written by John and Paul, was inspired by a New York City doctor who gave feel-good drugs and vitamin B-12 injections to his upscale patients. There was also a London dentist who John and George had visited and, unbeknown to both Beatles, the dentist slipped LSD into their tea. "Doctor Robert" begins with George's crunchy guitar part and Paul bouncing along with his bass line. John sings the first verse, then Paul harmonizes with John on the following verses and throughout the rest of the song. During the bridge, you are "well, well, well" and "feeling fine" as John plays the harmonium. "Doctor Robert" does everything he can to make you a new and better man.

The lyrics in Beatles songs during 1963–1964 had the following key words: *love, touch, hold, kiss, dream*—all focused on you, the listener. They used these words in a variety of ways that spoke directly to millions of Beatles fans. As the Beatles evolved as song writers, their creativity enabled them to go beyond love and romance themes. Their lyrics became more introspective and thought provoking. Some might say this had to do with the Beatles getting turned on to smoking pot in 1965. While that may have been a contributing factor, given the high level of creativity, it was their collective talents more than any outside stimulant that led to the Beatles creating new songs. With the songs on *Rubber Soul* and *Revolver*, the Beatles' creativity appeared to have no limits. Their lyrics and music got deeper. The listener's experience with the Beatles is full of sonic surprises, emotional riches, and a musical experience like no other. The Beatles were, and still are, addicting.

In 1966, the Beatles were in the high-end wealthy tax bracket in England. They had to pay a staggering 95 percent tax rate on their income. As a creative response, George wrote the song "Taxman," which is the first song on *Revolver*. George sings the lead vocals about getting taxed on everything from your seat to your feet. When listening to the song, you will hear John's and Paul's background voices sing "Mr. Wilson" and "Mr. Heath." Harold Wilson and Edward Heath were British politicians at the time of the recording. Before the music begins, George counts off the song with a rather low voice, saying, "One, two, three, four," mixed in with guitar noises and a cough. George plays sharp-hitting guitar chords on the second and fourth beats and alternately on the first, second, and fourth beats. Ringo crashes his cymbals on the first and second beats with George's guitar. Ringo's bass drum is tightly locked in with Paul's bass line. On "Taxman," Paul plays a cutting lead guitar, which is extraordinary, considering that George wrote the song, sings lead vocals, and is known as the Beatles' lead guitarist. After the lead guitar solo, Paul doubles his infectious bass line on his electric guitar. During the bridge, Paul plays an upward glissando bass line, while John and Paul harmonize, singing *ifs*. George finishes the sentences with what will be taxed. The song ends with a repeat of Paul's wailing guitar solo. Surprisingly, John doesn't play guitar on "Taxman," but he does play tambourine and sings background vocals. Knowing how outspoken John was, he must have had something to say about the gouging English taxman. I'm sure he enjoyed singing "Mr. Wilson" and "Mr. Heath."

The inspiration for the song "She Said She Said" comes from an August 1965 party that the Beatles hosted while they were renting Zsa Zsa Gabor's house in Beverly Hills. Those who attended included David Crosby and Roger McGuinn, members of the folk-rock band the Byrds, and actor Peter Fonda. John, George, Ringo, and Peter had taken some hallucinogenic drugs, and Peter repeatedly said to John that he knew what it was like to be dead. That was the last thing that John, who wanted to have a good time, wanted to hear. In so many words, John told Peter to shut up. Fortunately, thanks to Peter Fonda and what "he said," John wrote "She Said She Said."

When the Beatles were in the studio working on "She Said She Said," something unusual happened. Paul stormed out of the recording session after having a heated argument with John. As a result, two "first" occurrences happened. For the first time in the Beatles' recording history, Paul is not on a Beatles recording, and in Paul's absence George plays bass for the first time on a Beatles song. "She Said She Said" begins with George playing a distorted electric-guitar riff. Then Ringo comes crashing in along with George's bass part and John's rhythm guitar. George sings harmony with John's lead vocals for most of the song. More than likely, Paul would have sung the harmony if he hadn't left the recording session. The rhythm is complex during the bridge. After maintaining a four-four time in the verses, it changes to three-four time. Once the bridge ends, four-four time is restored. John mixed meter and time signatures with many of his songs during the 1966–1967 time period. John emphasizes the lyrics "when I was a boy" in the bridge, which was a time when "everything was right." Ringo's drum fills are outstanding and plentiful throughout, except for the bridge section, where he plays steady downbeats during the time changes. The song breaks into double time during the short fade-out ending, where John and George sing, "I know what it's like to be dead" and "I know what it is to be sad," overlapping each other.

"Good Day Sunshine," written by Paul, is a piano-centric, happy song about being in love. Inspired by the song "Daydream" by the Lovin' Spoonful, released in March 1966, "Good Day Sunshine" begins with Paul playing the piano and builds dynamically with drums coming in before Paul's lead vocals. The phrasing and meter in the chorus is three beats followed by five beats, which is unusual for a rock song in 1966. George Martin plays the tremolo-styled piano solo. All four Beatles clap, matching Ringo's snare-drum hits, starting with the piano solo. "Good Day Sunshine" is another song on *Revolver* in which John doesn't play any instruments, but he and George do sing background vocals on the choruses. The song ends with the chorus raising up a full pitch and fades out with vocal harmonies singing "Good Day Sunshine" in a round, overlapping each other.

"I Want to Tell You" is another song written by George that appears on the *Revolver* album. The song fades in with George's melodic, syncopated guitar riff, followed by Ringo pounding his snare drum on the second and fourth beats. Paul plays a prominent piano part throughout song, and at the end of each verse, he plays a dissonant piano chord—an unusual sound for a Beatles recording. Similar to "Taxman," John doesn't play guitar on "I Want to Tell You," but he does play tambourine and sings backing vocals with Paul. George sings that he wants to tell you but the words slip away. He feels hung up, and he doesn't know why. Perhaps it's because the lyrics are drug induced. George took numerous LSD trips in 1966. He was overwhelmed with an abundance of thoughts but was unable to articulate them. "I Want to Tell You" ends with George's opening guitar riff, along with George, John, and Paul singing, "I've got time." In the fade-out, Paul's vocal wails with a cascading variety of pitches on the word *time*.

What the Beatles had created with *every* song on the *Revolver* album was a masterful, innovative, artistic achievement. *Revolver* thrust the Beatles to a heightened position as the leaders of the rock and pop music world. In comparison with other recording artists at that time, no one was doing what the Beatles were doing. Those who came close were following or trying to follow the Beatles' lead.

Take a look at the *Revolver* album cover and you will see the Beatles' faces drawn in black ink, with smaller photos of the Beatles superimposed. The album cover was created by German artist Klaus Voormann, who became a friend of the Beatles when they met in Hamburg during the early 1960s. If you look closely at the top right of George's head, you will see a small photo of Klaus along with his name. With millions of fans blown away by *Revolver*, in 1967 the Beatles went on to outdo themselves with "Penny Lane," "Strawberry Fields Forever," and the entire *Sgt. Pepper's Lonely Hearts Club Band* album. The Beatles reinvented themselves and further established themselves as the most in-credible band of rock/pop musicians on earth. In 1967, the Beatles blew the hats off millions of heads, and the heads were filled with songs from *Sgt. Pepper's Lonely Hearts Club Band*.

Suggested Listening: "Cry for a Shadow"; "I Want to Hold Your Hand"; "She Loves You"; "Please Please Me"; "Think for Yourself"; "Day Tripper"; "She Said She Said"

3

NEVER TOO MUCH

More Rock-and-Roll Originals

1967

The *Sgt. Pepper's Lonely Hearts Club Band* album begins with sounds from an awaiting audience and an orchestra tuning up. Decades later, the Beatles are still able to transport you into their audience. Sgt. Pepper's Lonely Hearts Club Band is really Paul McCartney's band. He conceived the idea of an alter ego band, a reinvention of the Beatles named Sgt. Pepper's Lonely Hearts Club Band, who wear dayglow-colored marching band costumes. The album cover, created by Jann Haworth and Peter Blake, is a visual spectacle. The letters in the Beatles' name are composed of red flowers, articulating the popularity of flowers with love-in, flower-power hippies in 1967. There are eight Beatles on the cover—the former mop-top Beatles and the reinvented Sgt. Pepper's Lonely Hearts Club Band Beatles. Surrounding the Beatles are more than sixty characters, including W. C. Fields, Marlon Brando, Mae West, Lenny Bruce, Karlheinz Stockhausen, Edgar Allan Poe, Fred Astaire, Bob Dylan, Marilyn Monroe, Stan Laurel, Oliver Hardy, James Joyce, Karl Marx, Stu Sutcliffe, Albert Einstein, Shirley Temple, Lewis Carroll, and many others. This varied cast of characters strikes both a serious and funny tone. On a sweater that a Shirley Temple doll wears are the words "Welcome the Rolling Stones," which signifies the Beatles' friendship with the Rolling Stones. Most of the characters on the cover went along with it; however, Mae West didn't want to belong to a "lonely hearts club." Once it was explained to her that it was the name of the album and not a real club, she no longer objected. The album title begs the question, why a *lonely* hearts club band? Are the people depicted on the cover lonely members of the club? Not really. The possible answer to the question is that the title is a reference to the song "Eleanor Rigby," which was released in 1966, before the *Sgt. Pepper* album was created. Eleanor was lonely, and in the song the chorus addresses all the lonely people and asks the question, "Where do they all belong?" The answer: in a lonely hearts club.

The band begins by playing a new song written by Paul, "Sgt. Pepper's Lonely Hearts Club Band." Paul and George play lead and rhythm guitars. Paul sings the lead vocals in his upper register, and even though they are a "new" band, he tells the audience that they were formed over twenty years ago and that they're the band the audience has known for years. As if the band includes a group of French horn musicians, a quartet of horn players play an instrumental passage. The audience cheers and laughs with approval. Next John, Paul, and George, singing harmony, announce their new identity and hope the audience will enjoy the show and ask them to "let the evening go." With the French horn quartet, Paul and John sing in unison, saying that the Pepper Band would love to take you, the audience, home with them. In the closing verse, Paul introduces the audience to Billy Shears, the singing drummer, who is really Ringo.

With no pause after "Sgt. Pepper's Lonely Hearts Club Band," John, Paul, and George announce "Billy Shears," along with a pulsating organ, sounds from the audience, and an introductory guitar riff from George. Ringo sings "With a Little Help from My Friends," written for Ringo by John and Paul. This feel-good song is about friends helping each other and getting by and high with them. The sound of Ringo's ringing solo drum fills and the tone of Paul's syncopated, extremely melodious bass line are an audio production that is hard to beat. What's really astounding is that this song, and all of the songs on the *Sgt. Pepper's Lonely Hearts Club Band* album, were recorded using only a four-track recording device. Given the fact that overdubbing and adding additional tracks to the songs were prevalent on this album, George Martin did a masterful job of recording more than four tracks by mixing tracks together and freeing up a track so instruments or vocals could be added in order to satisfy the Beatles' audio vision.

The lyric structure of "With a Little Help from My Friends" is based primarily on John and Paul asking Ringo questions. They ask Ringo if he's sad to be alone, and Ringo says, no, he gets by with a little help from his friends. In the bridge, John and Paul sing harmony and ask Ringo if he needs anybody. Ringo needs somebody to love, and he believes in love at first sight. John and Paul hadn't finished all of the lyrics when the recording session began, and they finished them in the recording studio. In the first verse, instead of the lyrics, "Would you stand up and walk out on me?" the original words were "Would you throw tomatoes at me?" Ringo refused to sing that line, so the lyrics were changed. After several hours of recording the basic music tracks, Ringo was exhausted and wanted to go home. But John, Paul, and George, with their positive support, convinced Ringo to stay and sing his lead vocals. Ringo did, and he does get by with a little help from his friends—John, Paul, and George.

"Fixing a Hole," written by Paul, who sings the lead vocals, begins with George Martin playing the harpsichord. Paul wants to fix a hole to stop his mind from wandering. The sound of George Harrison's electric guitar, which glistens at the end of the verses, possesses a chiming quality. His guitar solo soars above the harpsichord, bass, and drums. Ringo plays the song's slow shuffle rhythm mostly on the hi-hat, which blends in well with the plucking sound of the harpsichord strings. John and George sing distant background vocals. According to Paul, the lyrics in the bridge, "wondering why they don't get in my door," are about fans who hung around his house and never got inside. The song's take-away message is it doesn't matter if you're wrong or you're right, because where you are is exactly where you belong.

"Lovely Rita," another song written and sung by Paul, is about a meter maid who writes up tickets for expired parking violations. Supposedly, the inspiration for writing the song was Paul getting a parking ticket when he parked his car outside of Abbey Road Studios. After the piano and guitar introduction, and before the piano solo played by George Martin, Ringo plays a drum pattern similar to what he plays in "With a Little Help from My Friends." The chorus, sung by John and George Harrison, happens before the first verse. The strange sound that happens after Paul sings "Nothing can come between us" and "made her look a little like a military man," was created by Paul, John, and George humming on a comb with tissue paper. Because Rita is so lovely, the lyrics are about trying to "make her"—in other words, be intimate with her. One of the voices singing three-part harmony is American musician Shawn Phillips. This is a curious addition since the Beatles could have easily overdubbed one of their own voices to sing the third harmony part. In the chorus after the last verse, Paul plays a leaping octave bass line, similar to what he played in the first chorus. Toward the end of song, you will hear breathing, moans, and *ahs*. "Lovely Rita" ends with an abrupt "leave it" and a fast glissando down the piano keyboard.

Paul counts off, "One, two, three, four," and in the background John says, "Bye," introducing the song "Sgt. Pepper's Lonely Hearts Club Band (Reprise)," which includes audience sounds. The tempo moves at a quicker pace compared with the opening "Sgt. Pepper's Lonely Hearts Club Band." Unlike the opening song, John plays a distorted electric guitar while George plays a distorted lead guitar part, and Ringo added tambourine and maracas to his drum track. All four Beatles sing the entire song. They hope you enjoyed their show, but it's getting late and it's time for the band to go. But not before they thank you for attending the show. The reprise makes the album thematic and concludes the show. However, the album continues with another song, "A Day in the Life," which I cover in chapter 10, "Orchestral Dimensions: Strings, Woodwinds, and Brass Songs."

With "Hello, Goodbye," written by Paul, the lyrics are about opposites: yes–no, stop–go, high–low, and of course, hello–goodbye. In John's "Strawberry Fields Forever," some of the lyrics are similar: "I mean it must be high or low." Paul sings the lead vocals and plays the piano and bass guitar in "Hello, Goodbye." The chord progression in the chorus is similar to the chord progression in another Paul song, "For No One"; however, the melody is different. In "Hello, Goodbye," George plays a high, suspended but short electric lead guitar riff in the verses and an ascending eight-note C major scale in the choruses. The ascending guitar line juxtaposed with the descending bass line creates contrary motion in the choruses. This harmonic counterpoint is more akin to classical music than it is to rock and roll. John plays a Hammond organ and sings backing vocals with George. After the second verse, the backing voices sing George's climbing and falling guitar part in the chorus. During the middle of the song, violas play with voices soaked in reverb, which ask, "Why do you say, goodbye, goodbye?" George Martin added the two viola parts to the song based on Paul's melody, which accompany his vocals. "Hello, Goodbye" ends with John and George singing a repetitive "hey, la, hey, bay, lo, ah" while the band plays in double time, which is twice as fast as the song's tempo. Paul improvised a lead vocal during the ending double-time section. "Hello, Goodbye" was a chart-topping number one hit single in several countries, including the United Kingdom and the United States, at the end of 1967 and the beginning of 1968.

1968

The Beatles formed the parent company Apple Corps Ltd. and Apple Records in 1968 as a way of providing themselves with a more beneficial tax structure and with more control of their recordings. The "Hey Jude"/"Revolution" single and *The Beatles* (*White Album*) were the first recordings released on Apple Records. On side one of the recordings is a green Granny Smith apple label, and when you turn the record over, the label on side two is the apple sliced in half.

In 1968, the Beatles released two rock-and-roll singles: "Lady Madonna" and "Revolution." The Beatles used pianos in many of their songs, but "Lady Madonna" showcases the piano. Written by Paul, who plays the piano and sings lead vocals, "Lady Madonna" signals the Beatles' return to rock and roll after a year of psychedelic songs. The style of Paul's vocals and piano playing are influenced by the early rock-and-roll recording artist Fats Domino. The song is about a woman with children who is trying to make ends meet. Paul's moving bass part parallels his left-hand piano playing. After the first bridge, George comes in with his electric guitar on the chorus, playing along with the piano riff, which is also doubled on the bass. Then the recurring riff is reinforced by saxophones—two tenor and two baritone saxes. A tenor saxophone solo played by Ronnie Scott takes place, with background vocals sung by John, Paul, and George, during the bridge section of the song. The saxophone quartet also plays on the last chorus. Ringo does double-duty drumming on "Lady Madonna." In addition to his drumming with sticks, he overdubbed playing his drums with brushes, snapping the rhythm along. "Lady Madonna" was a number one hit in the United Kingdom and reached the number four chart position in the United States in March 1968.

"Revolution" is a powerful, moderate-paced rock-and-roll song written by John, who sings strong words at the time of the Vietnam War, when protests against the war were taking place throughout the world. John was the Beatle who took a political stand while the others didn't. The exception is George Harrison's "Taxman." Beginning with blistering lead guitar parts played by John and George and continuing throughout "Revolution," the guitars are distorted to the point that they peaked beyond the acceptable audio levels at Abbey Road. The rollicking electric piano part, which is prominently displayed in the middle solo and the last chorus, is played by Nicky Hopkins. Having Nicky play the piano is unusual, considering it could have been played by Paul, John, or George Martin. Nicky was a popular London recording-session player who played on records with several recording artists, including the Rolling Stones, the Kinks, and the Who. When I first heard "Revolution" in 1968, like most people I figured the piano was played by one of the Beatles. However, this was not the first time that a musician other than a Beatle played on a Beatles recording. You can read about the other musicians in chapter 11, "Gifted Extras: Guest Musicians Revealed." In "Revolution," John screams after the guitar introduction and screams "Alright!" repeatedly at the end of the song. Lyrically, John was noncommittal. Regarding a revolution, he was both "in" and "out."

Written by John with some assistance from Paul, "Hey Bulldog," originally titled "Hey Bullfrog," is another piano-dominant song. Starting with a syncopated low-register piano riff played by John, George comes in playing the same riff an octave higher on his electric guitar along with Ringo pounding out the syncopated rhythm on his drums. Then Paul plays the riff an octave lower on his Rickenbacker bass. Paul plays a dancing syncopated bass line during the verses. John sings the lead vocals and Paul sings harmony with John on this powerhouse rocking song. "Hey Bulldog" features a piercing fuzz-toned lead guitar solo played by George. In the "you can talk to me" chorus, the high note in the piano chords keeps climbing up, peaking on the word *lonely*. This creates a moving chromatic counterpoint to John's vocals. During the ending chorus of the song, with the piano riff repeating, John and Paul have lots of fun. They talk, bark like dogs, scream, and laugh. Then Paul instructs John to be quiet. As the song fades out, John and Paul sing, "Hey bulldog."

It's time to time travel and go back to early December 1968. . . . Snow is falling lightly, dusting the ground as you and your girlfriend drive to the Christmas tree farm. As always, the car radio is turned on. "Hey Jude" fills the interior of your Volkswagen Beetle. Even though it had been played on local radio stations for three months, you still love hearing the positive message of the song. After choosing a tree and tying it to the Beetle's roof, you drive over the accumulating snow to your house. While setting up the tree on a stand, your girlfriend puts a record on the hi-fi. The sound of a roaring jet taking off cross fades with electric guitars, bass, and drums. Surprised, having never heard the song before, you ask your girlfriend, "What's that amazing song?" "It's 'Back in the U.S.S.R.' on the Beatles' new album. Happy birthday, love!" Thanks to her, it was a happy birthday, and every December you always play the Beatles' White Album, *whether it's snowing or not.*

After returning from India, where the Beatles studied meditation with the Indian yogi the Maharishi, recording sessions began for *The Beatles* album, also known as the *White Album*. The Beatles had written and compiled so many songs that they followed in Bob Dylan's footsteps, who had released the double album *Blonde on Blonde* in 1966. With *The Beatles* album, the band released their one and only double album. The first song on the album is "Back in the U.S.S.R." Written by Paul, who sings lead vocals, plays a banging piano, lead guitar, and bass, he also plays the drums. Where was Ringo? Ringo, who felt as though he wasn't contributing much to the band and didn't feel included or appreciated, had temporarily quit the Beatles. He went sailing on Peter Sellers's yacht in the Mediterranean Sea. Since the remaining three Beatles had a production schedule that they wanted to keep, in Ringo's absence Paul picked up the drumsticks. The recording process that happened in "Back in the U.S.S.R." is extraordinary. On this rare occasion, not only does Paul play drums, but John and George also recorded a drum track. While Paul's drumming is the loudest, there are three drum tracks on the song. And there are three bass players on "Back in the U.S.S.R."—John, Paul, and George. The first bass part was played by John on a Fender six-string bass, then Paul overdubbed a bass part, and George also played a bass part on the six-string bass. Because the Fender bass has six strings, George played some chords when laying down his bass part. The triple-Beatle overdubbing didn't stop. In addition to Paul's lead guitar part, John and George recorded lead guitar parts. Furthermore, George Martin got in on the overdubbing process and recorded a second piano track. When you add all of the instrument overdubs together, you get an eleven-piece band. Therefore, "Back in the "U.S.S.R." has a dense, multilayered sound. The song begins and ends with a roaring jet. Ever since "Yellow Submarine," sound effects were a popular addition to some of the Beatles' arrangements. The song has a Beach Boys style to it, especially the bridge, where John and George sing low- and high-pitched background vocals. It just so happened that Mike Love of the Beach Boys was with the Beatles in India, where Paul wrote the song. Rather than singing about and complimenting girls from the United Kingdom, the United States, or different parts of the world, "Back in the U.S.S.R." raves about Ukrainian and Russian girls.

"Glass Onion," written by John for the most part, begins with Ringo executing two hard hits on his snare drum. In England, a glass onion is a slang phrase used to describe a monocle. The lyrics in this song incorporate titles and lyrics from earlier Beatles songs. Listen to "Glass Onion" and see if you can pick all of them out. When John mentions the song "The Fool on the Hill," a recorder is played by Paul. The recorder is a featured instrument in "The Fool on the Hill." In "Glass Onion," John declares that Paul was the walrus, which contradicts John singing that he, John, is the walrus in the song "I Am the Walrus." Was John just playing with listeners' heads and having fun? Probably. John certainly enjoyed playing with words and lyrics. The sound of Paul's bass has both a booming bottom low end and a bright top end. This is another illustration of the Beatles' endless desire to get new sounds with their instruments and on their recordings. Uncharacteristic with the rock style of the song, "Glass Onion" has a double string quartet mixed into it, arranged by George Martin. After the rocking Beatles stop playing, "Glass Onion" ends with the isolated strings, complete with a pizzicato cello part.

"Happiness Is a Warm Gun," written by John, is a medley of three different songs woven together. Prior to the third part, which is the song's title, the lyrics are abstract, intriguing, and metaphorical. For instance, who is "Mother Superior"? What is "the velvet hand like a lizard on a windowpane"? Could "I need a fix" be heroin related? Can "finger on your trigger" be construed as being a sexual reference? Only John knows the answer to these questions. This is not the first time John wrote abstract lyrics. The lyrics in "I Am the Walrus," which I cover in chapter 9, "Recording Studio Wizardry: Psychedelic and Electronic Songs," are abstract as well. John was inspired to write "Happiness Is a Warm Gun" after seeing the cover of a rifle magazine in the recording studio. The song begins rather quietly, with John fingerpicking his guitar and singing about a girl who doesn't miss much. Then the song gets heavier when John sings about a man with multicolored hobnail boots. The music moves on to the second song, switching to three-four time with a snarling electric guitar. John and Paul sing in octaves about needing a fix and Mother Superior jumping the gun. After she jumps the gun, happiness begins. The style of the "happiness" song is rooted in traditional 1950s rock and roll, except for when the bridge goes back to three-four time. When the music retards before the final chords and Ringo's thumping drums, John sings a high falsetto "gun." The background "happiness" and "oh yeah" voices, sung in harmony by John, Paul, and George, are superb. Even though the Beatles were quarreling with each other during the *White Album* recording sessions, when they sing "happiness" together, they really do sound happy.

With "I'm So Tired," written by John, he delivers a slow, sleepy vocal and then leaps high before singing the chorus. In the chorus, John sings that he's going insane and is willing to give up everything for peace of mind. Paul harmonizes with John on the choruses. After the first chorus, John returns to a drowsy second verse. "I'm So Tired" is a dichotomy—John is so tired, but he can't sleep. The tired parts are the verses; the can't-sleep parts are the choruses. The musical arrangement, which includes John playing acoustic and electric guitars and organ, George playing electric guitar, and Paul playing bass and electric piano, underscores the difference between the verses and choruses. The music is light during the verses; the music is heavier and rocks out on the choruses. Ringo plays drum fills on the repeated ending chorus. After the music stops, John says something that sounds like gibberish. When played backward, it sounds like he is saying, "Paul's a dead man, miss him, miss him." John was especially fond of backward recording techniques. A year later in 1969, something known as the Paul McCartney death hoax caused quite a stir in the media and fueled record sales. Clues about Paul's supposed death were pointed out in lyrics, on album covers, and with backward messages. The Beatles denied that they had planted the clues deliberately, but I believe they did and were just having fun and being creative. Did Paul really die? Some people believe so. Last I heard, Paul's traversing the globe and performing concerts with his band for thousands of fans.

When Paul was in India, he saw two monkeys having intercourse in a road and as a result wrote "Why Don't We Do It in the Road?" Musically, this song is simple, built on a three-chord progression, and has minimal repetitive lyrics. What makes "Why Don't We Do It in the Road?" interesting is Paul's voice. His vocal tone is similar to his Little Richard style of singing, but in this song he pushes the envelope. Paul's vocals are gritty. He also hits a high falsetto leap and ends with a growl. "Why Don't We Do It in the Road?" is another instance on the *White Album* where Paul plays most of the instruments, except for the drums, played by Ringo. Increasingly, the Beatles were functioning more as solo artists rather than a band. This evolution was an unconcealed sign that led to the Beatles' eventual demise.

"Birthday" has a jam-session quality about it. The song is built on an electric guitar riff, which is answered by George's melodic bass line and then with lyrics in the verses. This happy-spirited song was written primarily by Paul, who plays the piano part. John plays lead guitar on "Birthday." A high-energy rocker with Paul screaming vocals in his upper register, John sings a lower harmony part with Paul. Ringo plays eight measures of drums before the song goes into the "going to a party, party" middle section, followed by a chromatic ascending and descending guitar and keyboard lick, with voices singing, "I would like you to dance." An instrumental section, based on the opening riff, takes place, followed by a variation of the main guitar riff doubled on the bass, which goes into the middle section one more time. "Birthday" ends with the energy-packed guitar riff and charged vocals. The high background vocals are a unique combination of singers. Yoko Ono, who by this time was constantly at John's side, and George's wife Pattie, sing on the word *birthday*. All present recorded handclaps, including the Beatles' road manager Mal Evans. While it is a favorite birthday song with many fans, John considered "Birthday" to be a piece of garbage.

"Yer Blues" is a raw, bare-bones blues song written and sung by John. The lyrics to this song are frightfully sad and depressing when John sings repeatedly that he wants to die, feels suicidal, and hates rock and roll. A rhythmically diverse song, in one of the verses, John sings, "Just like Dylan's Mr. Jones," which is a reference to Bob Dylan's 1965 song "Ballad of a Thin Man." The blues movement was happening in England in 1968, with musicians such as John Mayall and Eric Clapton playing and singing the blues. "Yer Blues" can be interpreted to be a tongue-in-cheek parody of a blues song. Lead guitar parts are played by John and George. Ringo provides a splashy drum track and outstanding fills around John's vocals. The first lead guitar solo, played by John on his low strings, is manically repetitive, followed by George's stinging solo. John's recorded low-level vocals, which he sang when recording the music, can be heard as the song fades out. This "ghost" vocal track bled onto microphones that recorded the instruments and could not be removed. The minimal production sound of "Yer Blues" is a precursor to what John did with most of the songs on his first solo album, *Plastic Ono Band*, in 1970.

"Everybody's Got Something to Hide Except for Me and My Monkey" is the longest title in the Beatles' song catalog. The working title was much shorter: "Come on, Come On." Written by John, who sings the screaming lead vocals, he claimed that the song is about him and Yoko. "Everybody's Got Something to Hide Except for Me and My Monkey" begins with a bright electric guitar playing on the first, second, and third beats. A lead guitar riff played by George, which happens over the course of seven beats, occurs between the verses. The song has a rattling bell played by Paul during the verses and ending. Before the song ends, a series of uneven layered voices say "come on," followed by Paul's syncopated bass line and a repetitive distorted guitar. Then you hear the "come on" voices again during the fade-out. Some people believe that "Everybody's Got Something to Hide Except for Me and My Monkey," which contains the lyrics "the deeper you go" and "the higher you fly," is about heroin. Given that *monkey* was a slang word for heroin, the association makes even more sense.

After returning from India, John wrote "Sexy Sadie." A moderate-tempo song with a lead vocal by John that goes higher than his usual range, "Sexy Sadie" is not about a sexy woman. Instead, it's about the yogi Maharishi. John was disillusioned and felt duped by the Maharishi, who allegedly made sexual advances toward Mia Farrow, who was with the Beatles at the Maharishi's meditation retreat. When John told the Maharishi that he was leaving the ashram, the Maharishi asked why.

John responded by saying, "If you're so cosmic, then you'll know why." A rather obscure song by the Beatles, Paul and George sing sweeping background vocals, Paul plays a dance-like piano part, and George plays note-bending guitar riffs. There are a lot of chords in "Sexy Sadie," and the chord progression is unlike most Beatles songs, which makes "Sexy Sadie" all the more intriguing.

Paul was inspired to write "Helter Skelter" after reading an article about Pete Townshend claiming that his band the Who had recorded the hardest, loudest, dirtiest rock-and-roll song, titled "I Can See for Miles." Paul figured he and the Beatles could top the Who. "Helter Skelter" demonstrates Paul's hard-rock vocals, as he laid down one of his best-ever rock vocal tracks. "Helter Skelter" is an aggressive, screaming rocker with blistering guitar parts and abundant sound effects. The song is cacophonous and dissonant—at times the music sounds like it is colliding with itself. Paul, George, and John play electric guitars, and John also plays a busy bass part on a six-string bass. When listening to "Helter Skelter," you will hear the chaotic, slippery, spiraling music fade out toward the end of the song, and then it fades back in. This is the same fading technique they used with "Strawberry Fields Forever." The Beatles had spent many hours recording this intense song, and at the end of the eighteenth version, which is the one that's on the *White Album*, Ringo screams, "I've blisters on my fingers!" followed by a cymbal crash. Listen to "I Can See for Miles" and "Helter Skelter" and decide for yourself if the Beatles outdid the Who.

1969

It's October 1969, and you walk up a black metal spiral staircase to a living room with wooden, vaulted ceilings. In the four upper corners, where the walls meet the ceiling, are speakers. Your friend has a surprise for you. You sit in the black leather beanbag chair while she puts an album on the turntable, part of a new stereo system. You hear a deep, rolling melodic bass line along with a series of drumrolls. Wait, is someone saying "shoot me"? As soon as you hear "here come ole flat top," you recognize John's voice. Your friend hands you the album cover and you see John, Ringo, Paul, and George crossing a street. The images of the Beatles are so well known that the name Beatles doesn't appear on the front cover. Their photograph is all that is needed. The songs from the Beatles' new album, Abbey Road, resonate off the wooden ceiling and reverberate in your head for the rest of the year.

John wrote the opening song on *Abbey Road*, "Come Together." This chart-topping single is rooted in Paul's melodic bass line and Ringo's quick rolling drum pattern, which he plays in the introduction, between the verses, and after the choruses. During the instrumental section and in the long chorus fade-out, Ringo plays his entire kit with drumrolls and crashing cymbals. The inventive, electric piano part was created by Paul but played by John on the recording. Another example of the developing solo-Beatle atmosphere at the time of this July 1969 recording is that Paul wanted to sing with John on the chorus, but John told Paul that he would do the vocal overdubs. Paul does sing harmony with John on some of the verses. The middle instrumental section highlights John's piano playing and George's lead guitar part. The abstract lyrics make references to "I Am the Walrus," Yoko, Muddy Waters, and shooting Coca-Cola. Unfortunately, John got in copyright trouble for using a melody in "Come Together" that is too similar to a melody that Chuck Berry used in his song "You Can't Catch Me." To further complicate matters, John also used some of Chuck's lyrics. A law suit was settled by John agreeing to record some of Chuck's published songs, which resulted in John recording his 1974 *Rock and Roll* album. During the opening bass riff and drum pattern in "Come Together," John does say "shoot me." Given the horrific, senseless killing of John, which occurred on December 8, 1980, eleven years after "Come Together" was released, John's words are both eerie and tragically prophetic.

Tapping his Fats Domino rock-and-roll roots, Paul wrote and sings the rhythm-and-blues-styled "Oh! Darling." His vocals are ferocious during the bridge as he sings his heart out. Paul recorded his lead vocal part for several days until he was satisfied with it. John was not impressed with Paul's lead vocals and thought that he himself would have delivered a better vocal performance. George and John sing background vocals that are barely audible. Like he did on many Beatles songs, George strikes chords on the second and fourth beats. He also plays an electric guitar arpeggio part during the bridge. One would think that Paul plays the piano on "Oh! Darling," having written the song. But no, it's John who plays the pounding piano. I'd be surprised if he didn't break a string or two when banging on the instrument. George ends "Oh! Darling," playing a series of electrified descending tremolo notes.

A harmonically sophisticated piano part, played by Paul, introduces his song "You Never Give Me Your Money," which is actually a series of different songs woven seamlessly together. The songs in the medley on side two of *Abbey Road*, an innovative form at the time, are songs that John and Paul stitched together. John had said that the medley was a good way to "get rid" of his songs. The medley, which was Paul's idea, begins with "You Never Give Me Your Money." Paul sings about "funny money," a reference to the financial problems the Beatles were having with their Apple Corps. company. Beginning with the piano, subtle electric guitars accompany Paul's vocals. Beautiful light harmonies sung by John and George join Paul on the second verse. The song segues into an up-tempo, boogie-woogie second section, where Paul sings, "All the money's gone." The third "magic feeling" and "nowhere to go" section happens, followed by contrapuntal electric guitar parts played by George and John, with background vocal *ah*s. Then a climbing electric guitar solo, with Ringo pounding out accents, brings the listener into the "one sweet dream" section, about stepping on the gas and getting away. The lyrics "step on the gas and wipe those tears away" refer to getting away from the business problems that the Beatles were having. All three Beatles sweetly sing, "One, two, three, four, five, six, seven, all good children go to heaven," adorned with a guitar solo and arpeggios played on guitars, along with Paul playing a descending bass line, topped off with his high-octave notes. The song ends with bells, wind chimes, birds, chirping crickets, and the sound of bubbles, which segues into the next song, "Sun King."

"Sun King," the second song in the medley on side two of *Abbey Road*, features exquisite multitracked vocal harmonies sung by John, Paul, and George. At the beginning of "Sun King," John and George play dreamy-sounding electric guitars, which move from right to left and back again across the stereo spectrum. Paul's bass notes are perfectly placed between the guitar parts. George Martin plays the organ, which is one of the last times he played keyboards on a Beatles recording. A positive, mellow song written by John about everybody being happy and laughing, "Sun King" has ending harmony vocals sung in a combination of different languages that mean nothing in particular. Thematically, John's "Sun King," with the lyrics "here comes the sun king," ties in nicely with George's "Here Comes the Sun." Both songs are on side two of the *Abbey Road* album.

"Mean Mr. Mustard," the third song in the medley written by John, is about a miserly man. After nearly four years since "Think for Yourself," Paul once again plays a fuzz bass line. After the first verse about a man who shaves in the dark, Paul joins John's lead vocals with tight harmony. John plays rhythm guitar, organ, and maracas on "Mean Mr. Mustard." George chimes in with lead guitar lines. Unlike the rest of the song, which is in four-four time, the last chorus is in three-four time and segues directly into the fourth song, "Polythene Pam."

Another short, rocking song written by John, "Polythene Pam" is about a girl dressed in polythene whom John met. This quick-paced song is guitar dominant. John plays a big-sounding, twelve-string acoustic guitar, and George displays lead guitar punches and a solo, which he plays after John says, "Hit it mate!" Ringo plays a busy driving drum part and also plays the tambourine. John, Paul, and George sing "yeah, yeah, yeah," the same lyrics they sang in "She Loves You." John was not fond of "Polythene Pam" and "Mean Mr. Mustard." In *The Beatles Anthology*, he said they were "a bit of crap I wrote in India." A descending guitar riff at the end of "Polythene Pam" provides a musical transition to "She Came in through the Bathroom Window."

The fifth song in the medley, "She Came in through the Bathroom Window," was written by Paul. "She Came in through the Bathroom Window" was inspired by avid female fans, also known as Apple Scruffs, who got into Paul's house by climbing up a ladder and going through the bathroom window. The lyrics about stealing are based on the girls who stole some of Paul's photographs and his clothes. Paul sings the lead vocals and harmonizes with himself on the chorus. John and George sing distant harmonies in the background. During the second verse, where Paul sings about the dancer who "worked in fifteen clubs a day," you can hear the sounds of a whip, played by Ringo. Paul's bass playing in the second verse is rhythmically outstanding. John plays his twelve-string acoustic guitar, and George weaves his lead guitar lines between Paul's lead vocals.

Released as a Beatles single in 1969, "The Ballad of John and Yoko" is an autobiographical story about what was going on in their lives at that time. Even though the recording was released as a Beatles single, it is actually not the Beatles; it's only John and Paul. John sings lead vocals, plays lead guitar and rhythm guitar, and Paul plays piano, bass, drums, and maracas on this "getting back to their rock-and-roll roots" song. Paul sings harmony with John and on part of the bridge, where they sing, "When you're dead, you don't take nothing with you but your soul." The two of them sing the last verse and chorus together. Even though some American radio stations banned the song because of the lyrics "Christ you know it ain't easy" and "crucify me," "The Ballad of John and Yoko" was a number one hit in the United Kingdom and a Top 10 hit in the United States.

George wrote and sings lead vocals on "Old Brown Shoe," the B-side to "The Ballad of John and Yoko." He plays lead guitar, organ, and a fast-paced bass part, especially on the bridge. Paul's contribution to the song is playing the tack piano part and singing backing vocals. John doesn't play any instruments on "Old Brown Shoe," but he does sing backing vocals with Paul. Similar to the lyric structure of "Hello, Good-bye," the lyrics in "Old Brown Shoe" deal with opposites: right and wrong, up and down, and smile and frown. George's flashy lead guitar solo leaps and soars. You can hear Paul and John wailing high notes as they sing on the fade-out.

"I Me Mine," another song written by George, is significant in Beatles history. It marks the last time Paul, George, and Ringo worked together as a band in the recording studio, which occurred on January 3, 1970. By this time, John had unofficially quit the Beatles and was traveling outside of England. George sings an emotional lead vocal and plays acoustic and electric guitars. Paul plays bass, organ, and electric piano, and like an anchor, trusty Ringo plays his drums. "I Me Mine" has two distinctly different sections. The verses are in three-four time; the choruses rock out in four-four time. The transition from three-four to four-four time is maneuvered by Ringo's shuffle rhythm played on his cymbal and drums. Paul sings harmony with George on the rocking choruses. Getting back to three-four time after the chorus, the song takes on a heavy waltz feel. Producer Phil Spector, known for his "wall of sound" production techniques, added strings and brass to the three-Beatle recording, which you can hear on the original *Let It Be* album. "I Me Mine" is a sad song about George perceiving John and Paul as being selfish and his interpretation of the breakup of the Beatles.

The scope and range of the songs in these two rock-and-roll originals chapters are truly a definitive testament to the Beatles and their mammoth creative output. But there's so much more, as you will read about in the chapters that follow.

Suggested Listening: The entire *Sgt. Pepper's Lonely Hearts Club Band* album; "Sexy Sadie"; "Helter Skelter"; "Hey Bulldog"; "You Never Give Me Your Money"

4

PLAYING AMERICA'S HEART STRINGS

Love Songs

The Beatles wrote many love songs. Some of them are ballads; some of them are rockers. The Beatles' love songs go beyond being appealing—they became timeless classics. Some of the songs are lush with vocal harmonies, while others feature solo vocals by one of the Beatles. The melodies, chord progressions, and lyrics that evolve beyond the simplicity of boy meets girl and falls in love are what makes these love songs extraordinary classics.

"Love Me Do," one of the first love songs written primarily by Paul when he was sixteen, is straightforward, simple, with effective lyrics. John plays a bluesy harmonica, starting with the opening riff, repeated throughout the song, plus a harmonica solo. When John was a child staying at his aunt Mimi's house, Mimi's acquaintance Harold Phillips gave John his first harmonica. "Love Me Do" is the first original song on which John played harmonica, but he played it and recorded it on many songs during the next several years. John and Paul harmonize together on the verses, reminiscent of the Everly Brothers' perfectly blended singing voices. The recording of "Love Me Do" happened on three different dates. On June 6, 1962, with Pete Best on drums, the Beatles recorded their first version. Record producer George Martin was not happy with Pete's drumming, and he made it clear that going forward he would not record the Beatles with Pete Best. George Martin's remarks about Pete's drumming had a significant impact on John, Paul, and George Harrison. They were at a crucial point in their music career, and the three Beatles could not afford to jeopardize their relationship with Martin. Pete was replaced by Ringo Starr, and the Beatles recorded the song again on September 4, 1962. George Martin and Paul were not satisfied with Ringo's drumming. Another recording date was set for September 11. Not willing to take his chances recording the song with Ringo a second time, Martin and engineer Ron Richards brought in studio drummer Andy White. Ringo was relegated to playing the tambourine, and you can be sure that he was not pleased about Andy playing the drums. The recording with Ringo's drumming was released as a single in the United Kingdom in October 1962. The version with Andy White on drums and Ringo playing tambourine was released in the United States in April 1964. This was a bumpy start for Ringo's recording relationship with George Martin, but things quickly improved. At the recording session in November 1962 for their next single, "Please Please Me," Ringo had secured his position as drummer, and the classic Beatles formation was set. In their wildest dreams when they initially recorded this song, the Beatles could not have imagined the magnitude of the millions of fans throughout the world who would soon love them. The Beatles certainly got what they asked for and much more.

The B-side to the "Love Me Do" single, released in the United States in April 1964, is "P.S. I Love You," written by Paul when he was in Hamburg, Germany, in 1962. "P.S. I Love You" is a love song with a brisk cha-cha beat. The lyrics are about long-distance treasured love written in a letter. In the verses, John and George sing harmony with Paul on the first few words of each sentence. All three Beatles sing together on the choruses and on the last verse. When Paul sings "I love you," he emphasizes the word *you* by repeating it. When you listen to Paul sing that word, it sounds personal, as though he is singing to you. Once again, it's Andy White playing the drums, with his drumstick placed across the snare drum and hitting the drum's rim. Recorded the same day that Andy and the Beatles recorded "Love Me Do," Ringo's only contribution to the song is playing maracas.

"Do You Want to Know a Secret?" was written by John for the most part. His inspiration to write the song was influenced by "I'm Wishing," a song from the Disney film *Snow White and the Seven Dwarfs*. When John was a young boy, his mother, Julia, would sing "I'm Wishing," which contain the lyrics "Want to know a secret?" and "Promise not to tell?" George sings the lead vocals, and John and Paul sing background vocals bathed in reverb. "Do You Want to Know a Secret?" is a bouncy love song about whispering and falling in love. During the bridge, Ringo plays percussion along with the snare drum, accentuated by a reverb effect, which makes the arrangement more interesting. Recorded in February 1963, Paul's moving bass lines in "Do You Want to Know a Secret?" demonstrate his natural tendency to play melodic bass lines. The continuity and the powerful effect of singing the word *you* in so many early Beatles songs is part of the magnetic emotional appeal that attracted millions of listeners to the Beatles. "Do You Want to Know a Secret?" was a Top 10 hit single in the United States in the spring of 1964 and was the first hit single sung by George.

Let's travel back in time when singles and albums were sold in record shops. . . . You drop a quarter into the coin box on the bus heading downtown. You're a little nervous and excited because you will be meeting your new girlfriend at the record shop, where you both will buy the Introducing the Beatles *album. Once inside the shop, you meet your girlfriend and hold hands while strolling through the record bins. Then you see it and your eyes light up. There they are—the Beatles— smiling at you on the cover of their new album. After purchasing it, you look at the list of songs on the back of the album cover. Your girlfriend tells you that "P.S. I Love You" is her favorite song. You tell her that "Do You Want to Know a Secret?" is yours. You ask her if she wants to know a secret. She does, and you whisper in her ear that you love her. Beatles songs take you to a place where you can go, a place where you feel the passion and excitement of the Beatles. They are now a big, exciting part of your life, and you begin to live and experience what the Beatles are singing about.*

While George asks, "Do You Want to Know a Secret?," John doesn't ask any questions. When John sings "All I've Got to Do," his crooning, sexy voice underscores the passionate desire to kiss. Written by John, the song begins with a soft, altered chord played by George. "All I've Got to Do" has a seductive nature that pulls you into the song. Paul and George sing background *ahs* and sing harmony on the song's title and on the lyrics "You just gotta call on me." During the verse fade-out, John hums the melody instead of singing lyrics. With the lyrics in this song, John makes it sound so easy. To get a kiss, all he has to do is make a phone call and whisper in her ear.

The slow, sultry sounds of "All I've Got to Do" fade away and make room for the exciting song "All My Loving." Written by Paul when he was on a tour bus in England in 1963, this song arouses the desire to kiss. Unlike most of his songs, with "All My Loving" Paul wrote the lyrics first. Invariably, he writes music first and then comes up with the lyrics. Featuring similar "letter" lyrics as "P.S. I Love You," "All My Loving" sends love in a letter to a faraway girl. John does something different with his rhythm guitar in this song. He plays a rapid, strumming guitar during the verses, which supports Paul's lead vocals. Paul plays a walking bass line, and George plays a rockabilly guitar solo. During the last verse, Paul overdubbed a higher harmony part to his lead vocals. Paul declares that his loving will be true. In a 1980 *Playboy* interview, John praised "All My Loving," saying, "It's a damn good piece of work."

In 1964, telephones with a rotating dial were commonplace in most homes. . . . The beige phone hangs quietly on the wall in the kitchen. You met a cute girl the other day, and you bravely gave her your phone number. She smiled at you and said she would call you. You want to speak with her. You want to whisper in her ear. And you really want to kiss her. All she has to do is call you. How you wish you could be like John. How you wish it could be so easy, just pick up the phone and call her. But you can't because you don't have her phone number. Eventually, she calls you and she invites you to her house, where together you listen to Beatles records and hold hands. You're listening to "All My Loving" through a four-inch speaker on the hi-fi. Now it's time to meet each other's lips. She closes her eyes. You kiss her. The Beatles were writing the script for an entire generation, and you were captivated, driven to follow that exciting, sensational script.

In 1963, while the Beatles were on tour in England, John wrote "This Boy" with Paul. The clean sound of John strumming his Gibson acoustic guitar takes you in, followed by the full band and the vocals. "This Boy" is modeled after the song "To Know Her Is to Love Her," a cover song the Beatles played during their Cavern Club days. The tight three-part harmonies, sung by John, Paul, and George, are warm and move along with the chord progression. Paul sings and weaves in some suspended passing notes. Ringo plays the perfect rhythmic pattern on his hi-hat, matching George's guitar playing. The band opens up on the bridge as it shifts to a different chord progression to match John's emotionally charged lead vocals about how he could be happy, and it peaks on the word *cry*. "This Boy" is a song about competitive, determined love, and this boy prevails.

Fueling fantasies about young love, the fast-paced love song "It Won't Be Long" gives hope to those waiting to be loved. The song begins with the dynamic chorus in which John sings emphatically and repeatedly that it won't be long before he belongs to you, as Paul and George answer him affirmatively, singing, "Yeah, yeah, yeah." There are those Beatle *yeah, yeah, yeah*s again. John endures the waiting, convinced that he will be yours and rejoices singing that "you're coming home" at the end of the bridge. A clever play with the words *be long* and *belong*, the lyrics "be long" will surface again three years later in George's song "Blue Jay Way." In "It Won't Be Long," George's low-string guitar riff provides the perfect musical break in the verses. The song ends with three-part harmony on the word *you*. Once again, the Beatles were singing directly to their audience, telling every boy and girl that it won't be long before they belong to the Beatles.

"I'll Get You," the B-side to "She Loves You," covered in chapter 2, starts with the confident "oh yeah," then instantly gets your attention with the opening lyric that asks you to imagine that "I'm in love with you." The song contains a lyric variation of "yeah, yeah, yeah" from "She Loves You." John and Paul both sing the lead vocals, sometimes in unison (singing the same note), and other times they harmonize on two different notes. John plays the harmonica throughout "I'll Get You," except during the bridge. His harmonica playing demonstrates why the harmonica is also called a mouth organ. John plays long, held sustained notes, like an organ does, which provides a contrast to the vertical rhythm of the song. The Beatles told you that they would get you, and they certainly did.

One of the earlier, obscure love songs, in 1962 John presented "Ask Me Why" to Paul. John was inspired to write this song, having been influenced by the American rhythm-and-blues recording artists Smokey Robinson and the Miracles. "Ask Me Why" begins with the lyrics "I love you." John sings the lead vocals and reaches up to his falsetto voice at the end of the verses. During the bridge, John and Paul emphasize the lyrics "Can't conceive of any more misery." Paul and George sing background vocals and extend the last word in the first line in the verses, such as "you-ooh-ooh-ooh-ooh" and "true-ooh-ooh-ooh-ooh." George plays a bouncy, rhythmic lead guitar part while Ringo provides a cross-stick cha-cha beat. Recorded on November 26, 1962, "Ask Me Why" spotlights John, Paul, and George's vocals.

Moving on from being influenced by Smokey Robinson, a fine example of the Beatles' innovation is the beginning of "Eight Days a Week." The song begins with a fade-in, as if coming from a distance, and gradually reaches full volume just before John sings the opening lyrics, telling you that he needs your love. Paul harmonizes with John on the choruses and bridges. George plays a syncopated, rhythmic lead guitar part, and all four Beatles overdubbed handclaps. The song ends with the same opening chords played over Paul's repetitive single-note bass line. This infectious song's title was what a driver had said to Paul when he was driven to John's house for a writing session. Paul asked the driver how he was, and the driver replied, "Working eight days a week." Like the lyrics say, "Hold me, love me." Seven days in a week was not enough, so the Beatles made it eight. "Eight Days a Week" was a number one hit in the United States in March 1965.

Instead of days, weeks, or months, John reflected on his life when he wrote "In My Life." Written mostly by John, this is a retrospective song with a moving melody that perfectly matches the lyrics as he remembers people and places from his past. John opens up with lyrics that give the listener insights into what he was thinking when the Beatles recorded the song as part of their *Rubber Soul* album. A personal song, John sings about people in his life, some who are living and some who are dead. Even though he loved them all, there is no one compared to *you*—John loves you more. Just before the song ends, John's vocal jumps up to his falsetto voice, and he sings, "In my life" and repeats that he loves you more. Paul and George harmonize with John on the verses and bridges. Ringo's drum patterns during the verse and bridge perfectly complement the rhythm of the melody. On the bridge, Ringo adds tambourine to his ringing ride cymbal. George Martin plays a baroque-styled piano solo, giving the song a classic character. Paul and George sing the beautiful backing vocals. The gentle music and sincere vocals make "In My Life" one of the most popular Beatles songs.

"It's Only Love," written by John and Paul, is on the American *Rubber Soul* album. The song is filled with profound lyrics about the complexities and challenges of a loving relationship. While the sight of her lights up the night, the couple fights every night. It's only love, but it's so hard. When I first heard this song in December 1965, I didn't understand the lyrics. How could love be hard? Naively, I thought that love was easy and what everyone wanted. Many years later, I realized what the lyrics meant. John plays an acoustic rhythm guitar and sings the vocal track. The soaring melody peaks in the chorus on the word *love*. George gives "It's Only Love" a distinct sound with his lead guitar riff played with a tremolo effect. Several years after the recording of "It's Only Love," in a 1980 *Playboy* interview, John said, "I always thought it was a lousy song. The lyrics are abysmal. I always hated that song." John was highly critical of himself and his songs.

The complexities of love disappear with Paul's song "Michelle." An acoustic guitar song, "Michelle" is a tender love song that originally was an instrumental written by Paul. He was inspired to write the song after attending parties in France. John suggested that Paul write some lyrics to the instrumental. Not knowing how to speak French very well, Paul asked the Beatles' friend Ivan Vaughan if his wife, Jan, who was a French teacher, could help him. Jan came up with the phrase "Michelle, ma belle," which are the opening lyrics that Paul sings. John wrote the bridge section with the repetitive "I love you." Aside from the "Frère Jacques" background vocals in "Paperback Writer," "Michelle" is the only Beatles song that has lyrics in French. Paul, John, and George play acoustic guitars. John plays a nylon-string classical guitar, and George plays a twelve-string acoustic. The nylon-string guitar has a softer tone than steel-string acoustic guitars. George's lead guitar part is unusually mellow in tone, adding to the tenderness of the song.

With "Here, There and Everywhere," Paul claims that life is better when he's with his love. His love when he wrote the song in 1966 was actress Jane Asher. Paul was inspired to write this vocally rich love song after hearing the Beach Boys' album *Pet Sounds*. While waiting for John to wake up for a songwriting session, Paul wrote "Here, There and Everywhere" sitting by the outdoor swimming pool at John's house. There are only a few instruments played on the recording. John doesn't play anything, but in addition to singing background vocals with George, John does snap his fingers occasionally. George plays a dreamy electric guitar melody during the bridge. The chord progression in "Here, There and Everywhere" works its way through different tonal centers. When Paul sings, "I want her everywhere" leading into the bridge, the song moves into another key. John and George sing the soft-toned rising and falling backing vocals. In the autobiographical book *Paul McCartney: Many Years from Now*, written by Barry Miles, Paul said that "Here, There and Everywhere" is one of his favorite Beatles songs. John said the same in his 1980 *Playboy* interview.

"All You Need Is Love" is a highly influential, idealistic song written by John, who sings the lead vocals. Coming off the heels of the critically acclaimed, top-selling *Sgt. Pepper's Lonely Hearts Club Band* album, "All You Need Is Love" was the anthem for the 1967 summer of love, when love-ins were happening in parks at major cities in the United States, the United Kingdom, and throughout Europe. Long-haired hippies came together wearing tie-dyed clothing, some with flowers in their hair and peace signs painted on their bodies, and professed peace and love. This message song encapsulates the spirit of the "flower power" peace/love movement that exploded in 1967. Teenagers throughout the world were enraptured with the euphoria of love, and "All You Need Is Love" was their theme song. The song was premiered on the first live global television broadcast, titled *Our World*, on June 25, 1967. Musically, it's complex. The song begins with a brass ensemble playing the French national anthem, "La Marseillaise," followed by John, Paul, and George singing, "Love, love, love." The verses alternate between a bar of four-four time and three-four time. Lyrically, the song is irresistibly positive—John sings that you can do anything as long as you have love. He also sings that love is easy. This an about-face from him singing that love is hard in "It's Only Love." George plays a note-bending guitar solo, mimicking the opening "love, love, love" melody. Paul invites everyone to sing along with the Beatles when he says, "All together now" and "everybody" in the last chorus. (That three-word phrase is the title to the song "All Together Now," which was recorded approximately five weeks *before* "All You Need Is Love." "All Together Now" was eventually released as part of the soundtrack to the *Yellow Submarine* movie in July 1968 and on the *Yellow Submarine* album in January 1969.) Creating a party-like atmosphere and celebration, many of the Beatles' "beautiful people" friends attended the live-televised broadcast, and they happily complied with Paul's invitation to join in the singing. Mick Jagger, Keith Richards, Eric Clapton, Keith Moon, Graham Nash, Jane Asher, Pattie Boyd, and Paul's brother, known as Mike McGear, sang "love is all you need" and clapped during the ending chorus. Paul sings "she loves you" on the long fade-out. The "she loves you" addition cleverly ties one of their first love songs with this 1967 love anthem. Innocently, "All You Need Is Love" is what many teenagers believed to be true. It was a wonderful ideal, which unfortunately couldn't last. But the song and its love message do stand the test of time.

Trans World Airlines was a popular airline in 1967, and one of their popular destinations was San Francisco. . . . You had saved up enough money from working as a waiter at the local sandwich shop to buy an airline ticket. A big love-in was going to be happening in San Francisco, so you go to the nearest Trans World Airlines ticket counter and buy your ticket to ride. "All You Need Is Love" was playing endlessly in your head, and the San Francisco love-in was where you belonged. Once in San Francisco, it didn't take long to find the Haight-Ashbury section of the city. As if being pulled by a magnetic force, you follow a crowd of hippies to Buena Vista Park. You had heard rumors that one or two of the Beatles were going to be in San Francisco. You wondered if you were dreaming and then thought, dreams do come true. You hear a band playing "Sgt. Pepper's Lonely Hearts Club Band." That's a good sign. Suddenly, in the distance you see someone wearing heart-shaped sunglasses strumming a guitar. He looks familiar. You make your way through the crowd surrounding him and hear him singing "With a Little Help from My Friends." It was George Harrison! You try to get closer, but George abruptly stops playing and quickly vanishes into a haze of smoke. Some dreams do come true.

In 1968, John had left his wife Cynthia and began an intimate relationship with Japanese artist Yoko Ono. Paul, who had been friends with Cynthia for years, went to visit her and Julian, Cynthia and John's son. Feeling sorry for little Julian, whose father had left him, Paul said, "Hey Jules, don't make it bad." Paul was giving Julian some emotional support and wanted him to believe that things would get better. As Paul was driving home, he put some of those words to a melody that he had in his head, which would become "Hey Jude." Initially, it was "Hey Jules," but Paul changed it to "Hey Jude" because he thought Jude sounded better. John didn't realize that Paul wrote the song about his son. Instead, John thought Paul wrote the song about him and interpreted the lyrics "go out and get her" as Paul telling John it's okay to be with Yoko.

The Beatles had used pianos on many of their recordings, but with "Hey Jude" the piano became the centerpiece and featured instrument in the song. The huge popularity of guitars had happened largely because of the Beatles and their guitar-dominated songs. With "Hey Jude," pianos and piano ballads became a sudden craze. The song begins with Paul singing "Hey Jude, don't make it bad," along with his piano accompaniment. The tone of Paul's vocals are warm and inviting. John and George enter the song on the second verse, singing background *ahs*, and harmony on the word *better*. John plays acoustic guitar and Ringo plays tambourine in the second verse. On the transition into the first bridge, Ringo plays a series of drum patterns, and in the bridge Paul begins his overdubbed bass part. During the bridge, Paul sings, "Don't carry the world upon your shoulder," and sings about a fool who plays it cool and makes his world a little colder. George's electric guitar playing in "Hey Jude" is minimal, but you can hear him playing in sections of the bridges. John and George sing more harmony with Paul's lead vocals in the third and fourth verses. "Hey Jude" illustrates the Beatles using dynamics effectively. By gradually adding instruments, harmonies, and ultimately a thirty-six-piece orchestra, "Hey Jude" builds dynamically and peaks during the end chorus. The first song to be released on the Beatles' Apple Records label, "Hey Jude" was number one for a staggering nine weeks on the U.S. singles charts from September to November 1968. Its popularity was due in part to the Beatles' desire to be innovative. "Hey Jude" is a remarkable seven minutes, eleven seconds long. The ending chorus runs four minutes, with Paul scatting a variety of screaming vocals soaring above the orchestral arrangement conducted by George Martin. But primarily, the song's appeal is about its positive message—turning a sad situation into something better.

Perhaps you have had the unfortunate painful experience of being dumped by a lover. . . . Your girlfriend, who you had intended to marry, had suddenly dropped you when you went out of town for a week. It was a crushing blow, having been committed and dedicated to her for two years. Feeling depressed, you lay in bed, the bed where you made love with her countless times while listening to every Beatles record you own. Tossing and turning, you lament your loss and try unsuccessfully to get her out of your mind. Then you turn on the radio and hear Paul singing a ballad about taking something sad and making it better. Paul's timely words of wisdom comfort and embrace you. The Beatles and "Hey Jude" make you feel better, better, better.

Soon after the release of "Hey Jude," the short song "I Will" was released on *The Beatles (White Album)*. Paul had the melody in his head for quite some time and worked on the song when he was in India. But he wasn't happy with the lyrics. In September 1968, inspired by his new relationship with Linda Eastman, Paul wrote the love lyrics. Being a perfectionist, Paul kept recording the song until he was satisfied and recorded it a staggering sixty-seven times. Paul plays acoustic guitars, sings the lead vocals, and harmonizes with himself during the bridge and at the end of the song. The sound of the acoustic lead guitar parts glisten in "I Will." Ringo and John play percussion, while George is absent from this recording. If you listen very carefully, you will hear an innovative vocal bass line sung by Paul. A vocal bass line? Yes, and it's extraordinary.

"Julia," a tender love song written and sung by John with a dreamy voice, is about his mother, Julia, who was killed by a drunk driver when John was seventeen years old. You can be sure that the death of John's mother had a long-lasting, devastating effect on him. As an emotional release, he was able to express some of his feelings in the song. But "Julia" is not only about John's mother. Some of the lyrics are about John's newfound love for Yoko Ono. When translated from Japanese to English, Yoko means "child of the sea." John paraphrases those words with the lyrics "ocean child." A number of songs on *The Beatles* were performed by solo Beatles. "Julia" is a rare solo performance by John, who fingerpicks the strings on his acoustic guitar. He learned how to play fingerpicking guitar from singer-songwriter Donovan. Donovan was with the Beatles when they were all together studying meditation with the Maharishi in India, and that's where John wrote "Julia."

A year later, the song "Because" tantalizes your ears with classical sounding music played on an electric harpsichord by George Martin. Then the same musical notes are doubled on an electric guitar played by John. John, Paul, and George softly sing "ah" before the first verse. "Because," written by John, is one of the last love songs recorded by the Beatles and appears on the *Abbey Road* album. The three-part harmony sung by John, Paul, and George is breathtakingly beautiful. Creating a lush, layered effect, they overdubbed their voices twice. George Harrison plays a synthesizer solo toward the end of the song. In 1969,

George had recently acquired a Moog synthesizer and used it on a number of songs on *Abbey Road*. Love may be old, love may be new, but the bottom line is that love is you. A return to personalizing their lyrics, as they did with their earlier love songs, the emphasis is on you, the listener. As if unwilling to end the song, the final chord doesn't resolve; it leaves you suspended on an unresolved chord. But it does serve as a segue to "You Never Give Me Your Money" on *Abbey Road*.

With the prevailing dominance and abundance of John's and Paul's songwriting output, in comparison, George contributed only a few songs per album. As the Beatles were falling apart in 1969, due in part to growing business differences after the death of their manager, Brian Epstein, George wrote "Something." Initially, George had presented "Something" to John and Paul during the Beatles' "Get Back" sessions in January 1969, but John and Paul were not enthused. That all changed when the Beatles got back together for the last time to work on the *Abbey Road* album. Knowing that it would be their final recording as a four-piece group, their mood and temperament toward each other improved and was amicable. George's opening lyrics are the same as the song title "Something in the Way She Moves," a different song written by James Taylor, who at the time was an Apple recording artist. Pattie Boyd, George's wife in 1969, claims that the lyrics are about her. Initially, George said they were, but years later, after they had divorced, he denied it. "Something" was released as a double-sided A single in October 1969, along with John's "Come Together." Harmonically, "Something" is in two entirely different keys, which dramatically delineates the verse from the bridge. The verses and guitar-riff chorus are in C, while the bridge is in A. There is no harmonic relationship between the two different keys, yet the Beatles weave them together seamlessly. The way the Beatles play their instruments on "Something" demonstrates their superb musicianship. George's critically acclaimed lead guitar solo is considered to be one of his best ever. Paul's melodic bass part is brilliant—very busy yet perfect with the chord progression and doesn't step on George's vocals. Ringo's drum fills are perfectly placed throughout the song, and his rapid hi-hat playing during the bridge adds to the drama of not knowing if love will grow, as George sings the highest notes in the song. John plays a dramatic descending low piano part after George sings "I don't know" in the bridge. After the second time John plays it, the song returns to the verse in the key of C, where George plays his heartfelt guitar solo. Adding to the song's arrangement, Billy Preston played the organ and George Martin wrote and conducted an orchestral score. Frank Sinatra said "Something" was the best love song ever written by John and Paul, not realizing that George had written it. George finally received his long-overdue success as a songwriter with the Beatles and achieved his first number one Beatles hit single.

Suggested Listening: "All My Loving"; "This Boy"; "In My Life"; "Here, There and Everywhere"; "All You Need Is Love"; "Hey Jude"; "Because"; "Something"

5

LIVE BEATLES

The Ed Sullivan Show and Live Concert Songs

In the northeast part of the United States, January 1964 was a frozen, dreary month. After the holidays in December, which were muted because of President John F. Kennedy's recent assassination, everything seemed to be quiet, dull, and depressed. Little did American teens know that their world would dramatically change one month later when the Beatles came to America for the first time.

The Pan Am jet slowly taxied to the gate at John F. Kennedy International Airport on February 7, 1964. Thousands of fans were waiting in the cold winter air for the Beatles to arrive. Four young men emerged from the jet with mop-top hairdos. They smiled and waved to the screaming fans. That was the first time the Beatles set their Cuban heeled boots in America. Their music, charm, wit, and winning personalities would soon do exactly what they had set out to do—conquer America.

In advance of their arrival, Capitol Records released *Meet the Beatles!* Shrewd businessman Brian Epstein knew that the best way for the Beatles to reach millions of American teenagers was for them to perform on *The Ed Sullivan Show*. In 1964, *The Ed Sullivan Show* was the most popular television program on Sunday nights, having established a wide demographic of millions of dedicated viewers. On February 9, the Beatles performed on *The Ed Sullivan Show* and played the following songs from *Meet the Beatles!*: "All My Loving," "Till There Was You," "I

Saw Her Standing There," and "I Want to Hold Your Hand." They also performed "She Loves You," which was released as a single on the Swan Records label. On the CBS television stage, the Beatles exuded explosive positive energy. They looked different from American recording artists at the time. Elvis, the Everly Brothers, Chuck Berry, and the Beach Boys wore their hair combed back, away from their faces. The Beatles combed their hair down, covering their foreheads, and believe it or not, in 1964 the Beatles' hair was considered to be long. And they sounded different. Most bands in the United States played Fender or Gibson guitars, but John played a black, solid-body Rickenbacker guitar, George played a Gretsch Country Gentleman guitar, and Paul played a Hofner bass. But more important, the songs and their singing voices didn't sound like American songs and singers. The Beatles sang with Liverpudlian accents, and their original songs, "All My Loving," "I Want to Hold Your Hand," and "She Loves You," had more than the typical three or four chord progressions used in most rock-and-roll songs at the time.

In early February 1964, radio stations and newspapers were all abuzz about the Beatles. . . . "I Want to Hold Your Hand" was playing on radio stations and photos of the Beatles popped up in newspapers along with announcements that they would be performing on The Ed Sullivan Show. *Sitting on the couch won't do; you have to get closer to the black-and-white Philco television set, so you sit on the floor. Filled with anticipation, you are beyond excited. After watching some dancing dogs and a comedian, Ed says, "Ladies and gentlemen, the Beatles!" The audience erupts with screams. The Beatles are all smiles, and then Paul, holding a bass guitar shaped like a violin, sings, "Close your eyes and I'll kiss you." John strums his electric guitar, George picks his electric guitar strings, Ringo sways on his drum stool, and "All My Loving" ignites your fascination with the Liverpudlian band. Beatlemania instantly takes hold of you. The next day, you go to school with your hair combed down on your forehead and turn the lapels of your sport coat inside, trying to look like a mop-top, collarless Beatle.*

Ed Sullivan's studio audience was packed with teenage girls who could barely stay seated. A flood of screams rushed toward the Beatles. Polished, experienced, and riding on a wave of successful tours in England and Europe, the Beatles performed with confident, professional ease. Girls in the audience felt as though the Beatles were singing to them, and they became infatuated with the Beatles. Every time the Beatles sang high-pitched notes and shook their long-haired heads, the audience went wild and screamed. Not only was this sensational, emotional impact affecting the live studio audience, in millions of homes throughout America, teenage girls and boys were mesmerized and knocked out by the Beatles' performance. The band gave American teenagers something hopeful and exciting, something new, something that they could be a part of—a new-sounding Beatle band that would be their very own.

When the Beatles performed at concerts, they had perfected a set list of songs that built to a climatic frenzy. Their first U.S. concert happened in Washington, DC, on February 11, 1964. A snow storm blanketed the northeastern coast, grounding flights at New York City airports. After their wildly successful *Ed Sullivan Show* performance, where reportedly a staggering seventy-three million people tuned in, the Beatles traveled by train from New York City to Washington, DC, to perform their first concert in America at the Washington Coliseum. The stage, which was a reconfigured boxing ring located in the center of the Coliseum, presented a challenge for the Beatles. Inevitably, at different times during the show, some of the audience didn't see the Beatles' faces—they saw only their backs. To appease the crowd and do their best to accommodate all four sides of the audience, after playing a number of songs, the Beatles and stage crew moved the microphones and Ringo's drum kit around. Fortunately, Ringo's drums were on a rotating circular platform. The Beatles' Vox amplifiers remained facing one side of the audience. The Beatles' historic performance knocked out the crowd, and all sides of the audience loved the show.

As soon as the Beatles came on to the center stage, the crowd of eight thousand excited fans erupted with screams. The Beatles began their twelve-song set and played "Roll Over Beethoven," with George singing lead vocals. Instantly, the Beatles were bathed in a burst of flashbulbs from cameras documenting this historic event. Unfortunately, George's microphone wasn't working properly, so he dashed over to John's microphone, which picked up his voice and sent it into the Coliseum. Most of the audience had seen the Beatles on *The Ed Sullivan Show* and had already accepted them with wide-open arms. Seeing them live in person was thrilling, and the key word is *seeing* the Beatles. The PA systems in 1964 weren't built to overcome and cut through massive waves of screaming fans, so hearing the Beatles was difficult. Seeing the Beatles rather than hearing them would become the norm. That, along with other factors, would eventually lead to the end of the Beatles' live concert performances.

For their second song, the Beatles performed "From Me to You." John and Paul sang together on the same microphone. Because Paul is left handed and plays a left-handed bass, his instrument didn't point at John, and John's right-handed guitar pointed away from Paul. Visually and physically, they fit perfectly together, like bookends. Their voices also fit together as well, singing in unison and harmonizing with a distinct Liverpudlian blend. The Beatles had everything the audience wanted—true hearts and lips that want to kiss "you." Ringo's drumming in "From Me to You," and throughout the entire concert, was forceful and provided John, Paul, and George with the rhythmic percussive foundation while never overplaying or stepping on their vocals. At times, Ringo attacked the drums with so much intensity it's surprising his drums didn't go flying off the circular platform. Paul's posturing onstage was readily apparent. Clearly, he was the director, counting off the beginning of songs, turning toward and prompting George during George's guitar solos, and speaking to the audience between songs. Even though it was John's band from the very beginning days of the Quarrymen, his first band, Paul was the spokesman and leader onstage.

Paul asked the crowd to clap their hands and stamp their feet, and then the Beatles played a riveting "I Saw Her Standing There" before the enthralled crowd. During George's lead guitar solo, Ringo fiercely pounded his drums. When John harmonized with Paul on the chorus, they sang together on one microphone. The girls in the audience could not contain themselves, and the unrelenting screams continued.

The Beatles got quieter when they played "This Boy," which features John, Paul, and George in three-part harmony. They sang together on one microphone and portrayed a physical closeness as a unified trio of singers as their voices blended together. Then they performed another love song, "All My Loving," the first song that they had played on *The Ed Sullivan Show*. As if scripted, when George harmonized with Paul on the last verse, deafening screams erupted.

The spotlight was put on Ringo when he sang "I Wanna Be Your Man." Quite remarkably, one of the two microphones on straight stands was given to Ringo and placed between his face and drum kit. It didn't have a boom extension, so Ringo had to juggle his way around the microphone while singing, and fortunately his drumming was not hampered at all. Compared with today's standards, audio equipment in 1964 was primitive. With each Beatle being featured as a singer, the audience members became enraptured with their favorite Beatle. When three or four of them sang together, the audience was driven over the top and became emotionally overwhelmed.

While performing their songs, some of the fans threw jelly beans at the Beatles. During a TV interview that George gave in England before the Beatles came to the United States, George said that he loved jelly babies, which are softer than the hard-coated American jelly beans. He would have preferred to have received them as a gift, but instead some fans brought jelly beans to the concert. Throwing them at the Beatles while they performed was distracting and potentially dangerous if a jelly bean had hit their eyes. When the Beatles started playing "Please Please Me," George got stung by jelly beans by a girl sitting in the front row who flung them at the stage. Fortunately, the Beatles were facing the opposite audience so it was only George's back that got hit.

Slowing down the pace and catching their breath, the Beatles played "Till There Was You." Even though this show-tune ballad, which Paul sang, was quieter than the rockers, the screams continued. With four more songs to play, the Beatles began their perfectly crafted crescendo finale and played "She Loves You," accompanied by earth-shattering screams from the out-of-control audience. The personal lyrics of "She Loves You" and "I Want to Hold Your Hand" drove the audience into fits of hysteria. At the beginning of "I Want to Hold Your Hand," John played the wrong chord. George was very surprised and laughed. Since there was no response from Paul, he more than likely didn't hear it. Before they played "Twist and Shout," John danced a few funny steps while Ringo accompanied him with some drumbeats. The crowd loved this zany side of John, and he would use this funny-dance bit throughout their touring years. They played twelve songs, packed into one thirty-five-minute set, and the set list was constructed in a way that built to a frenzied, pandemonium-filled climax with Paul belting out "Long Tall Sally." During the last chorus of "Long Tall Sally," Ringo, like a wild man, smacked the drums with a ferocious, thundering drum pattern. With so many years of performing experience under their belts, the Beatles knew exactly how to work an audience to the boiling point.

Infectious Beatlemania exploded at the Coliseum, and the Beatles were thrilled to be performing their first U.S. concert. The amount of energy that they put out came back at them a thousandfold. Anyone who was fortunate enough to attend the concert saw that the Beatles were hard-working musicians who had polished and perfected their performance skills. With manners, the Beatles bowed to the audience at the end of this amazing performance.

Transistor radios were popular in 1964, and this is what is was like to hear the Beatles on those battery-operated products. . . . You are thrilled when you listen to your transistor radio and hear Beatles song after Beatles song. You see the Beatles' faces in newspapers and maga-zines. You hear their voices during interviews on the radio. The Beatles are everywhere, and you are determined to see them perform while they are in New York City. Being one of the lucky ones, you get a ticket to see them at Carnegie Hall at their first show at 7:30 p.m. The plush, ma-roon-seated hall is packed with an overflowing crowd. You take your seat, a good seat, eighth row center. Much to your surprise, to accom-modate the overflowing crowd, dozens of chairs are on the stage, and people are sitting on them. You wonder who those extremely lucky peo-ple are. Could they be friends and relatives of the Rockefellers, celeb-rities, and local politicians? A constant, exciting buzz fills the hall as everyone anxiously awaits the Beatles coming onstage.

Hardly catching their breath after their exhilarating concert in Washington, DC, the next day, on February 12, the Beatles performed two concerts at New York City's prestigious Carnegie Hall. Concert promoter Sid Bernstein booked the Beatles to play two shows at Carne-gie Hall before getting approval from Brian Epstein. That's how confi-dent Sid was, and sure enough, tickets for both shows quickly sold out. The Beatles were whisked away in a taxicab from where they were staying at the Plaza Hotel and snuck backstage at Carnegie Hall. On-stage, the Beatles performed the same twelve songs in their set list as they had performed the night before in Washington. It was an unprece-dented night at Carnegie Hall. The Beatles were surprised and uncom-fortable with people sitting just a few feet away from them onstage. The stage had always belonged to the Beatles; fans were never allowed on-stage—they belonged in the audience. When the Beatles performed, people in the audience stood up. Those sitting in the rows behind them couldn't see the band, so they stood on their seats and armrests. Undeterred, yet not pleased with the circumstances, the Beatles repeated their Washington, DC, show with professional ease and the audience was thrilled. Unfortunately, the excited audience caused damage to the seats and armrests. Carnegie Hall is not suitable for rock-and-roll shows; it was built and designed for more refined, controlled classical concerts. Wanting to capture the Beatles' performance, George Martin, their London record producer who was in New York, wanted to record the concert at Carnegie Hall, but the local New York musicians' union wouldn't allow it. George Martin was disappointed, and the Beatles were not happy with the Carnegie Hall experience. But Sid Bernstein was very pleased with the overflowing crowd, and he had another Beatles concert in mind. He spoke with Brian Epstein and tried to convince Brian to let him book the Beatles at Madison Square Garden while they were still in New York. Sid was sure that with the Beatles' huge popularity, he could easily sell all the seats in Madison Square Garden. Brian turned Sid's offer down, but their relationship would result in the biggest concert the Beatles would ever play the following year at Shea Stadium.

Moving at a fast clip, the Beatles flew to Miami to make their second appearance on *The Ed Sullivan Show*, broadcast from the Deauville Hotel. When Brian had met with Ed Sullivan in November 1963, a two-Beatles-appearance deal was made, plus an additional prerecorded segment to be broadcast on February 23. Given the nasty cold weather in New York and Washington, DC, and the dreary cold weather back home in England, the Beatles loved sunny, warm Miami. On Sunday, February 16, the Beatles performed "She Loves You," "This Boy," "All My Loving," "I Saw Her Standing There," "From Me to You," and "I Want to Hold Your Hand." Wanting to see and hear more of the Beatles, seventy million viewers watched them on their home television sets. On February 23, Ed Sullivan once again presented the Beatles, with their prerecorded performance of "Twist and Shout," "Please Please Me," and "I Want to Hold Your Hand." Collectively, it was a one, two, three knockout performance that positioned the Beatles as the hottest and most popular music group in America. On television and at their concerts, the Beatles performed with exciting high energy, and the excitement from the audience rushed back to the Beatles. It was the perfect relationship that fed and grew on each other.

The Beatles were a hardworking band, having performed approximately 365 concerts in twenty countries during the 1960s. Since this book is focused primarily on the Beatles' U.S. record releases and performances, I will highlight some of their concerts that took place in America during the summer months of 1964, 1965, and 1966.

1964

The Beatles embarked on their first North American tour in August 1964. It was a staggering twenty-four-city tour over the course of thirty days. The Beatles' set list consisted of twelve songs: "Twist and Shout," "You Can't Do That," "All My Loving," "She Loves You," "Things We Said Today," "Roll Over Beethoven," "Can't Buy Me Love," "If I Fell," "I Want to Hold Your Hand," "Boys," "A Hard Day's Night," and "Long Tall Sally." The first performance took place at the Cow Palace in San Francisco on August 19. As soon as the Beatles started playing, deafening screams from the audience began. This would be the case at every venue they played, and while it was exciting for the Beatles and the audience, the unrelenting screams caused a problem. The audience couldn't hear the Beatles, and the Beatles could barely hear themselves.

On August 23, the Beatles performed their twelve songs at the world-famous Hollywood Bowl in Los Angeles. The acoustics of the band shell were so good that the Beatles actually were able to hear themselves for a change. Radio personality Bob Eubanks and radio station KRLA promoted the concert. Eubanks was so sure that the Hollywood Bowl would be sold out, he mortgaged his house to pay the Beatles their $25,000 fee. Tickets were sold out in three and a half hours and Eubanks was more than pleased. Capitol Records recorded the concert with hopes of releasing a "live" Beatles album.

This whirlwind tour had an unexpected stop—an unscheduled performance in Kansas City on September 17. Charles O. Finley, a local businessman and owner of the Kansas City Athletics baseball team, eventually persuaded (or bribed) Brian Epstein to add the concert date by offering the Beatles an unprecedented $150,000 to perform at the Kansas City Municipal Stadium. Finley's first offer was $50,000, which Epstein turned down, followed by $100,000, which still Epstein refused. Finally, Brian accepted the $150,000. For this concert, the Beatles added a thirteenth song to their set list and began the concert with "Kansas City/Hey, Hey, Hey, Hey," which was a crowd pleaser with the local fans. Finley actually lost money on the concert. He set the ticket prices too high ($8.50 for the best seats, which was the highest ticket price on the tour). He had a questionable reputation with local baseball fans because of his intentions to relocate the Athletics to another city. Furthermore, many people thought it was in bad taste that he put his photo, wearing a Beatles' wig, on the back of the tickets with the quote "Today's Beatles fans are tomorrow's baseball fans." While the Beatles did take the money and run to the next tour stop in Dallas, in retrospect they probably would have preferred to have had the day off.

As part of this 1964 summer tour, the Beatles performed in New York City three times. On August 28 and 29, they played at the Forest Hills Tennis Stadium in Queens. Then as their last stop on the tour, the Beatles returned to New York on September 20 and played a United Cerebral Palsy benefit concert at the Paramount Theatre in Manhattan. Because it was a benefit concert for a good cause, ticket prices were set at $100. Graciously, the Beatles performed for free. After the performance, the Beatles spent the night at the Riviera Hotel near JFK airport. That night, the Beatles had a visitor. Robert Zimmerman, more commonly known as Bob Dylan, stopped by to spend some time with the Beatles. It was during this meeting at the Riviera Hotel that Dylan turned the Beatles onto marijuana for the first time. The Beatles and Brian Epstein got very stoned that night. Paul claimed to have discovered the "seven levels" of life, and Brian felt as though he had risen to the ceiling. From that night forward, pot would have an impact on the Beatles and their songwriting.

1965

On August 15, 1965, the Beatles began their second U.S. concert tour. Their first performance was at Shea Stadium in Flushing, Queens, New York. The largest audience ever assembled came to Shea Stadium, and it was the Beatles' biggest money-making concert. Approximately fifty-six thousand people attended, and ticket sales totaled $304,000. From Manhattan, the Beatles traveled by helicopter and landed on top of the World's Fair building in Queens. From there, the Beatles were ushered into a Wells Fargo armored bank truck, given Wells Fargo agent badges, and rushed to the stadium. The Beatles, adorned with the badges on their military-style beige jackets, waited for their introduction. Sid Bernstein, who promoted the concert, introduced Ed Sullivan. Since Ed was closely associated with the Beatles, the crowd started screaming when Ed started speaking. Then he said, "Here they come!" The Beatles ran across the baseball field toward the stage and the audience went berserk. Once onstage, the Beatles were visibly thrilled by the size of the crowd and launched into "Twist and Shout." With all the shouting coming from the audience, it was an appropriate opening number. During the songs "She's a Woman," "I Feel Fine," "Dizzy Miss Lizzy," and "Ticket to Ride," the Beatles bounced up and down, smiled, and laughed as they thrilled the sold-out audience. After George sang "Everybody's Trying to Be My Baby," Paul pointed to the different sections of the audience and asked everybody to clap their hands to the next song, "Can't Buy Me Love." Some in the audience clapped, and most of them screamed. Some girls fainted or cried while others broke through barricades, ran toward the stage, and were carried away by policemen. Continuing to appreciate the audience and show them respect, the Beatles bowed after each song. When John introduced "Baby's in Black," he spoke some gibberish while watching more girls try to rush the stage. The waltz-like "Baby's in Black" contrasted with the otherwise up-tempo songs.

Fortunately for Ringo, microphone stands had evolved. When he sang "Act Naturally," there was a boom attachment on the stand, which made it much more comfortable for Ringo to play the drums and sing. Afterward, John stepped up to the microphone to introduce the next song and suddenly spoke in some indefinable foreign language. He then threw his arms up in the air and looked up to the night sky. Talking about the Shea Stadium concert in *The Beatles Anthology* documentary, Ringo said, "I feel that on that show that John cracked up." Perhaps John was blown away and overwhelmed by the size of the adoring crowd that exuberantly screamed nonstop attention toward him and the Beatles. The Beatles launched into "A Hard Day's Night" followed by "Help!" Paul thanked the frenzied crowd and announced that the Beatles would be playing their last song, "I'm Down." John took off his guitar and played a Vox Continental organ. Paul screamed the lead vocals while George and John answered Paul, laughing and singing,

"I'm really down." Demonstrating a new technique, John played an organ solo with his elbow! The Beatles bowed one more time, waved at the crowd, and ran off the stage. They got into a white station wagon, which drove across the field and out of the stadium. It was an astonishing concert at the time when the Beatles were on top of the world during the summer of 1965. They were basking in the success of their second feature-length film, *Help!*, and soundtrack album; the "Ticket to Ride" and "Yesterday" smash-hit singles; and performing before record-breaking crowds.

The Beatles returned to the Hollywood Bowl for two shows on August 29 and 30. Once again, Bob Eubanks and KRLA promoted the concerts. The concerts were sold out with an overcapacity crowd of 17,600 screaming fans at each performance. The screaming fans at the Hollywood Bowl caused a problem for Capitol Records. At this 1965 concert, as well as the one from the previous year, Capitol recorded the concerts with the intent of releasing a "live" Beatles album. Even with the best recording equipment available at that time, the Beatles were almost drowned out and their sound was significantly obscured by the crowds' screams. Nonetheless, in 1977, when the Beatles were no longer a band, Capitol Records gave the tapes to George Martin with hopes that he could clean them up and present an acceptable album. Martin did a remarkable job and was able to bring the vocals and music up above the waves of screams. Since this is the only official live recording of the Beatles that was deemed good enough to be released, listen to *The Beatles Live at the Hollywood Bowl* and you will hear and feel the live energy that the Beatles unleashed at the peak of their concert-performance period. On the recording, the sounds of the fanatical screaming audience ebbs and flows from song to song. John, Paul, and George's personalities come through as they banter between songs. Because of the high energy of the Beatles onstage mixed with the overwhelming excitement from the audience, the tempos of the songs are quicker than their controlled studio recordings. It is astounding that the Beatles sounded this good considering that there were no audio monitor systems onstage. *The Beatles Live at the Hollywood Bowl* is a necessary listening experience for everyone who wants to feel the sensation that the Beatles created with their live performances. In doing so, you will be putting yourself in a seat at the Hollywood Bowl at a Beatles' "live" concert. The songs on *The Beatles Live at the Hollywood Bowl* are a mixture of the Beatles' performances at the Hollywood Bowl in 1964 and 1965. The songs are "Twist and Shout," "She's a Woman," "Dizzy Miss Lizzy," "Ticket to Ride," "Can't Buy Me Love," "Things We Said Today," "Roll Over Beethoven," "Boys," "A Hard Day's Night," "Help!," "All My Loving," "She Loves You," and "Long Tall Sally."

While the Beatles were in Los Angeles during the summer of 1965, a once-in-a-lifetime event happened. They met their idol, Elvis Presley. A secret meeting for the superstars was arranged between Brian Epstein and Colonel Parker, Presley's manager. Meeting Elvis for the first and only time, the Beatles were speechless and just stared at him. After several minutes, Elvis said with so many words that if the Beatles were not going to say anything, then he was going to go to bed. That got the Beatles talking. They talked about touring and the movies that Elvis had made. Eventually, a few guitars were passed around and the Beatles and Elvis played songs together. Most unfortunately, as prearranged by the managers, this historic meeting was not recorded and no photographs were allowed to be taken. Certainly a significant meeting in the annals of rock-and-roll history, this rare occasion was uncomfortable for Elvis. Surely he didn't show it, but given the fact that the Beatles had dethroned Elvis from being the "King of Rock and Roll," Elvis could not have been happy to be replaced by them.

1966

By the time 1966 rolled in, the Beatles were growing tired of touring even though their popularity hadn't waned. Things were about to change and hurt the Beatles. In an article published on March 4, 1966, in the *London Evening Standard*, John said, "Christianity will go. It will vanish and shrink. I needn't argue about that. I'm right and I'll be proved right. We're more popular than Jesus now. I don't know what will go first, rock 'n' roll or Christianity. Jesus was all right but his disciples were thick and ordinary. It's them twisting it that ruins it for me." John's remarks didn't seem to bother anyone in England. However, a few months later in the United States, DJs on radio stations in the southern Bible Belt were offended by what John had said. The DJs sounded the alarm and convinced Beatles fans to burn their Beatles records. Bonfires were held, and hundreds of teenagers threw their

Beatles albums into the fire. Brian Epstein was extremely concerned about the mess, and in order to keep the Beatles out of harm's way, he was willing to cancel the tour. Brian spoke with his attorney friend Nat Weiss in New York City and asked him what would it cost to cancel the tour. Nat said $1 million. Without hesitating, Brian would have written a check in that amount, but after speaking with the Beatles, they decided they wanted to go ahead with the tour. The Beatles didn't want to be seen as a group that could be intimidated and denied their tour because of John's statement, which they believed was taken out of context. When the Beatles came to the United States for their last U.S. tour, Brian persuaded John to make an apologetic statement at a press conference in Chicago. John felt terrible about what had happened, and while he didn't retract what he had said, John did try to explain the context of his words and put an end to the firestorm. "I'm not anti-Christ or anti-religion or anti-God. I'm not saying we're better or greater, or comparing us with Jesus Christ as a person, or God as a thing or whatever it is. I just said what I said and was wrong, or taken wrong, and now it's all this. If I had said television is more popular than Jesus, I might have got away with it. In reference to England, we meant more to kids than Jesus, or religion at the time. I wasn't knocking it or putting it down. I was just saying it as a fact and it's true more for England than here."

Prior to starting their 1966 U.S. tour, the Beatles performed in Japan and the Philippines. They encountered problems when they played at the Nippon Budokan in Tokyo. Some Japanese people were offended and protested the Beatles' performance because they felt as though the Budokan was built for martial arts and not for rock-and-roll performers. Aside from the protests, nothing more serious happened. Things got worse when the Beatles went to the Philippines. Imelda Marcos, the First Lady of the Philippines, invited the Beatles to attend a breakfast reception at the presidential palace. Brian Epstein declined the invitation, and as a result, much to his dismay, the Beatles no longer had police protection. When the Beatles went to the airport, they were victims of violent behavior. Demonstrators hit and spat at them, and the Beatles' road manager Mal Evans was physically attacked. It was a disturbing experience for the Beatles, and with these two out-of-the-ordinary events in their minds, they flew to the United States, where there was a growing number of teenagers who no longer loved or wanted to see the Beatles.

The Beatles 1966 U.S. tour started on August 12 in Chicago with two performances at the International Amphitheatre. Overall, ticket sales on this tour were not as good as what they had been a year earlier. The empty seats were attributed to John's comments about Jesus, which incited some former fans to boycott the concerts.

Despite death threats coming from Memphis, the Beatles played at the city's Mid-South Coliseum. During the show, there was a loud explosion. Paul, George, Ringo, and the Beatles' entourage quickly looked at John, fearing that he had been shot. To their great relief, it wasn't a gunshot. Someone had thrown a firecracker onto the stage. The Beatles were not accustomed to this type of rude behavior and were feeling on edge and uncomfortable. Nonetheless, they continued with the tour.

On August 23, the Beatles returned to Shea Stadium in another concert promoted by Sid Bernstein. Unlike a year earlier, the concert was not sold out. Much to Sid's and the Beatles' surprise, there were thousands of empty seats in the stadium. The difference between the 1965 concert and this one was striking and had a chilling effect on the Beatles. They clearly saw that their mass appeal in live-concert venues was wearing off.

After playing two shows in Seattle, the Beatles performed at Dodger Stadium in Los Angeles on August 28. Bob Eubanks and radio station KRLA promoted the concert, like they had done for the Hollywood Bowl concerts in 1964 and 1965. For this concert, tickets were nearly sold out, but problems ensued as the Beatles tried to get out of the stadium. There was no clearly defined exit. The audience rushed onto the field and threw themselves on the series of vehicles that tried to usher the Beatles safely out of the stadium. Fights broke out between the fans and the police. Several teenagers were hurt and twenty-five were arrested. As a last-ditch resort, the Beatles quickly rushed into the dugout and were trapped in the Dodgers' team dressing room. John was outraged by the experience. Eventually, the Beatles got out of the stadium in an armored vehicle. But the collective frustrations had drained them. It had become too difficult and was no longer fun for them to keep touring. When you put all of these negative events together, it's no surprise that the Beatles decided to make their concert at Candlestick Park in San Francisco their last paid public performance.

No one other than the Beatles and their inner circle knew that their Candlestick Park performance would be their last one. This concert was poorly attended, with nearly 40 percent of the seats left unsold. At one point during the show, Ringo got off his platform and took photos of John, Paul, and George. Then they all took photos of each other, memorializing their last concert. If the general public knew that this was going to be the Beatles' last performance, surely it would have been sold out, with thousands of fans packed into Candlestick Park. Their final set list, which they played at all the venues on this U.S. tour, consisted of the following songs: "Rock and Roll Music," "She's a Woman," "If I Needed Someone," "Day Tripper," "Baby's in Black," "I Feel Fine," "Yesterday," "I Wanna Be Your Man," "Nowhere Man," "Paperback Writer," and "Long Tall Sally." With so many songs for the Beatles to choose as their last live closing number, they chose "Long Tall Sally," a song that they had been playing for several years. This high-energy song was a good way for the Beatles to say good-bye, with the upbeat, positive lyrics "we're gonna have some fun tonight." At the last minute before going onstage, Paul asked Tony Barrow, the Beatles' press officer, to record the concert on his cassette tape recorder. Tony did, and Paul has the original recording. Somehow, Tony's copy of the tape was stolen. As a result, there is a bootleg of the recording on the Internet. While the recording did capture the Beatles' final concert performance, the audio quality leaves a lot to be desired. They *still* sounded tight and good, but at times the tempo of some songs dragged on, and some of the vocals sounded haggard and tired. At this point in time, the Beatles *were* tired of putting on these shows. After the concert on the flight to Los Angeles, George Harrison said to a reporter, "That's it. I'm not a Beatle anymore."

With the Beatles agreeing to no longer do concert tours, this caused a problem for Brian Epstein. Booking the Beatles' performances was Brian's principal activity. Furthermore, Sid Bernstein was planning on having the Beatles return to Shea Stadium in 1967. That would never happen, as the Beatles retreated to the recording studio and put all of their creative energy into their recordings. Brian had little to do with the Beatles in the recording studio. This big change in the Beatles' activities may have been a major contributing factor in Brian overdosing on prescribed drugs in September 1966. Fortunately, Brian survived the overdose, but his life would never be the same, and a year later he would be dead. On August 27, 1967, Brian was found dead in his bedroom having overdosed on a mixture of barbiturates and alcohol. In a December 1970 *Rolling Stone* magazine interview, John talked about Brian's death and said, "After Brian died, we collapsed. That was the disintegration. I was scared. I thought, 'We've fuckin' had it.'" Brian was the one who made the Beatles superstars, and they depended on Brian for all of their business affairs. Brian knew that the strength of the Beatles was their combined talents and unique personalities; it was always about the band, not four individuals. Without Brian, the individual personalities of John, Paul, George, and Ringo started to surface. The Beatles began to function as individuals rather than a unified band, and that was the beginning of the end.

What caused the Beatles' downward turn? Had they lost their magical charm? Could it solely be attributed to John's comments about Jesus? They were no longer selling out all of the seats at the concert venues, but their record sales were still strong. In 1966, "Paperback Writer" was a Certified Gold Record, having sold a million copies, and the double A-sided single "Yellow Submarine"/"Eleanor Rigby" was a top-selling hit record. "Yellow Submarine" hit the number two spot on the *Billboard* record chart; "Eleanor Rigby" reached number eleven. In the autumn of that year, rumors circulated that the Beatles had disbanded. They did leave each other and go off on individual projects. John went to Spain to act in the film *How I Won the War*, George traveled to India to study sitar with Ravi Shankar, Paul was busy composing soundtrack music for the film *The Family Way*, and Ringo visited John in Spain. It was a quiet time for the Beatles as a band, but the rumors of them splitting up would be completely squashed in February 1967 when the Beatles released their groundbreaking single "Penny Lane"/"Strawberry Fields Forever."

Selected Listening: "Long Tall Sally"; "I Saw Her Standing There"; "Roll Over Beethoven"; "Rock and Roll Music"; "Nowhere Man"; "I'm Down"

6

A LIGHTER SIDE

Folk-Rock and Country-Rock Songs

Folk music was popular in the early 1960s, with several successful recording groups, including the Kingston Trio, the Weavers, and Peter, Paul and Mary, as well as solo artists such as Woody Guthrie, Joan Baez, and Bob Dylan. The groups used three- or four-part vocal harmonies accompanied by acoustic guitars, while soloists accompanied themselves on acoustic guitars and sometimes with other instruments like the harmonica. In England during the mid-1950s, skiffle music was a popular craze with young musicians, including John Lennon and his band the Quarrymen. Influenced largely by the Scottish singer-songwriter Lonnie Donegan, skiffle music, like folk music, was played on acoustic instruments. In addition to guitars, skiffle also included homemade instruments such as washboards and thimbles, which created a percussive scrapping sound, and tea-chest basses, made with a broom handle and string attached to a wooden tea chest. When the skiffle craze began to fade, the Quarrymen, who in 1958 included John, Paul, and George, began their love affair with rock and roll.

As early as 1964, the Beatles were recording some of their songs using acoustic instruments. At a time when they were well known as a rock-and-roll band, having had huge successes based on their chart-topping singles such as "She Loves You," "I Want to Hold Your Hand," and "Can't Buy Me Love," their desire to write new, non–rock-and-roll songs gave birth to a new genre of music called folk rock. Adding drums, electric bass, and electric guitars to folk music's standard acoustic guitar ensemble is what made folk music rock. This new folk-rock genre was a clear indication of the Beatles' pioneering spirit to expand their songwriting styles and evolve as a creative band.

"I'll Be Back," written for the most part by John, is one of the first folk-rock songs recorded by the Beatles. While Paul played electric bass, John and George put down their electrics and played acoustic guitars. George also played a classical nylon-stringed guitar. Stylistically, "I'll Be Back" was a sign of things to come and would usher in a folk-rock movement a year later. Harmonically, this song is innovative, going back and forth between major and minor keys, bridged together by a recurring guitar riff played by George. During the verses, a jarring overdubbed acoustic guitar plays against the even rhythm of the song. The bridge has a descending guitar line falling beneath John's lead vocals as he sings the word *I* with a long, sustained note that is not in the backing chord. This is unusual and creates a harmonic suspension and uncertainty as John sings he "thought" you would realize. Conflicting lyrics say he wants to go but he hates to leave, which parallels the vacillating major/minor chord exchange. The lyrics "if you break my heart I'll go, but I'll be back" pose the question: Coming back for more heartache? The song fades out with harmonic uncertainty as the band continues to play major and minor chords. While John said he'd be back, Paul had different things to say.

"Things We Said Today," written by Paul, is a brisk-paced song about the future and looking back on things that were said in the present tense. Paul wrote this song in May 1964 while on a yacht cruising the Caribbean Sea with his girlfriend Jane Asher. "Things We Said Today" has a similar chord structure as "I'll Be Back." However, with "Things We Said Today," the verses are based on A minor chords, while the middle bridge of the song shifts to a parallel-modulation A major chord. The song also contains additional major chords in the bridge, which match the more positive lyrics. The identifying sound that makes this song unique is the pronounced open A string plucked by John on an acoustic guitar at the beginning of the song, between the verses and on the ending fade-out. This open string reverberates and sustains over the underlying rhythm. The same note is reinforced on the piano, played by John. George plays electric guitar mixed in with John's big rhythm-guitar sound. Paul sings the lead vocals and harmony overdubs on

"Things We Said Today." Being on a yacht in the Caribbean Sea would be an ideal place to write a song about the sun. But instead, Paul wrote "I'll Follow the Sun" at home in Liverpool.

"I'll Follow the Sun," one of the first songs that Paul wrote when he was sixteen years old, is about moving on from a failing relationship and seeking brighter times. Sung by Paul, this song demonstrates Paul's acoustic guitar abilities. John also plays acoustic guitar while George provides a sliding electric guitar solo, mirroring the melody in the verses. Rather than starting on the root chord (usually the first chord of a song that matches the key of the song) the verses in "I'll Follow the Sun" start on a dominant cord, which is a chord that generally occurs later in a song. This harmonic surprise gets your attention and perks up your ears. The chorus begins on the root chord and then the bridge moves to another chord sequence, with harmony sung by John. Instead of Ringo playing the drums, he provides percussion by slapping out a rhythm on his knees. A musically light song, "I'll Follow the Sun" is early Beatles folk rock.

A different kind of Beatles song, "Baby's in Black" has a six-eight time signature and sounds like a moderate folk-rock waltz. George starts the song playing a country-styled, low-string guitar riff, which reoccurs at the end of the choruses and at the end of the song. He also plays the lead guitar solo in the same style. John and Paul sing the harmonizing melody throughout the song. John's best friend from his Liverpool College of Art days was Stuart Sutcliffe, a talented painter who played bass guitar with the Beatles in 1960 and 1961. While in Germany with the Beatles, Stuart met Hamburg photographer Astrid Kirchherr. The Beatles and Astrid became close friends, and Stuart and Astrid fell in love with each other. Wanting to be with Astrid, Stuart decided to quit the Beatles and stayed in Hamburg. Soon afterward, Stuart experienced severe headaches, and in 1962 he collapsed and died on his way to the hospital. The sad lyrics about "she dresses in black" and "he'll never come back" can be interpreted as Astrid mourning Stuart's death.

"I Don't Want to Spoil the Party," the B-side to the "Eight Days a Week" single, is written by John. Adding to the folk-rock character of this song is the style of George's lead guitar solo. The lyrics in "I Don't Want to Spoil the Party" are about being stood up at a party. Not wanting to ruin a good time for the others, the rejected character chooses to leave. During the verses, rather than Paul singing the harmony, John harmonizes with himself. This solo Beatle vocal-overdubbing recording technique was used by the Beatles in 1965. Later in their recording career, individual Beatles frequently overdubbed their vocals. Paul sings the high harmony part during the bridge, and even though the lyrics are a downer, the music is quick and bright, as if the song were driving the main character to get moving and leave the party.

Having met Bob Dylan in 1964, the Beatles were aware of what Dylan was doing in the recording studio and with the songs on his 1965 *Bringing It All Back Home* album. Dylan's album contained songs played on acoustic guitar and harmonica, plus electrified folk-rock songs. Influenced by Dylan, Lennon wrote the song "I'm a Loser." This song marks a significant change with John's songwriting. Not containing lyrics about love and romance, John actually sings that he is not what he appears to be. With Paul harmonizing with him, the song begins with John proclaiming that he is a loser. Most listeners at the time thought that the self-deprecating lyrics of "I'm a Loser" could not be about John. In 1965, John and the other Beatles were perceived to be the antithesis of being losers; in the eyes of the general public, they were the biggest winners in the pop/rock music world. Yet John was telling us that he wasn't the big winner we believed him to be. Paul plays an up-and-down walking bass line during the chorus and harmonizes with John. After John's harmonica solo, George picks a lead guitar solo. The song ends with John playing his harmonica and George picking his strings on the fade-out. Another way of feeling like a loser is not getting a response.

"No Reply" is a dramatic song about cheating on someone. Written mostly by John, the rhythm of the song is syncopated. Ringo plays cross stick and hits his snare drum on downbeats and upbeats during the verses. On the chorus, John and Paul scream "I saw the light" and the dramatic lyrics "I nearly died," with cymbal crashes from Ringo. With the same intensity as the chorus, John and Paul sing the bridge's lyrics, declaring their love is greater than that of any other guy. Still, there's no reply, and being replaced by another man cannot be tolerated. Another big rhythm-guitar song, John and George play acoustic guitars, and that's all George plays because there's no guitar solo in "No Reply." Even though there's no reply, John and Paul want to know what you see.

"Tell Me What You See," a song written by Paul on the *Beatles VI* album, is more folk rock than rock and roll. The song is built primarily on John's rhythm guitar and percussion instruments. Ringo plays the tambourine and claves, and George plays a guiro, a gourd-shaped Latin instrument that makes a clicking sound when scraped with a stick. "Tell Me What You See" showcases harmony and lead vocals sung by Paul and John and also highlights the Hohner Pianet, played by Paul at the end of each chorus and at the end of the song. A clever play with the word *part* are the lyrics "we will never be apart, if I'm part of you." The vocal line is rhythmically syncopated during the verses, bouncing in between the even downbeats. After the Beatles sing the words "tell me what you see," you hear the electric piano followed by drums and bass, a musical answer to the inquiring lyrics. When you open your eyes and ears, what you see and hear are the Beatles. The lyrics "trying to get to you" are the same as the title to a 1956 Elvis Presley single titled "Trying to Get to You," illustrating how Elvis made a lasting impression on the Beatles.

In 1965, the Beatles continued to develop their rock-and-roll songs. "Ticket to Ride" demonstrates the use of electric guitars and a dynamic syncopated drum track, which makes the song rock and roll. During the same time period, John, Paul, and George wrote several folk-rock songs. Some of these songs do not include drums or electric guitars. A few of them are featured in their movie *Help!* and accompanying soundtrack album.

In the opening sequence in the Beatles' second feature-length film, *Help!*, John plays an acoustic Gibson guitar. However, on the studio recording John plays an acoustic twelve-string guitar. The song "Help!" is written by John as the title song for the movie. While the title is perfectly appropriate for the film in which Ringo clearly needs help escaping from East Indians who are trying to kill him, John was honestly crying for help. No one in 1965 could have known that was the case since the Beatles appeared to be on top of the world. Even though John and the Beatles wanted worldwide fame, John was no longer happy with stardom and felt trapped by his celebrity status. Regardless, "Help!" was a number one hit on record charts throughout the world. Wasting no time, the song begins with an abbreviated chorus and a screaming plea for "help!" During the verses and chorus, John's voice sounds emotionally pained and exclaims that he's down and feeling insecure. At the end of the full chorus, articulating the dramatic cry for help, John, along with harmony from Paul and George, sing the highest notes in the song on the word *please*. Contrary to the "down" lyrics, the music is driven by a quick, bright tempo. George plays a cascading guitar riff at the end of the choruses, which sets up the verses. While it was a perfect song for the movie, "Help!" had a hidden truth for John, who was looking for a way out.

Another folk-rock song in the movie *Help!* is "You've Got to Hide Your Love Away," written and sung by John. He plays a Framus Hootenanny twelve-string acoustic guitar in the song's film sequence and on the soundtrack album. "You've Got to Hide Your Love Away" is believed by some to be about Brian Epstein having to hide the fact that he was homosexual. In Great Britain at that time, it was against the law to be a homosexual, thus one had to hide his love. The introspective lyrics were inspired by Bob Dylan and his song "I Don't Believe You (She Acts Like We Never Met)," which contains the lyrics "I can't understand, she let go of my hand, and left me here facing a wall." In "You've Got to Hide Your Love Away," John sings, "Here I stand, head in hand, turn my face to the wall." At the beginning of each chorus, John gets your attention by belting out a high-pitched "hey." Instead of there being a harmonica solo, which would have been appropriate for a folk song, the Beatles do something different. A flute solo occurs during the last chord progression. This is another example of how the Beatles were surprisingly unpredictable and innovative. In addition to playing the tambourine, Ringo plays his snare drum with brushes. The brushed drum sound blends perfectly with John's rhythm guitar strumming, and on the chorus Ringo plays maracas.

In October 1965, the Beatles finally had a break from their hectic touring schedule and retreated into the recording studio at Abbey Road, where they recorded their *Rubber Soul* album. Look at the *Rubber Soul* album cover and you will see what appears to be a stretched, tilted photo of the Beatles. This occurred by accident when photographer Robert Freeman projected an image of the photo on a piece of cardboard and the cardboard tilted backward, thus giving the image an elongated look. You will also see that their hair is longer and that they are dressed in casual clothing and wear brown suede jackets. For the first time on a Beatles album, their name does not appear on the cover. By late 1965 when *Rubber Soul* was released, their images were so well known that the band's name was not needed to identify the faces on the album cover. The cover photo indicates that the Beatles' physical appearances had changed along with the style of their songs. The influence of this landmark album, recorded in about four weeks' time, popularized the folk-rock music scene that was happening in the United States. Folk-rock songs by Bob Dylan, the Byrds, the Mamas and the Papas, Simon and Garfunkel, and the Lovin' Spoonful dominated the record charts.

The U.K. *Rubber Soul* album included the songs "Drive My Car," "Nowhere Man," What Goes On," and "If I Needed Someone," which were released in the United States on the *Yesterday and Today* album. On the U.S. *Rubber Soul* album, "I've Just Seen a Face" is the first song. This song perfectly tied in with the folk-rock scene that was exploding in America. Written by Paul, this all–acoustic guitar, fast-paced song is about falling in love. The song begins with a descending twelve-string guitar part followed by ascending guitar lines beautifully played by George, who also plays the guitar solo. John also plays an acoustic guitar on "I've Just Seen a Face," and there is no bass part on the recording. Paul harmonizes with himself during the chorus. Ringo plays his drums with brushes and propels the song forward. Only two minutes, seven-seconds long, "I've Just Seen a Face" rushes by in a flash, and with "I'm Looking Through You," Paul sees more than a face.

As demonstrated with the lyrics in Paul's song "I'm Looking Through You," his songwriting had evolved beyond love songs. The lyrics in this song are pointed at Paul's deteriorating relationship with his girlfriend Jane Asher. He felt as though she was no longer the same as she used to be. Jane had a full-fledged acting career that pulled her away from Paul. He was looking through her and saw that Jane had changed. Paul went so far as to say that love disappeared overnight. That's a far cry from "I give her all my love," which he sings in "And I Love Her." John sings harmony with Paul in the "you have changed" choruses and plays a driving acoustic guitar throughout the song. George plays the lead guitar riffs in "I'm Looking Through You." That's Ringo playing two notes on the Hammond organ on the first and second beats during the chorus, plus he keeps the rhythm moving along by tapping on a box of matches and hitting his thighs.

"Wait," written by Paul, has prominent tambourine and maracas throughout the song, played by Ringo. Paul and John sing the lead vocals in harmony in the verses and choruses. In the bridge, it's solo Paul singing the vocals, with George and John playing pulsating guitars beneath Paul's voice. The lyrics address separation, feeling lonely, and being away from home. Given the fact that the Beatles were traveling a lot in 1965, the lyrics seem autobiographical. Some of the lyrics in the bridge are "as good as I can be." If you can't be good, then what? Not be good? But wait, unless your heart breaks, and if your heart's strong, then hold on. John and Paul end the harmony-rich "Wait" with "I've been alone," and George caps off the song with low guitar notes. Not willing to be alone, Paul believed that differences between lovers could be worked out.

The optimistic Paul wrote the verses and chorus to "We Can Work It Out." John wrote the bridge, citing that life is too short and there's no time for fussing and fighting. At a time when Paul's relationship with Jane was problematic, he more than likely wrote this song about hoping to work things out with her. In the bridge, on the lyrics "fighting my friend" and "ask you once again," the song switches to a three-four waltz feel. Released as a double A-sided single along with "Day Tripper," "We Can Work It Out" has only three Beatles performing on the recording: Paul sings lead vocals and plays bass; John plays acoustic guitar and a harmonium keyboard and sings a lower harmony with Paul on the bridge of the song; Ringo plays drums and the tambourine. Since John plays the guitar and the arrangement didn't include a lead guitar part, George is not on the recording. In January 1966, "We Can Work It Out" and "Day Tripper" were hits on the U.S. record charts. "We Can Work It Out" was number one for three weeks, and "Day Tripper" hit the number five spot.

The Beatles' influence on aspiring musicians and newly formed bands was powerful. A lot of those musicians had to have the same guitars that the Beatles played. . . . You finally put together a rock-and-roll band that could play Beatles songs. Your lead guitar player and drummer are from Manchester, England, not far from Liverpool. The bass player is from Manchester, Connecticut, so you think of naming the band the Manchesters. But that doesn't sound Beatle enough, so you name it the Batles, which is the Beatles minus an e. Kenny, the drummer, has a Ludwig drum set that looks like Ringo's. Jimmie, the bass player, has a Hofner, like Paul's, and Lenny, the lead guitar player, has a Gretsch Country Gentleman, like one of George's guitars. You have to have a twelve-string Rickenbacker like George's so you can strum full-sounding rhythm chords with the band. So you go to the music store where all the famous musicians buy their instruments—Manny's in New York City. After riding the train from Hartford to Grand Central Station in Manhattan, when you arrive at the music store on West Forty-Eighth Street, it is jam-packed and bustling with long-haired musicians. The first thing you notice is the wall behind the cash registers. It's completely covered with band photographs. Your eyes scan the wall and you see photos of the Rolling Stones, the Lovin' Spoonful, and the Young Rascals. Then your eyes rest and focus on a photo of the Beatles dressed in their collarless jackets smiling at you. You smile back. Getting on with your quest, you look up at hundreds of guitars hanging from elevated racks, and you spot a red sunburst electric twelve-string Rickenbacker. With the utmost care, you take it off the rack and hold it in your hands. It feels like the beautiful guitar should belong to you and was waiting for you to claim it. You take your nylon guitar pick out of your blue jeans pocket and strum the Rickenbacker. It being a semihollow guitar, even without amplification, the twelve strings ring out with a clean, cutting tone. Impressed and excited, you don't bother to plug it into a nearby amplifier. You are sold, and after haggling with a salesman about the price, with the twelve-string Rickenbacker in its new silver case, you walk down Fifth Avenue to Grand Central Station with a satisfied grin on your face. As you approach the station, you wonder what will be the first song you'll play on your new guitar. Considering that it's a Rickenbacker twelve-string, the perfect song pops into your head.

"If I Needed Someone" is a bright, electric Rickenbacker twelve-string song written by George. This song was influenced by the American folk-rock band the Byrds and their guitarist Roger McGuinn. Roger also played an electric Rickenbacker twelve-string and used it on many of the Byrds' recordings, including "Mr. Tambourine Man," written by Bob Dylan. The twelve-string guitar riff in "If I Needed Someone" is modeled after the Byrds' recording of "The Bells of Rhymney," written by Pete Seeger with words by Welsh poet Idris Davies. In addition to George's ringing Rickenbacker, "If I Needed Someone" has lush three-part harmony sung by George, Paul, and John. Also notable is Paul's prominent repetitive bass line during the verses while John's rhythm guitar chords move up and down the neck. George sings the vocals by himself on most of the first verse and in the bridges. While George didn't need someone, John needed to write a song for an upcoming recording session.

John was wracking his brain trying to write a song, but he couldn't come up with anything. At that moment, in terms of writing John was nowhere. Only after stopping and giving up did the song come to him. "Nowhere Man" has a sweeping melody and beautiful three-part harmonies. The sound of the recurring electric guitar riff, played by John and George, is extremely bright, due largely in part to their Fender Stratocaster guitars, which are known for their high-end, cutting tone. John plays the lead guitar solo on his sonic blue Stratocaster, and the three-part vocals match the brightness of the multiple guitar parts. The vocals immediately get your attention as they are isolated without backing instruments at the beginning of the song. In the bridge, Paul and George sing the "ah, la, la, la, la" vocals in harmony behind John's lead vocals. On the last vocal line, Paul's voice jumps up to a note higher than what he had sung in previous choruses.

The lyrics in "Nowhere Man" are introspective and philosophical. John brings the listener into the song by saying that the nowhere man is like you and me. After all, sometimes we might feel as though we are nowhere. In the movie *Yellow Submarine*, animated Beatles sing the song to a busybody character who seems to be going nowhere named Jeremy Hillary Boob, PhD. "Nowhere Man" is a fine example of how John's songwriting had evolved in two years' time, from writing songs such as "I Feel Fine" to the more insightful "Nowhere Man."

With so many bands emerging in 1966, battle of the bands competitions were popping up everywhere. . . . Now that your band, the Batles, are playing at the best music clubs in New England and attracting jam-packed audiences, it's time to enter a battle of the bands competition. You happen to see an advertisement in the local paper announcing a band competition offering to pay the winning band $100. John Jamison, who manages the Thundering Outlaws, is staging the competition and thinks that no one can beat his band. The Batles are one of four bands on the bill. After two local bands perform to lukewarm responses from the audience, it's time for the Batles to play. Standing in front of the band's Vox amplifiers and holding guitars exactly like the Beatles had, the Batles open with "If I Needed Someone" and close with "Nowhere Man." The crowd enthusiastically cheers, while some girls actually *scream. Next, the Thundering Outlaws play. They sound okay but don't get the crowd excited. Jamison comes up to the microphone and asks the crowd to clap after he names each band. The first two bands receive polite applause from the audience. Then he says, "What about the Batles?" The crowd roars with approval. Finally, Jamison asks, "How about the amazing Thundering Outlaws?" The crowd claps, but it is nothing like the reaction the Batles had received. "Well, I guess the Batles win," said Jamison. You and the band thank the crowd and begin to pack up your instruments. Then you look around the hall and notice that Jamison is nowhere to be found. You go outside and see him sitting in the backseat of a Lincoln Continental with his window rolled down. Running to the car, you say, "Hey, John, where's our money?" Jamison rolls up the window and the Continental speeds away. What? Your band had won fair and square and Jamison took off like a crook. In retrospect, you should have been wary of Jamison. After all, the name of his band is the Thundering Outlaws. If you needed someone, it was a manager like Brian Epstein who would prevent you from getting ripped off again.*

There's only one song in the Beatles catalog written by John, Paul, and Ringo, and that's "What Goes On." John had written an early version of the song when he was with his first band, the Quarrymen. In 1965, the Beatles dug it up and dusted it off. Paul wrote a few extended verses, and Ringo added new words to the original lyrics. The new version, with Ringo singing the lead vocals, became the B-side to the "Nowhere Man" single released in December 1965. This rockabilly-styled song begins with the chorus asking questions about "your heart" and "your mind." In the verses, Ringo sings about getting torn apart and being lied to. The songs' lyrics questioning a lover's cheating behavior could only come from John's heart and mind. John's guitar playing stands out in "What Goes On." He plays a chunky syncopated part predominately on the third and fourth beats. George plays an appropriate country-picking guitar solo. Paul's bass playing during George's guitar solo is a moving walking bass line. There's a lot going on with this obscure Beatles song.

As you can readily hear when listening to "The Fool on the Hill," one of the songs in the Beatles' 1967 *Magical Mystery Tour* film and on the accompanying album, Paul's songwriting continued to evolve with his use of philosophical lyrics. The song is about a wise man who is considered to be a fool by those who don't understand him. The sole vocal track is sung by Paul, and he plays nearly all of the instruments. He uses different chords in "The Fool on the Hill," beginning with a D major 6 chord. When the chorus begins, a minor chord accompanies Paul's voice. The musical arrangement uses harmonicas and flutes, and Paul adds to the light-spirited song by playing a recorder. In addition to John and George playing harmonicas, so do Ray Thomas and Mike Pinder, two members from the rock band the Moody Blues. There are three flute parts on the song, played by freelance studio musicians. Ringo plays finger cymbals, maracas, and some drums. Just before the song ends, after the words *spinning 'round*, you can hear a rustling, shimmering sound move across the stereo spectrum. Is that the sound of the world spinning around or a flock of birds flying by? With its unusual chord changes, "The Fool on the Hill" takes folk music to a level that goes beyond simple folk roots.

Several of the songs on *The Beatles* album, also known as the *White Album*, are folk oriented. This is due in part to the fact that when the Beatles were in India studying meditation with the Maharishi, they brought acoustic guitars with them. Electric guitars and amplifiers would not have been welcomed or appropriate at a meditation retreat. Staying indoors in your designated hut and meditating every day was the primary activity at Maharishi's ashram, located in Rishikesh, India, along the Ganges River. But that didn't mean that John, Paul, and George had to stop writing songs. Far away from the noise and distractions of busy city life, the meditation setting was an ideal place to be creative, focus with no interruptions, and write a new batch of songs.

One of the songs that John wrote in India was "Dear Prudence." Along with the Beatles, several other musicians and celebrities, including Mia Farrow and her sister Prudence, attended the ashram. John was trying to entice Prudence to come out of her hut and "play," "greet the brand new day," and "look around" instead of meditating all of the time. You can hear a noticeable change in the way John plays his guitar on the recording. Musician friend and successful recording artist Donovan had also brought his acoustic guitar to India, and he taught John and Paul a fingerpicking guitar technique. "Dear Prudence" begins with John playing a fingerpicking guitar riff before settling in on a repetitive, drone-like pattern during the first verse. On the chorus and following verses, Paul plays a descending melodic bass line. Background voices float in, contributing to the hypnotic feel of the song. During the "round, round" bridge and the last verse, George plays bright guitar fills between John's vocals. The "round, round" lyrics are the same as the lyrics in "The Fool on the Hill," recorded about a year earlier. Listen carefully to the last chorus and you'll hear that the bass part has become edgier, with a top-end punch to it along with some tasty drumming. But much to everyone's surprise, it's not Ringo. That's Paul playing the drums and playing a rapid tremolo piano part. Paul played the drums because Ringo had temporarily quit the band for a few weeks. John, Paul, and George didn't want to wait and see if and when Ringo would return, so Paul filled in on drums. While John wanted Prudence to come out of her hut, he was also intrigued about a tiger-hunt incident.

"The Continuing Story of Bungalow Bill" is a song about tigers and elephants. Written by John when he was in India, the song was inspired by a young, wealthy American named Richard Cooke, who along with his mother had visited the meditation center in Rishikesh. Richard and his mother went out of the compound to hunt tigers while riding elephants. A tiger attacked an elephant and in order to save the elephant, Richard shot and killed the tiger. Hearing about this, John wrote "The Continuing Story of Bungalow Bill," changing Richard's name to Bill, as in Buffalo Bill. The song begins with all four Beatles singing the chorus, along with Ringo's first wife, Maureen, and Yoko Ono. The verses are twice as slow as the chorus, and in the verses John tells the story about the tiger hunt on elephants. The end of the song is unusual. What sounds like a bassoon solo is accompanied by a group of handclaps, and then the song abruptly ends.

Yoko was in the studio for the recording of "The Continuing Story of Bungalow Bill" and during most of the 1968 recording of the *White Album*. Her presence added to the friction going on within the Beatles. Paul, George, and Ringo didn't want Yoko in the studio, but their protests fell on deaf ears because John insisted that Yoko be with him. Even though John's first wife, Cynthia, was with him in India, Yoko was sending telegrams to John every day while John was at the ashram. The seeds of love between John and Yoko were planted, and soon after John returned from India, while Cynthia was vacationing with her mother in Italy, John and Yoko consummated their relationship. The impact Yoko had on John was like nothing he had ever experienced. Yoko was an educated conceptual artist who came from a wealthy Japanese family.

John was looking for something new, something different, and Yoko satisfied his desires on multiple levels—artistic, intellectual, political, and physical. While Yoko's constant inclusion in John's life forever changed him, it also created resentment, further dissent, and division among the Beatles. Many people believe that Yoko broke up the band. While Yoko being in John's life was a contributing factor, it was the Beatles who ultimately broke up the Beatles. They had grown apart and behaved as separate individuals who wanted to do different things. John, Paul, George, and Ringo no longer worked together as a close-knit band. Even though the Beatles had spent weeks meditating and perhaps finding inner peace, tensions were particularly high while recording the *White Album*, which caused the group to splinter, and in a number of instances, solo Beatle recordings took place. Such is the case with "Blackbird."

When Paul was in India, he heard the sound of a blackbird calling, which was the inspiration for writing "Blackbird." Playing acoustic guitar, singing, and tapping his feet on the recording studio floor, "Blackbird" is a solo performance by Paul on the *White Album*. The guitar part is influenced by the German baroque composer Johann Sebastian Bach's composition "Bourrée," which was written for the lute. Paul's "Blackbird" takes flight, seeking light and freedom. If Paul had written and recorded this song in 1965, it's probable that he would have recorded "Blackbird" as a band arrangement with the other Beatles. On the same album, Paul contrasts the poetic "Blackbird" with a gun-slinging "Rocky Raccoon."

"Rocky Raccoon," written by Paul while in India, is a parody of a western saloon "show down" gun battle over a girl named Lil—or was her name Nancy? Rocky's girlfriend had left him for another man. In a hotel room at the saloon, Rocky gets shot by Nancy's new boyfriend, Dan, but Rocky survives, saying, "It's only a scratch." Adding to the grit, Paul's opening acoustic guitar sounds slightly out of tune. The honky-tonk, sparkling piano part is perfectly played by George Martin. John contributes a lot to "Rocky Raccoon" and sings some background vocals and plays the six-string bass, harmonium, and harmonica. This is the last time John played harmonica on a Beatles song. However, he did return to the harmonica as a solo artist and played it on "Oh Yoko!" on his *Imagine* album. George's participation on "Rocky Raccoon" is nominal, only singing some background vocals with John toward the end of the song. Paul shines in the spotlight in "Rocky Raccoon" and has fun spoofing on an Old West folk singer.

Once again it's solo Paul on the *White Album* with "Mother Nature's Son." Inspired by a lecture given by the Maharishi in India, the song explores the wonders and pleasures of nature. John contributed a few lyrics, but the majority of the song was written by Paul, who sings and plays acoustic guitars, timpani, and distant-sounding drums. George Martin wrote the tranquil brass accompaniment to "Mother Nature's Son." If Paul had recorded the song with the other Beatles, it might have sounded something like an updated "I'll Follow the Sun," with a more developed guitar part and harmony sung by John and George. While Paul's song is about Mother Nature, John's song is about a mother's child.

Toward the end of 1967, John wrote "Cry Baby Cry," a song rooted in a driving acoustic guitar played by John with lyrics that come across like a nursery rhyme. John also plays piano and organ on the recording and harmonizes with his own lead vocals. Paul sings a high falsetto vocal part during the chorus, and his bass part in the first verse is unique. He plays a pulsating *woo, woo, woo*, which fades in and out. The song has some sound effects going on in the background, and a harmonium is played by George Martin. It was during the recording sessions of "Cry Baby Cry" that the Beatles' recording engineer Geoff Emerick quit. After working with the Beatles for more than two years, Geoff had had enough of the ongoing bickering and outright cursing that was going on among the Beatles.

Even though it is not officially referred to as a Beatles song, at the end of "Cry Baby Cry," you will hear Paul sing, "Can you take me back?" Paul plays acoustic guitar while John plays maracas and Ringo plays the bongos. On the *White Album*, this short musical transition segues into "Revolution 9."

The cover of *The Beatles* is completely white, including the name "The Beatles" in raised print, thus the name *White Album*. This double album is the most diversified album recorded by the Beatles, containing a wide range of songs in many different musical idioms, including the bizarre electronic music piece titled "Revolution 9," created by John. The eclecticism of musical styles is the result of the Beatles exploring other genres as individual writers and recording artists instead of a unified creative team. Geoff Emerick's departure and Ringo's temporary split from the band signaled that the Beatles were beginning to fall apart.

In late August 1968 at Abbey Road Studios, while the Beatles were working on "Back in the U.S.S.R.," Ringo walked out on the band. He said in the Beatles' 1995 *Anthology* documentary that he left because he felt like an outsider and wasn't playing his drums well. So he went to Sardinia and sailed on Peter Sellers's yacht for a few days. While on the yacht, Ringo asked for fish and chips. He got chips, but instead of fish, it was octopus. The captain of the yacht told Ringo about octopuses and how they make gardens under the sea. Ringo found that to be fascinating, and it inspired him to write "Octopus's Garden," a fun country-rock song. The recording of "Octopus's Garden," a song on the *Abbey Road* album, captured a positive spirit with the Beatles. They knew they were recording their final album and gave the songs the energy and attention they deserved. Paul's and George's smooth, floating harmonies support Ringo's lead vocals. Adding to the underwater theme of the song, during George's lead guitar solo, Paul's and George's voices are heavily processed to create a rippling underwater effect. Additionally, George blows through a straw in a glass of milk and makes bubble sounds. John's contribution is playing a fingerpicking guitar part throughout the song. In the repeat ending chorus, Ringo's drum fills are perfectly intertwined with George's lead guitar riffs. It's George's lead guitar playing that makes "Octopus's Garden" a country-rock song. While the sun shines brightly in Sardinia, it occasionally shines in England.

The opening song on side two of the *Abbey Road* album is "Here Comes the Sun." George wrote the song in Eric Clapton's garden with an acoustic guitar on a spring day. When you listen to "Here Comes the Sun," you will hear its sunny, cheerful nature with overall bright sounds from the guitars and George's vocals emphasizing that "it's alright." In addition to guitars, George also plays a synthesizer part. At the end of the verses and during the "sun, sun, sun" bridge in the middle of the song, rapid successive eighth notes are played on guitars in a combination of three beats followed by two beats. This creates a propelling rhythm and implies that the sun is coming, as if the sun is rising on the horizon. George Martin added a wind and string arrangement to "Here Comes the Sun." John is not on this recording as he was in a hospital recuperating from a car accident. He was not a good driver and had smashed up his car while driving in the Highlands in Scotland.

Paul performs a solo act again on the short, little, folksy ditty titled "Her Majesty." Only twenty-three seconds in length, "Her Majesty" was originally part of the medley of songs on side two of *Abbey Road*, placed between "Mean Mr. Mustard" and "Polythene Pam." Paul wasn't satisfied with it and asked that it be removed from the album. George Martin instructed studio engineer John Kurlander to never discard anything that the Beatles recorded, so Kurlander put "Her Majesty" at the very end of the master tape of the *Abbey Road* album. When the Beatles heard a test pressing of the album with "Her Majesty" at the very end, they liked it. Even though the album ends with "The End," "Her Majesty" is a surprise ending. Right up to the very end of their career as recording artists, the Beatles were still being cleverly innovative.

The song "Two of Us" appears on the *Let It Be* album, the final album released by the Beatles. Written by Paul, who plays lead acoustic guitar and sings the lead vocals, he has claimed that the lyrics are about him and his wife Linda. Some of them sound like they are. However, during the bridge when Paul sings lyrics about long-term memories, they don't quite fit with Linda since they had been together for only a little more than one year at the time of the recording. Those lyrics are likely about the longtime career and friendship Paul had with John, as well as verse lyrics about chasing paper and getting nowhere, which appear to reference the troubling business affairs plaguing the Beatles and their company Apple Corps. George plays a lead bass line on his six-string Telecaster guitar, giving the bass part a distinctive sound. At the end of the song, Paul says, "We're going home" and "better believe it," a statement that can be interpreted to be about the Beatles leaving each other and going their separate ways. A year after they recorded "Two of Us," when the *Let It Be* album was released in May 1970, the Beatles had officially split up. But before they disbanded, John was still writing in the Beatles' universe.

"Across the Universe," written and sung by John, is a dreamy song with stream-of-consciousness lyrics. Inspired by John's wife Cynthia rambling on and on about something, John came up with the lyrics "words are flowing out like endless wind." Initially recorded and produced by George Martin in February 1968 before the Beatles went to India, the first version of "Across the Universe" appears as the first song on the compilation album *Nothing's Gonna Change Our World*, a charity album benefiting the World Wildlife Fund. This compilation album was released in December 1969. The *Nothing's Gonna Change Our World* arrangement of "Across the Universe," which is faster than the two other recordings, begins with the sound of flying birds, and the birds appear again on the fade-out ending. John plays acoustic guitar and electric guitar through a Leslie speaker, Paul and George sing background *ahs*, and Paul harmonizes with John on the Indian mantra words "jai guru deva om." George plays a tambura, an Indian stringed droning instrument, and an electric wah-wah-sounding guitar. Paul supposedly plays piano, but it's buried in the mix, and Ringo plays maracas. Two Beatles fans, Lizzie Bravo and Gayleen Pease, were invited in to the Abbey Road recording studio to sing with John on the words "nothing's gonna change my world," singing an octave higher than John. The second released version of the song is on the 1970 *Let It Be* album, produced by Phil Spector. Phil used the slower-speed recording and added a vocal choir and orchestral strings. He also eliminated all background voices, including Paul's harmony and his piano track. Thus, Paul was eliminated from this version. In 2003 on the *Let It Be . . . Naked* album, a third version was released. This stripped-down "Across the Universe" features John singing solo and playing his acoustic guitar with George playing the tambura. Listening to the three different versions of "Across the Universe" reveals the differing arrangements and production techniques that occurred over the course of many years. In a 1970 *Rolling Stone* interview regarding "Across the Universe," John said, "It's one of the best lyrics I have ever written. In fact, it could be the best." He was never completely satisfied with the 1968 recordings but thought that Phil Spector did a good job on the 1970 version.

George wrote "For You Blue," a country-blues-folk love song, for his first wife, Pattie. The song features John on lap steel guitar. During John's guitar solo, George pays John a compliment and says, "Elmore James got nothing on this baby," a reference to blues guitarist Elmore James. George plays acoustic guitar and sings the lead vocals. Paul plays a "fixed" piano, with paper inserted between the piano strings, creating a brittle percussive sound. Ringo plays the drums, but surprisingly, Paul, George, or John didn't overdub a bass part. "For You Blue" was the B-side to "The Long and Winding Road," which was the last single released by the Beatles while John was still living. Due to the number one chart-topping success of "The Long and Winding Road," "For You

Blue" received a lot of radio airplay, and as a result the record was recognized as double-sided A single by the U.S. *Billboard* record charts.

Tapping back to their early roots and love for skiffle music, the Beatles recorded a short version of the traditional song "Maggie Mae." One of the songs that John, Paul, and George had played with the Quarrymen, "Maggie Mae" got a new lease on life when the Beatles were recording the "Get Back" sessions, which eventually became the *Let It Be* album. John and Paul play acoustic guitars and sing while George plays a bass line on his electric Fender Telecaster guitar, and Ringo plays the drums. Making a full circle, starting with skiffle, to rock and roll and rhythm and blues to folk rock to string quartets and brass ensembles and to psychedelic and electronic music, the Beatles ended their recording career by playing what they began with—skiffle and rock and roll.

One could say that "Act Naturally" is the most-definitive Beatles country song. As you had read in chapter 1, "Beatles Roots: Covering American Songs," "Act Naturally" was originally recorded by Buck Owens and the Buckaroos. And the Beatles do act naturally in their movies, as you will read about in the next chapter.

Suggested Listening: "I'll Be Back"; "I'll Follow the Sun"; "I'm a Loser"; "I Don't Want to Spoil the Party"; "You've Got to Hide Your Love Away"; "Dear Prudence"; "Blackbird"; "Across the Universe"

7

ACTING NATURALLY

Movie Songs

There are five Beatles movies available to enhance your visual and auditory experience, starting with *A Hard Day's Night*; followed by *Help!*, *Magical Mystery Tour*, *Yellow Submarine*; and ending with *Let It Be*. The Beatles wrote songs specifically for each of their films. The style of the songs range from rock and roll, folk rock, and ballads to psychedelic. This book is about experiencing the Beatles' music, but watching their movies will give you an even greater perspective on each of the Beatles' individual personalities. There is John's sharp-tongued wit, Paul's sweet charm initially and then his domineering personality in *Let It Be*, George's laid-back coolness in *A Hard Day's Night*, and Ringo's overall affable, go-along-with-anything charisma. Be sure to have lots of popcorn on hand. There are a lot of Beatles visuals to watch.

A HARD DAY'S NIGHT

The Beatles could not have been happier in the summer of 1964. Beatlemania was happening throughout the world, their records were number one hits, and their first feature-length film premiered on July 6 at the Pavilion Theatre in London. A black-and-white film produced by Walter Shenson, United Artists released *A Hard Day's Night* worldwide in the summer of 1964. The movie portrays a day in the life of the Beatles, traveling on a train, getting mobbed by fans, playing a concert before a live studio audience for a television show, and singing and playing their new original songs. The songs featured in the movie are "A Hard Day's Night," "I Should Have Known Better," "And I Love Her," "Can't Buy Me Love," "If I Fell," "I'm Happy Just to Dance with You," and "Tell Me Why," plus "She Loves You," the closing song in the television show segment. An orchestral version of "This Boy" arranged and conducted by George Martin underscores a scene where Ringo goes walking about and eventually gets into trouble.

The fast-paced film begins with fans chasing John, George, and Ringo. During the chase, George trips and falls, followed by Ringo falling on George. John looks back and sees them on the ground and laughs. Rather than reshoot the opening scene, director Richard Lester kept it as is, setting the exciting, and at times somewhat slapstick, tone of the movie.

George ignites the song "A Hard Day's Night" with a sensational, harmonically complex chord played on his newly acquired electric Rickenbacker twelve-string guitar. The same chord is doubled on the piano, played by George Martin, while John plays a D suspended chord on his acoustic Gibson guitar and Paul plays a high D on his bass. It was the first time that the Beatles used the electric twelve-string guitar so boldly. After a few suspenseful seconds, John sings the lead vocals, and the full band comes in on the word *hard*. The melody in the bridge was too high for John, so Paul sings that section of the song. George raises the bar when it comes to lead guitar solos and plays single notes followed by a rapid circular guitar riff. Ringo is busy on the recording of "A Hard Day's Night," playing drums and overdubbing bongos and cowbell. The song ends with George playing an arpeggio configuration of the opening chord, alternating between the high notes G and F. "A Hard Day's Night" ends positively with the lyrics "I feel alright." This dynamic, fast-tempo song written by John perfectly matches the highly energetic movie and was a number one hit single in many countries, including the United Kingdom and the United States.

Outdoor drive-in movie theaters were popular during the 1950s and 1960s. When A Hard Day's Night *was released, cars jam-packed the theaters. . . . There is a long line of cars at the entrance to the Lakewood Drive-In Theater. You sit in the passenger seat while your mother pa-*

tiently waits and eventually parks the car at one of the few remaining car slots. After rolling down the driver's side window halfway, your mother lifts the small metal-encased speaker with wires attached to the post in the ground and places it on the car's window. The hot summer sun had set, and you and everybody in all of the cars are anxious to see the new Beatles movie, A Hard Day's Night. *After watching a few commercials about buying food and drinks at the drive-in's concession stand, the giant screen goes black. Then suddenly you hear the opening chord to "A Hard Day's Night" along with the movie's title and opening scene. Seeing the much-larger-than-life Beatles dazzles your eyes, and even though it's only a two-inch speaker, their songs fill the inside of the car and electrify your ears.*

The timing could not have been better with the movie released in advance of the Beatles' 1964 world tour and North American tour. Produced by Walter Shenson, directed by Richard Lester, and released in the United Kingdom on July 6 and the United States on August 11, *A Hard Day's Night* fueled Beatlemania. The single "A Hard Day's Night" and B-side "I Should Have Known Better," as well as the other songs from the soundtrack album, dominated radio airwaves. The songs were played repeatedly on Top 40 AM radio stations throughout America. The Beatles had made a successful leap from recording artists and performers to acting on the big screen. They did so, for the most part, by being themselves, by acting naturally. In the movie, their charming personalities were turned up all the way and they were irresistible to Beatles fans. The plot is centered around Paul's grandfather's seemingly innocent troublemaking. Played by actor Wilfrid Brambell, the "clean old man" grandfather persuades Ringo to leave the television studio where the Beatles are scheduled to perform live, and Ringo goes off exploring and gets into trouble. After being followed by a policeman who is suspicious of Ringo's behavior, Ringo is taken to the police station, while the television director, played by Victor Spinetti, is on the verge of having a nervous breakdown. Ringo's solo "exploring" scene showcased his natural acting abilities and enhanced his growing popularity. There's another natural thing that happened during the filming of *A Hard Day's Night*. George met an uncredited actress named Pattie Boyd who played the role of a schoolgirl during a train sequence. Taken by her beauty, George asked her out on a date, but she turned him down as she already had a boyfriend. Initially miffed by Pattie's rejection, George continued to pursue her, and eventually Pattie became Mrs. George Harrison.

The first staged song performed by the Beatles in the film is "I Should Have Known Better." Written by John, this moderate-paced love song has a recurring harmonica part. John sings the vocals and plays the harmonica. The climbing melody in the verses tops on the words *do* and *more*. In the movie, the song begins with the Beatles playing a game of cards, cuts to them playing the song, and then cuts back to them playing cards. "I Should Have Known Better" looks like it was shot in a cargo section of a train. Actually, it was filmed in a decorated van that was shaken periodically to give the viewing audience the impression that it was part of a moving train. George shines when he plays the lead guitar solo, based on the melody of the verse, while John plays the harmonica in the background. The bottom-line ending love lyrics in "I Should Have Known Better" are "you love me too." After watching this scene, you'll probably love the Beatles, too.

Written for the most part by Paul, "And I Love Her" is a light love ballad. The song was used in the movie when the Beatles play the rehearsal for the upcoming televised broadcast. Paul is featured and sings the sweet, tender lead vocals. George made a significant contribution in the arrangement of "And I Love Her." He wrote the recurring low-string guitar riff, the arpeggio part during the verses, and the lead guitar solo based on the song's melody, all played on a nylon-string classical guitar. Right before George's guitar solo, a harmonic shift occurs—the music changes key and stays in the new key. Listen carefully to the ending lead guitar riff and you'll hear Paul hum the same guitar notes. The last chord is a surprise—a major chord after a series of minor chords. In keeping with the song's light-sounding quality, Ringo doesn't play drums. Instead he plays bongos and claves.

"Can't Buy Me Love" is groundbreaking in the way it was used in the movie. Using fast-paced editing techniques applied to film footage of the Beatles running, jumping, and dancing in an open field, the film sequence of "Can't Buy Me Love" is a precursor to what would be called a music video. Twenty years later, music videos would become immensely popular. This quick-tempo song written by Paul is musically quite simple. It's the high energy, combined with Paul's powerful lead vocals and lyrics, that make it exciting. Addressing materialism, the song confirms that you can buy lots of things with money, but you can't buy

love. It was George Martin's idea to have Paul sing the title to introduce
the song. Paul wrote "Can't Buy Me Love" when the Beatles were in
Paris in January 1964, and they recorded the song at the local EMI
studio. The Paris recording of "Can't Buy Me Love" had background
harmonies sung by John and George. Once back in London, overdubs
were added. Paul recorded a new lead vocal without John's and
George's harmonies, and George recorded a new lead guitar solo.
When listening to George's lead guitar solo, you will hear two overlapping solos—the initial one recorded in Paris combined with the overdubbed solo recorded at Abbey Road.

John wrote the love ballad "If I Fell" and sings the introduction,
which has an unusual chord progression that does not reoccur. Then he
and Paul sing the smooth two-part harmony throughout the song. On
his twelve-string electric guitar, George plays a light arpeggio guitar
part woven in beneath the vocals during the entire song. The cautionary
lyrics address the uncertainty of romantic relationships, with hopes that
new love will be true and won't be in vain. The key word *if* underscores
the uncertainty surrounding new love. During the film sequence of "If I
Fell," George leans against a Vox amplifier and it tilts backward, causing
him to nearly fall. Here again, rather than reshoot the scene, the director kept it in, adding to the real, natural feel of the movie.

John and Paul wrote "I'm Happy Just to Dance with You" for
George to sing and feature in the TV rehearsal sequence in *A Hard
Day's Night*. George plays a Gibson acoustic guitar, and if you watch
the film you will see that the surface of the guitar would have benefited
from a good polish. The song begins with accented chords that are
played in the bridge along with Ringo's crash cymbals and drum fills.
John's quick-paced rhythm guitar playing propels the song forward.
John and Paul harmonize, singing "dance with you" and "oh" background vocals. The high-note harmony "oh" underlines the excitement
of the song's dance rhythm. As was the case with many early original
Beatles songs, brevity was common. "I'm Happy Just to Dance with
You" is one of the shortest songs in the Beatles' catalog, being only one
minute, fifty-eight seconds long. Once the TV studio is filled with an
audience, the Beatles perform a medley of songs.

Listen to the lyrics to "Tell Me Why." If by now you're getting
familiar with John's lyrics, then you'll know "Tell Me Why" could only
have been written by John. The lyrics address being lied to, hanging

one's head, and moaning, yet he's still desperately in love. Containing conflicted, emotional lyrics, the song begins with punchy drums and electric guitars. "Tell Me Why" features three-part harmony vocals sung by John, Paul, and George. John's lead vocals are intense, and he leaps up to his falsetto voice in the bridge. The lyrics "I beg you on my bended knees" are almost word for word the same as "I begged her on my bended knees" from the song "One After 909." John and Paul wrote "One After 909," and the Beatles performed it in their 1970 *Let It Be* movie. The musical ending in "Tell Me Why" is a rhythmic variation of the beginning of the song. "Tell Me Why" was part of a medley of songs played during the live studio scene toward the end of the film.

As a true testament to its timeless appeal, *A Hard Day's Night* continues to be shown at selected movie theaters and on some television channels. If you want to see what the Beatles looked like, feel Beatlemania, hear them speak, and listen to some of their best songs from 1964, watch *A Hard Day's Night*.

HELP!

The Beatles second movie, *Help!*, originally titled *Eight Arms to Hold You*, premiered at the London Pavilion Theatre on July 29, 1965, and was released in the United States a month later. Again, the Beatles timed the theatrical release of their movie to coincide with the start of their 1965 American concert tour and their historic performance at Shea Stadium. *Help!* had a much bigger budget than *A Hard Day's Night* and was shot in color. The bigger budget allowed director Richard Lester to shoot the film in three different geographical locations: England, the Austrian Alps, and the Bahamas. The storyline is centered on Ringo, who wears a sacrificial ring. According to an East Indian cult, the ring is a necessary part in sacrificing a woman to the goddess Kali. A group of Indians, led by Clang, brilliantly played by actor Leo McKern, are determined to get the ring from Ringo. After numerous failed attempts to remove the ring, Clang discovers that the large ring is stubbornly stuck on Ringo's finger. Clang has no choice but to make Ringo the sacrificial victim. Two scientists, played by Victor Spinetti and the comedic Roy Kinnear, become aware of the ring's supernatural powers and are also determined to get the ring from Ringo. The pacing of *Help!*

is slower than *A Hard Day's Night*, but the cinematography and close-up color shots of the Beatles make up for the slower pace. The highlights of the movie are the songs, which are "Help!," "You've Got to Hide Your Love Away," "You're Going to Lose That Girl," "The Night Before," "I Need You," "Ticket to Ride," and "Another Girl." Similar to the way Lester used "Can't Buy Me Love" in *A Hard Day's Night*, the song segments in *Help!* are precursors to what would later be defined as music videos, especially the songs "Ticket to Ride" and "Another Girl."

The movie begins with a sacrificial ceremony taking place, only to be halted because the woman to be sacrificed isn't wearing the necessary ring. In the next scene, the Beatles, dressed in black turtleneck jerseys, play and sing "Help!" on a projected screen. Clang throws darts at the Beatles' images on the screen, and the mission to get the ring from Ringo begins.

"You're Going to Lose That Girl," a warning song written by John and Paul, is the second song in the movie, shot in a mock-up recording studio. The lighting and close-up shots of the Beatles in "You're Going to Lose That Girl" draw you into the film. This vocally rich song is filled with tight harmonies sung by Paul and George, who sing the song's title and repeat what John sings in the lead vocals. During the chorus, John's voice leaps up to his falsetto register on the word *lose*. "You're Going to Lose That Girl" has a surprise harmonic change when the key changes in the bridge, where George plays a tasty, note-bending lead guitar solo, and then slips back to the original key. To add to the rhythm of the song, Ringo plays bongos. At the end of this song sequence in the film, a funny thing happens. The recording engineer hears a buzzing noise. He asks if any of the Beatles are buzzing, and then suddenly Ringo and his drum set fall through a section of the floor that was cut with a buzz saw by the Indians.

During the film's "You've Got to Hide Your Love Away" song sequence, John sings and plays his acoustic twelve-string guitar. Ringo plays the tambourine while sitting alone in John's sunken bedroom. The actress Eleanor Bron, who plays the character Ahme, sits on a couch with George, who makes eyes at her while he plays a Gibson acoustic guitar. The ending flute solo is played by the Beatles' indoor gardener, who trims the faux grass-covered floor in their adjoining apartments. "You've Got to Hide Your Love Away" embodies the folk-rock music style that was becoming increasingly popular in 1965.

The film scene for "Ticket to Ride," a song written by John, was shot in the Austrian Alps. The Beatles are frolicking, sledding, skiing, and having lots of fun. They are also gathered around a grand piano in the snow, where they playfully mime the lyrics to the song. George looks especially cool wearing a nineteenth-century top hat. The song begins with George playing a recurring guitar riff on his electric twelve-string guitar. Then the full band comes crashing in. An overdubbed electric guitar part plays a droning open A string during the verses, giving the song a multilayered sound. Listen to "Ticket to Ride" and you will hear a unique syndicated drum part. While played by Ringo, it was Paul who came up with the drum pattern. In addition to playing bass and singing harmony with John's lead vocals, Paul also plays the lead guitar part after the bridge of the song and during the "my baby don't care" double-time, fade-out ending. "Ticket to Ride" was a number one hit in the United States and many other countries in May 1965.

There is only one George Harrison song in *Help!* and it's "I Need You," a love song that he wrote for Pattie Boyd. Filmed outdoors in a field on the Salisbury Plain, the Beatles are protected from Clang and his gang by military tanks and armed British troops. It was a cold, windy day, and Ringo shivers from the cold English air. This scene also reveals that the Beatles' hair has grown longer than it was a year earlier when they appeared in *A Hard Day's Night*. "I Need You" has a striking, characteristic lead guitar part played by George on his electric twelve-string, even though he plays a Gretsch electric six-string guitar in the film sequence. He plays suspended and resolved chords using a volume pedal when he sings the last two words of the verses, on the song's title, and on the music at the end of the verses. This recording has an unusual percussion ensemble with Ringo hitting a guitar case (or backside of a guitar) and John playing a snare drum. Adding variety to the percussion, Ringo overdubbed a cowbell in the bridges. Background vocals sung by John and Paul add tenderness to George's heartfelt "I Need You."

"The Night Before," written by Paul, was also filmed on the Salisbury Plain. The song begins with the prominent sound of a Hohner Pianet, played by John, who was particularly fond of the keyboard instrument in 1965. Paul sings the arcing lead vocal melody while John and George harmonize together, singing, "Ah, the night before." Paul wants things to be the way they were in the past rather than how they turned out to be. The lyrics in "The Night Before" are a clever way of addressing how quickly romantic relationships can change. Paul's vocal peaks on the word *cry*, adding a bit of a growl to his voice during the bridge. The note-bending lead guitar solo is played by George and Paul. They play the same part in different octaves, which gives the solo a layered texture. This octave guitar technique was a new sound for the Beatles in 1965 but was short-lived, except for when they used it again briefly in "Hey Bulldog." During the film sequence, Ahme tricks Clang into believing that the Beatles are directly above an underground cavity filled with explosives. Ahme did this by playing "She's a Woman" on a tape recorder hidden near explosives. Above ground, the Beatles are playing "The Night Before." Both songs are spliced together and interspersed with each other, matching the film's action. At the very end of "The Night Before," the planted dynamite ignites with a huge explosion. The Beatles run for cover.

Moving on to the Bahamas, "Another Girl," written by Paul, was shot on rocks by the ocean and on a coral reef. On the recording, the slippery lead guitar fills are played by Paul. In the film, the Beatles mime playing the song and exchange instruments. Paul pretends to be playing his bass on a bikini-clad actress, John mimes playing the drums, George plays the bass, and Ringo plays guitar. "Another Girl" is a fun-filled music segment in the film, in which the Beatles share a lot of laughs. The song begins with a strong declaration by Paul, proclaiming that he has another girl, and he has met quite a few. Through the course of the lyrics that repeat "another girl" sung in harmony by Paul, John, and George, many girls pose with them, reminding the audience that the Beatles were having no difficulty whatsoever getting girls' attention during their wild Beatlemania days.

The Beatles did a lot of laughing during the filming of *Help!* They were smoking marijuana and were high most of the time. The album design for the *Help!* soundtrack illustrates how much fun the Beatles were having with the movie. On the front cover, you will see George above the *H* as in Harrison, Ringo above the *E*, John above the *L* as in Lennon, and Paul above the *P* as in Paul. Three Beatles names match the *H*, *L*, and *P*. That left Ringo with the *E*. Perhaps in this case we can call Ringo "Ringe"? Open the album cover and you will see a photo of the Beatles, and Ringo has red paint on him. Why red paint? According to the Indian cult, the person being sacrificed needed to be painted red before the ceremony could take place. There was a lot of red paint flying around in the movie, and it was all targeted at Ringo.

Something life changing happened to George during the filming of *Help!* In the Indian restaurant scene where the Beatles are confronted by Clang, an arrangement of the Beatles' song "A Hard Day's Night" is played on Indian instruments. This was the first time that George heard Indian instruments. Indian music would have a major impact on George as he studied the sitar, Indian culture, and Hinduism. George's Indian music contributions to the Beatles are highlighted in chapter 8, "Broader Horizons: World Music Songs." It should also be noted that Ken Thorne composed the outstanding orchestral soundtrack to the film, which included Indian instruments.

The movie *Help!* is dedicated to Elias Howe, who invented the sewing machine. Why would the Beatles dedicate the film to Mr. Howe? In the closing credits, there is a screenshot of a Singer sewing machine. The logical explanation is that the Beatles are singers, and so is this sewing machine.

MAGICAL MYSTERY TOUR

By 1967, the Beatles' music had changed dramatically, as you can hear in the songs on the *Sgt. Pepper's Lonely Heart Club Band* and *Magical Mystery Tour* albums. On December 26, 1967, the Beatles released their self-directed and self-produced *Magical Mystery Tour* movie on television in the United Kingdom. This largely experimental, see-what-happens movie was Paul's idea and is very different from the scripted *A Hard Day's Night* and *Help!* movies directed by Richard Lester. Improvisational in nature, the loose plot is based on a group of varied characters, including the Beatles, who travel on a bus in the English countryside. Filming took place in September 1967, at the time when the Beatles were glowing with the critically acclaimed success of their *Sgt. Pepper's Lonely Hearts Club Band* album. A psychedelic glow glistened on the *Magical Mystery Tour*, but aside from the songs, the movie is more mysterious than magical. For some reason, Ringo continually argues with his aunt Jessie, and the bus conductor, Buster Bloodvessel, and Jessie fall in love with each other. A bizarre vehicle and foot race happens. John, dressed as a waiter, shovels pounds of gooey spaghetti onto Jessie's overflowing plate. A strip show takes place, backed by the Bonzo Dog Band, and the movie ends with the Beatles in white-tailed tuxedos dancing to the song "Your Mother Should Know." Something unfortunate, but funny, happened that was not included in the film. While the bus was traversing English country roads, it came upon a small bridge and proceeded forward. But not for long. The bridge was too narrow, and the magical bus got stuck on the bridge. Photographer Chris Walter traveled with the Beatles on their *Magical Mystery Tour* and took many photos of the Beatles at several locations. He happened to take a photo of the bus stuck on the bridge.

The *Magical Mystery Tour* movie was the Beatles' first creative flop for a number of reasons. The unscripted, experimental approach was too unstructured and lacked continuity, and the Beatles had no experience directing a film. The film was released in the United Kingdom on Boxing Day, when exchanging gift boxes, not boxing gloves, takes place. The movie was shot using color film, but the majority of television sets in the United Kingdom were black and white. As a result, the dynamic colors could not be seen and the black-and-white broadcast looked dull. If Brian Epstein had still been alive, he may have prevented the release of the movie and focused on the strength of the songs and the album. The movie includes six new Beatles songs: "Magical Mystery Tour," "The Fool on the Hill," "Flying," "Blue Jay Way," "Your Mother Should Know," and "I Am the Walrus."

On the *Magical Mystery Tour* album cover, the Beatles are dressed in animal costumes and surrounded by multicolored stars. Below a walrus, which references the song "I Am the Walrus," is the vibrant-colored album title. Unlike the lyrics in "I Am the Walrus," when John says that he is the walrus, during the song "Glass Onion," John sings, "The Walrus was Paul." Therefore, it's conceivable that Paul is dressed as the walrus on the album cover. The back cover is a multilayered collage photo of the Beatles dressed in white-tailed tuxedos from the "Your Mother Should Know" film scene. Side one of the album contains the six songs from the movie. Side two is a collection of the Beatles' 1967 singles: "Hello, Goodbye," "Strawberry Fields Forever," "Penny Lane," "Baby You're a Rich Man," and "All You Need Is Love." The style and production of the songs in the movie certainly parallel the trippy, psychedelic nature of the film.

It's time to get on the bus. "Magical Mystery Tour," the trippy title song to the movie, was written by Paul, with John contributing a few lyrics. Recorded less than a week after completing the *Sgt. Pepper's Lonely Hearts Club Band* album, the song begins with Paul's carnival-sounding voice announcing, "Roll up!"—as in roll a joint before getting on the bus? The Beatles were doing plenty of drugs in 1967—marijuana and LSD. A direct reference to an acid trip, during the bridge of the song, John says, "Mystery trip." Paul's brilliant bass playing during the bridge is out front and in your face. Sounds of the bus go rushing by with stereo panning. The trumpet ensemble adds a lot of sparkle to the song with rhythmic punches. John's and George's backing vocals are heavily processed with effects. The piano warbles during the ending fade-out, sounds stretched and trippy with some applied tape manipulation and tremolo and reverb effects. Opening the movie with this song, the Beatles extend an invitation to take you away, far away, into the world of their magical songs.

There are hundreds of thousands of hills in England, but none of them appealed to Paul. So he flew, without a passport, to Nice, France, where he found a hill that satisfied him. That's where the film segment for "The Fool on the Hill" was shot. When watching the footage, you will see many sides of Paul—spinning, dancing, jumping, and running on a hill. Paul says that the song is about someone like the Maharishi, but Paul is the only one on the hill. Certainly, Paul couldn't be the fool.

"Flying," composed of a simple three-chord progression, is one of the most unusual Beatles songs. Originally titled "Ariel Tour Instrumental," it's one of the few songs written by all four Beatles. The song is a rare Beatles instrumental with a "la, la, la, la, la" chorus and has no verses or bridges. John plays the organ and mellotron, an electronic keyboard instrument that plays prerecorded tape loops. The electric guitars are played by Paul and George. One of the guitars is heavily processed with a phasing effect and sounds choked or squashed. In contrast, the other guitar part has a mellow tone. The electronic sound effects at the end of the song, created by John and Ringo, are mindbending, improvisational in nature, and have nothing to do with the music that precedes it. Even though the Beatles are on the bus, they do get off the ground with "Flying."

"I Am the Walrus" is an amazing psychedelic, electronic, avant-garde, orchestral-backed pop song written by John. *Everything* about it is unlike any other Beatles song, and the same can be said for the "I Am the Walrus" scene in *Magical Mystery Tour*. The visuals in the film match some of the song's image-rich lyrics. The repetitive lyric "I am the egg man" is portrayed by John's head being wrapped in a white, egg-looking skull cap. There is a line of policemen holding hands on a high wall, bringing to life the lyrics "pretty little policemen in a row." Negative images of the Beatles playing their instruments are cut in and out of the film footage. The lyrics are intentionally abstract. Influenced by Lewis Carroll's poem "The Walrus and the Carpenter," a nursery rhyme, plus a considerable dose of LSD, John paints disjunctive, bizarre pictures with his words, such as "pigs from a gun," "crabalocker fish wife," "pornographic priestess," and "elementary penguin." For extra measure, John mixes in some nonsensical gibberish with "goo, goo, g'joob." What images do you see when you hear the lyrics to "I Am the Walrus"? Whatever they are, I'm sure they are colorful. You can discover more about "I Am the Walrus" in chapter 9, "Recording Studio Wizardry: Psychedelic and Electronic Songs."

In August 1967, George was staying at attorney Robert Fitzpatrick's home on Blue Jay Way, high up in the Hollywood Hills above the Sunset Strip in Los Angeles. Robert had been hired by Brian Epstein to handle some of the Beatles' and Brian's personal legal affairs. Robert was in Hawaii and offered his home to George, Pattie, and the Beatles' personal assistant Neil Aspinall while they were in Los Angeles. It was getting late, and having just flown in from London, George was jet-lagged and tired. But he wanted to stay awake because Derek Taylor, who was also in Los Angeles, was on his way to visit George. To stay awake, George started playing the small organ in Robert's home. As he played, George noticed that a fog was settling in on the city. That gave birth to the opening lyrics in the song "Blue Jay Way." An Indian-flavored droning song, "Blue Jay Way" documents the true account of George waiting for Derek to arrive. A month later, back in London at Abbey Road, George and the Beatles recorded "Blue Jay Way" for the *Magical Mystery Tour* film and accompanying album. In the film segment, George sits cross-legged, dressed in Indian-styled clothes with a colored chalk drawing of an organ on the concrete floor at his fingertips. "Blue Jay Way" spotlights the organ and doesn't include guitars. Paul and Ringo flesh out the sounds with bass and drums, which are processed with a flanging delay effect. "Blue Jay Way" begins with George playing long, sustained notes and the melody to the chorus on a Hammond organ followed by a solo cello, performed by an uncredited studio musician. George sings the first verse, which contains some backward music and fragmented voices. The rhythm is developed on the first chorus and second verse when Ringo plays his full drum kit, while George sings "Please don't be long" on the chorus. John and Paul sing background vocals on the second chorus, repeating George's "don't be long" vocals. The solo cello returns during the second chorus and continues throughout the song, chugging along and playing descending notes between the vocal passages during the ending chorus. Instead of repeating and answering George on the ending chorus, John and Paul harmonize with George. Perfectly replicating a late, foggy night in Los Angeles, the overall effect of "Blue Jay Way" is nocturnal and sleepy.

"Your Mother Should Know," written by Paul, is a throwback dance hall–styled song. This song was used as the closing number in the *Magical Mystery Tour* movie. The Beatles, dressed in white-tailed tuxedos, dance the same choreographed steps as they descend a large spiral staircase. John, George, and Ringo have red carnations attached to their jacket lapels. Paul is wearing a black carnation. A black carnation? Have you ever seen a black carnation? Why is Paul's carnation black? Paul claims it was simply a mistake. Some people think this was a clue that supports the Paul McCartney death hoax. According to conspiracy theorists, Paul died in a car crash on either September 11 or November 9, 1966. If you find the death hoax interesting, there is extensive coverage on this subject on the Internet, which details visual clues on Beatles albums covers and lyric clues in some of their songs.

Paul wrote "Your Mother Should Know" to acknowledge mothers in general, who know more about their children than their children realize. The arrangement of the song is quite simple: Paul sings lead and harmony vocals and plays piano and bass guitar, John plays the organ and sings harmony, George plays rhythm guitar and sings harmony, and Ringo plays the drums. The sound and texture of John's and George's background voices are similar to their voices in the bridge of "Lady Madonna," another one of Paul's songs, which was recorded a few months later. The lyrics are repetitive, but even so, "Your Mother Should Know" is an appealing, toe-tapping song.

From the albums *Meet the Beatles!* to *Sgt. Pepper's Lonely Hearts Club Band*, the Beatles' evolution as songwriters and as a band is unmatched. Starting with love songs using three or four chords and moving to complex lyrics and advanced, multichord progressions, the Beatles had raised the innovative creative bar so high that listeners expected every new Beatles album to be a new, evolutionary sound experience. The Beatles' soundtrack albums are a mix of songs from the movies, instrumental orchestral music, and prereleased singles. Only side one of the *Magical Mystery Tour* album can be considered a soundtrack, since side two is a collection of previously released singles, unrelated to the film. The *Yellow Submarine* soundtrack album, the Beatles' second album released on the Apple Records label, contains only four new songs on side one—"Only a Northern Song," "All Together Now," "Hey Bulldog," and "It's All Too Much," along with the previously released singles "Yellow Submarine" and "All You Need Is Love." Side two is made up of beautiful orchestral soundtrack music composed and conducted by George Martin. Unlike most Beatles albums, which contained wall-to-wall new songs, the *Magical Mystery Tour* and *Yellow Submarine* albums didn't equal the all new songs high standard the Beatles had set. Nonetheless, the *Yellow Submarine* movie was a critically acclaimed success, and it sent a powerful message that love can prevail against evil.

YELLOW SUBMARINE

You and your friends hear about the new animated Beatles' movie, which is going to be shown at the local movie theater. You wonder why it is an animated film, like a cartoon, and not a movie with the real, physical Beatles. Maybe the theater will be filled with kids wanting to see a new cartoon? When you and your Beatles pals walk into the theater, you are happy to see that the audience is filled with teenagers. Most of the guys have long hair, and the girls have long hair with bangs. The film takes you on a fascinating journey through Pepperland and a variety of seas, including the Sea of Holes and the Sea of Green. You also experience the scary Blue Meanies, who hate music. The Blue Meanies have ruined Pepperland and have frozen its citizens, draining them of all color and life. The Beatles come to the rescue, and with their music they overcome the evil Meanies and peace and love returns to Pepperland. Even the leader of the Blue Meanies has a change of heart and no longer threatens the music-loving people of Pepperland. At the end of the film, you are suddenly surprised when you see the real Beatles on the big screen. But after looking through a periscope, John announces that he sees Blue Meanies approaching the movie theater! The only way to stop the Meanies is to sing, says John. After the closing credits roll to the song "All Together Now," you and your friends walk out of the theater singing the song while holding hands. The Beatles restored peace and love in Yellow Submarine, *and you and your friends feel that love and believe it.*

The movie features brilliantly colored animated Beatles, created by animation directors Robert Balser from the United States and Jack Stokes from the United Kingdom. Watch *Yellow Submarine* and the wild, surreal animation will blow your mind and fill your heart with renewed love. In addition to the songs "Yellow Submarine," "Only a Northern Song," "All Together Now," "Hey Bulldog," "It's All Too Much," and "All You Need Is Love," the movie also includes "Eleanor Rigby," "Lucy in the Sky with Diamonds," "When I'm Sixty-Four," "Nowhere Man," "Sgt. Pepper's Lonely Hearts Club Band," immediately followed by a snippet of "With a Little Help from My Friends," and an excerpt from "Baby You're a Rich Man," which are not on the accompanying album. In addition to the songs, George Martin composed an orchestral soundtrack for the movie, which fills the entire second side of the *Yellow Submarine* album. John was critical of George Martin's score and didn't want it on the album. However, because the Beatles didn't have enough new material to fill the album, John had to accept the inclusion of the orchestral score. Without Martin's compositions, the movie and album would not have been complete.

The recording of the song "Yellow Submarine" is loaded with nautical sound effects, including bubbling water, a ship's bell, waves, whistles, and chains. The Beatles had a lot of fun talking through tin cans and shouting like sailors. Paul conceived "Yellow Submarine" as a children's song for Ringo to sing. A sing-along song with a big chorus of singers, the musical arrangement of "Yellow Submarine" is lean, with acoustic guitar, bass, drums, and tambourine. The marching band, sound effects, and big vocal chorus are what makes the song unique. A varied group of people sing the chorus: John, Paul, George, and Ringo; Brian Jones of the Rolling Stones; Mal Evans, who also bangs a bass drum; Pattie Boyd Harrison; recording artist Marianne Faithfull; plus extremely rare singing from George Martin, engineer Geoff Emerick,

Neil Aspinall, and Brian Epstein. As the number one hit single recorded and released in 1966 along with "Eleanor Rigby," two years later "Yellow Submarine" would give birth to the animated movie.

"Hey Bulldog," a powerful, piano-driven rocker written by John with a little help from Paul, was not included in the original U.S. release of *Yellow Submarine*. The movie's producer, Al Brodax, claimed that with "Hey Bulldog," the film was too long. But the song was included in the 1999 rerelease of the film. With doglike creatures in *Yellow Submarine*, "Hey Bulldog" is certainly a good fit. John had said in 1980, and is quoted in the book by David Sheff, *All We Are Saying: The Last Major Interview with John Lennon and Yoko Ono*, that the song "is a good sounding recording that means nothing."

"Only a Northern Song," written by George, contains an orgy of sounds, including George playing the organ and singing lead vocals, John playing the piano and glockenspiel, Ringo on drums, and Paul playing bass guitar and a trumpet. The song was recorded at the time when the Beatles were recording the *Sgt. Pepper's Lonely Hearts Club Band* album, when they experimented with new sounds in the recording studio. George Martin, John, and Paul decided not to include "Only a Northern Song" on the *Sgt. Pepper* album. When four new songs were needed for the *Yellow Submarine* movie, "Only a Northern Song" was one of the four that were chosen. The lyrics are both humorously on the nose and telling. George wasn't happy with the music-publishing agreement that he had with Dick Lewis and the music publishing company Northern Songs. The majority of monies received by the company went to John and Paul, while George's royalties were less than 1 percent. The song is filled with a dizzying array of electronic effects, backward tape loops, and dissonance, all of which mirror the lyrics "chords going wrong" and "out of key." "Only a Northern Song" was a musical vehicle for George to express his discontent with the publishing company and diminish the value of the song by stating that it didn't matter what chords he played or words he sang. George goes one step further and sings, "There's no one there," as if he is removing himself from the Northern Songs publisher. "Only a Northern Song" perfectly matches the psychedelic nature of the *Yellow Submarine* movie.

Sounding similar to "Only a Northern Song" in terms of production and use of instruments, George's second song contribution to the movie is "It's All Too Much." During the drug culture of the 1960s, a popular verbal phrase used to describe what happened when experiencing LSD was "too much." Intense, screaming guitar feedback ignites the song, along with the words "to your mind." Listening to this song can be a mind-expanding experience. The movie ends with "It's All Too Much," celebrating the defeat of the Blue Meanies with the positive force of love. You can read more about "It's All Too Much" and "Only a Northern Song" in chapter 9, "Recording Studio Wizardry: Psychedelic and Electronic Songs."

Concluding the animated part of the movie, "All Together Now" is a playful children's sing-a-long song written mostly by Paul. Acoustic guitars, played by Paul and George, along with ukulele and harmonica played by John, round out the skiffle style of the song. "All Together Now" exudes a spirit of bringing people together, making it a perfect closing credits song for the movie. At the end of the movie, translations of "All Together Now" appear onscreen in many different languages, indirectly asking people from different countries to be all together. After the first chorus, Paul sings a series of colors and finishes the lyric line with "I love you," suggesting an interpretation that differing races and cultures present no barriers to love and compassion. Paul sings the lead vocals and also plays the bass. Ringo plays the drums and finger cymbals. All four Beatles sing the chorus and clap their hands, along with some of their friends, which creates a party-sounding atmosphere. The last chorus accelerates and ends with clapping and a "honk-honk," which adds to the fun nature of the song.

The animated *Yellow Submarine* movie appropriately included the 1967 hit song "All You Need Is Love." After all, it was love that eventually overcame the Blue Meanies, turning them around and changing their hearts from being mean to lovable. More detailed information about "All You Need Is Love" is in chapter 4, "Playing America's Heart Strings: Love Songs," and chapter 10, "Orchestral Dimensions: Strings, Woodwinds, and Brass Songs."

LET IT BE

The *Let It Be* movie began as the "Get Back" recording sessions. The intent was to document the Beatles working on new songs for their next album without recording overdubs or building multiple tracks. These were songs that they would perform live. Starting on January 2, 1969, the Beatles met at Twickenham Studios in London to begin the project. Unfortunately, the tensions that existed during the recording of the *White Album* were still very much alive. John's relationship with Yoko Ono had grown deeper. She was constantly with John, and her presence at Twickenham exacerbated the deteriorating relationships among the Beatles. They tried to get back to their musical roots by playing some of their favorite rock-and-roll and rhythm-and-blues cover songs, including "Ain't She Sweet," "Blue Suede Shoes," and some of the songs they had played in Hamburg, Germany, and at the Liverpool Cavern Club, such as "That's All Right (Mama)," "What'd I Say," and "Be Bop a Lula." The Beatles played more than a hundred songs during the sessions, including new songs that ended up on the *Abbey Road* and *Let It Be* albums. As much as the Beatles tried to get back, they couldn't get back to where they once belonged, to borrow some of the lyrics from their single "Get Back." While there were some happy moments among the Beatles, to a considerable extent, the film documents the band splintering and coming apart. At one point early on in the sessions, George walked out and quit the band. And how did John respond? He said they should call Eric Clapton. "He's just as good and not such a headache," declared John, as quoted in the book *Luck and Circumstance: A Coming of Age in Hollywood, New York and Points Beyond*, written by Michael Lindsay-Hogg, who directed the *Let It Be* movie.

A month prior, John had performed with Eric Clapton in the *Rolling Stones Rock and Roll Circus*. At that performance, Paul didn't play bass and Ringo didn't play drums. Keith Richards of the Rolling Stones played bass, and Mitch Mitchell of the Jimi Hendrix Experience played drums. John's move to play with other musicians was an indication of his desire to be more than just a Beatle. So much so that in 1969, John formed a new band with Yoko called the Plastic Ono Band, which included a rotating roster of musicians such as Tommy Smothers, Eric Clapton, Klaus Voormann, and Alan White. While the Beatles were still officially together and working on the *Abbey Road* album, John released the single "Give Peace a Chance" by the Plastic Ono Band. Another loud and clear signal from John happened when the Plastic Ono Band released "Cold Turkey" in October 1969, the same month the Beatles released the "Come Together"/"Something" single. Ringo played drums on "Cold Turkey."

George's temporary departure happened for a number of reasons. He didn't like Yoko being at the sessions, he didn't like Paul telling him how to play the guitar and what to play, and he was frustrated with Paul and John having little interest in his songs. During the morning session, Paul was telling George how to play the guitar part in Paul's song "Two of Us." In this scene in the movie, George said to Paul with a frustrated tone, "I'll play what you want me to play, or I won't play at all if you don't want me to. Whatever it is that'll please you, I'll do it."

This was a sad and all-time low event in George and Paul's long relationship. Paul had brought George into the Quarrymen in 1958, and they had shared a close friendship and many years of good times playing together as the Beatles. But ever since the Beatles started work on their *Sgt. Pepper's Lonely Hearts Club Band* album, Paul had taken on a domineering, directorial role. Paul's proficiency with the guitar added to the tensions, which reached a boiling point on January 10, 1969, when George walked out on the Beatles.

The "Get Back" sessions were Paul's idea. John, George, and Ringo participated, but they did not appear to be enthused about it. In one scene in the film, Paul speaks to John about the project and John doesn't respond. He looks completely bored, says nothing, and just stares at Paul while smoking a cigarette.

The songs the Beatles play in the movie are "Don't Let Me Down," "Maxwell's Silver Hammer," "Two of Us," "I've Got a Feeling," "Oh! Darling," "One After 909," "Across the Universe," "Dig a Pony," "I Me Mine," "For You Blue," "Bésame Mucho," "You Really Got a Hold on Me," "The Long and Winding Road," "Rip It Up," "Shake, Rattle and Roll," "Kansas City," "Lawdy Miss Clawdy," "Dig It," "Let It Be," and "Get Back." The Beatles had many conversations about where they would perform the new songs. Possible locations for the performance included a concert hall in London, aboard a cruise ship, and at a Roman amphitheater in Africa.

The film begins with a shot of Ringo's bass drum with the Beatles' logo on it. As he had done for several years, the Beatles' trustworthy road manager Mal Evans moves instruments into place. Paul plays a classical composition by Samuel Barber on the piano with Ringo sitting nearby. A half-eaten Granny Smith apple is on top of the piano. Although not in the film, George enters Twickenham and says, "Hare Krishna," which is on the "Fly on the Wall" bonus disc released with the

Let It Be . . . Naked album in 2003. In the film, George comes in and smiles with Ringo. John and Yoko float in. Straightaway it's obvious that the Beatles are in different worlds. Paul appears to be interested in classical music; George is the only one immersed in the Indian culture and Hinduism; John is focused on himself and Yoko; and Ringo is about to act in the film *The Magic Christian* with Peter Sellers.

Once the Beatles settle in with their instruments, they begin to play John's new song about Yoko, "Don't Let Me Down." The Beatles work on the arrangement and rehearse and play the song during their impromptu rooftop performance. "Don't Let Me Down" begins with a chord, bass note, and cymbal crash followed by a guitar riff and a repeat of the opening musical arrangement that introduces the chorus. Then John emphatically sings, "Don't let me down," followed by Paul harmonizing with John on the repeated song title lyrics. While the song is in an even four-four time, the isolated vocals before each verse have five beats. Despite the odd time signature, the lyrics and melody flow and sound completely natural. The bridge contains a melodious countermelody played by George on guitar and an octave lower on the bass, played by Paul.

George thought it would be good to have keyboardist Billy Preston join the Beatles during the "Get Back" sessions. Billy was able to lighten the sour mood overshadowing the band as he played electric piano on "Don't Let Me Down" and performed with the Beatles at their rooftop performance. The only recording artist to have a name on a Beatles record, the "Get Back," and "Don't Let Me Down" single has "The Beatles with Billy Preston" printed on the record label. A peculiar omission by Phil Spector, who produced the *Let It Be* album, "Don't Let Me Down" is not on the album despite the fact that the song is in the movie.

The Beatles rehearsing Paul's song "Maxwell's Silver Hammer" is the next scene in the movie. Paul sings and simultaneously calls out the chord changes to John and George. During the chorus, Mal Evans bangs on an anvil with a hammer to the lyrics "bang, bang." "Maxwell's Silver Hammer" also was not included on the *Let It Be* album, but it is on *Abbey Road*. The dark lyrics about a fictitious character named Maxwell who goes around killing people with a silver hammer are strikingly juxtaposed to the bright, upbeat music. Paul tells the story about bad-boy Maxwell by singing the lead vocals and playing piano, electric guitars, and the Moog synthesizer. During the second and third verses, the synthesizer part harmonizes with Paul's lead vocals. George plays a rhythmic six-string bass part and acoustic guitar and sings background vocals along with Ringo, who plays the drums and bangs the anvil. You can hear Ringo's voice loud and clear mixed in with the ending "Silver Hammer" lyrics. John, who did not like the song, is not on the recording.

When you watch the documentary film, you will see how Paul's song "Two of Us" evolved. The first version is played as an up-tempo rock-and-roll song. During this film segment, John and Paul are having a good time singing and playing together. But Paul wasn't satisfied with the arrangement, so he replaced his bass guitar with an acoustic guitar and rearranged the song. The final version of "Two of Us" is performed by the Beatles in the second part of the film. Part two of the film takes place at the Beatles' recording studio in their office building on Savile Row. In the recording studio parts of the film, unlike the rehearsal sessions, where the Beatles are casually dressed, the Beatles dress up a bit more.

The Beatles rehearsed "I've Got a Feeling," and once again John and Paul were having a good time. The song is a combination of Paul's "I've Got a Feeling" and John's "Everybody Had a Hard Year." During the rehearsal, Paul tells John how he wants the descending lead guitar to be played, illustrating another example of Paul having fixed, definitive musical parts to his songs. The year 1968 had been a hard one for John. He had divorced Cynthia, Yoko had had a miscarriage, he was addicted to heroin, he was arrested for possessing drugs, and he was unhappy being a Beatle. In contrast with John's lyrics is Paul's uplifting "I've Got a Feeling." During the bridge, Paul screams passionately about years of trying to find the love of his life and finally meeting her. Unlike the rehearsal, it's George who plays the descending guitar part in the rooftop performance. During the last verse, John and Paul sing the lyrics to their individual songs together. With Billy Preston playing the electric piano on the recording and during the rooftop performance, one could say that in January 1969, he was the fifth Beatle.

George's growing discontent with the Beatles is clearly evident in the film when he presents his new song "I Me Mine" to Ringo and says, "I don't care if you don't want it." George sings a heartfelt lead vocal as he, Paul, and Ringo rehearse the song while John dances with Yoko. To further demonstrate John's disregard and lack of interest in George's song, when the Beatles recorded it for the *Let It Be* album, John didn't attend the recording session. George plays all the guitars on "I Me Mine," and Paul harmonizes with George on the rocking choruses. Ringo plays drums with the Beatles for what would be the last time while John was still alive.

At the beginning of part two of the film, the Beatles individually arrive at Apple headquarters on Savile Row. Underscoring their arrival is George's song "For You Blue," which segues to the Beatles playing the song in their recording studio. Yoko sits next to John as he plays the lap steel guitar. You can find out more about "For You Blue" in chapter 6, "A Lighter Side: Folk-Rock and Country-Rock Songs."

Going back to a song that the Beatles had recorded on a demo tape on January 1, 1962, the Beatles played a spirited cover version of the Spanish song "Bésame Mucho," written by Consuelo Velázquez. One of the lighter, fun performances in the film, Paul sings the song with an over-the-top operatic voice while John gives him a big smile.

Following the fun-packed rendition of "Bésame Mucho," George and Ringo sit at a grand piano, where they work on Ringo's new song "Octopus's Garden." George and Ringo worked well together as collaborative writers, and as a team after the Beatles had broken up, they produced Ringo's solo hit songs, "It Don't Come Easy" and "Photograph." While George and Ringo work on "Octopus's Garden," John gets on Ringo's drum kit and provides them with some rhythm while lighting up a cigarette.

Along with Billy Preston playing organ, the Beatles jammed for more than fifteen minutes on a song written by all four Beatles titled "Dig It." The three-chord song is loosely based on the chorus to Bob Dylan's song "Like a Rolling Stone." John actually sings the lyrics "like a rolling stone" during the jam session. With Paul playing the piano, John plays a six-string bass. George plays lead guitar with his Fender Telecaster, Ringo plays his drums, and George Martin, who did not officially produce the *Let It Be* album, makes an appearance and plays maracas. Less than one minute from the jam is included on the *Let It Be* album. On the album, "Dig It" ends with John saying, "That was 'Can You Dig It' by Georgie Wood, and now we'd like to do 'Hark the Angels Come,'" which is the introduction to "Let It Be," the next song on the album.

As much as Paul tried to keep the Beatles together as a band, the core of the apple had rotted. The Beatles had to call it quits and let it be. The philosophical lyrics in "Let It Be" are timeless. In troubled and difficult times, instead of putting up a fight, just let it be. These were troubling times for Paul and the Beatles. The band was falling apart, and their personal and musical differences were too far apart to bridge the distant holes in their relationship. John, George, and Ringo wanted Allen Klein to manage the Beatles' business affairs, but Paul wanted Linda's father, Lee Eastman, to manage them.

Engineer Glyn Johns had recorded the Beatles' "Get Back" sessions and presented mixes of the songs to Paul and John, who were not satisfied with what Glyn had produced. The unfinished album, originally titled *Get Back*, was shelved, and the Beatles moved forward and recorded and released *Abbey Road* in late September 1969. In March 1970, John and Allen Klein, who had become the Beatles' business manager, decided to bring in Phil Spector to take over what Glyn had put together. Phil rearranged and produced the songs from the *Get Back* album, which was renamed *Let It Be*. On the back cover of the album is the following statement: "This is a new phase BEATLES album. Essential to the content of the film *Let It Be*, was that they performed live for many of the tracks. In comes the warmth and the freshness of a live performance, as reproduced for disc by Phil Spector." Yes, some, or as stated, "many," of the songs are live. But contrary to it being a complete live album, Spector added strings and brass on "I Me Mine" and "Let It Be," plus a choir and harp on "The Long and Winding Road." The front cover has live-action photos of the four individual Beatles, boxed in separate squares. All have long hair, and Paul sports a beard. John and Paul are singing, Ringo looks sad, and George has a big smile on his face. It's ironic that George smiles, since he was the least-happy Beatle during the "Get Back" sessions. On the original albums released in the United States, the Apple label was a red apple. All previously released Apple recordings had the green Granny Smith apple label. A red apple, as in "stop, the end," signifying this is last Beatles album? While one could construe that was the reason the apple had turned red, it being red had to do with United Artists having the rights to the *Let It Be* film and accompanying soundtrack album. To differentiate the album from a Capitol recording, United Artists Records made the Apple label red.

The studio session of "Let It Be" in the movie has lots of close-up shots of Paul. After all, he wrote the song and sings it with a convincing voice. The ballad is immediately appealing, with piano chords that lay down the harmonic structure. In the book *Paul McCartney: Many Years from Now*, by Barry Miles, Paul had said that he had a dream about his mother, Mary, who reassured him that things would be alright. That was the inspiration for the song and the lyrics "when I find myself in times of trouble, mother Mary comes to me." During the film sequence, when Paul sings the chorus, he says, "There will be no sorrow," a variation of him singing, "There will be an answer." Billy Preston plays a gospel-sounding organ part. George's lead guitar solo is played through a Leslie speaker cabinet, which gives it a swirling, textured sound. John's contribution to the song is minimal. He sings background vocals with George and plays a six-string bass. However, on the single and album releases of "Let It Be," it's Paul who plays an overdubbed bass part.

The single version of "Let It Be," produced by George Martin, contains overdubbed background harmonies, which include a rare vocal performance by Linda Eastman and a subdued orchestral arrangement. On the *Let It Be* album, produced by Phil Spector, George Harrison plays a higher-pitched guitar solo, which continues in the last choruses. You can hear the lead guitar solo played by George on the single bleed through in the background. In addition to his organ part, Billy Preston also played electric piano. Phil Spector applied a delay effect on Ringo's hi-hat, and during the third verse, Ringo added a rhythmic tom-tom pattern. The arrangement and production differences between the single and album versions clearly illustrate the differing production touches and flourishes by George Martin and Phil Spector.

The last song to be presented in the recording studio section of the *Let It Be* movie, "The Long and Winding Road," written by Paul, has to be the saddest original song recorded by the Beatles. The Beatles had traveled on a remarkable, magical road, filled with record-breaking accomplishments and worldwide appeal, but ultimately the road became four individual paths. Along with Billy Preston playing a Fender Rhodes electric piano, the Beatles performed "The Long and Winding Road" on January 31, 1969, as a no-frills arrangement. Similar to the instrumentation in "Let It Be," the song features Paul singing lead vocals and playing piano, George playing a Leslie-treated lead guitar part, John playing a six-string bass, and Ringo on drums. The single, released more than a year later in May 1970, is based on a recording the Beatles made on January 26, 1969. "The Long and Winding Road" single, which was the Beatles' twentieth number one single in the United States, was produced by Phil Spector with a lush orchestral backing complete with a harp and a fourteen-part female choir. You can read more about this aspect of the song in chapter 10, "Orchestral Dimensions: Strings, Woodwinds, and Brass Songs."

There were to be no Beatles' performances on an ocean liner, at a Roman amphitheater, or in a concert hall in London. On the final day of the "Get Back" sessions, January 30, 1969, the Beatles used the rooftop of their office building on 3 Savile Row in London as the location for their performance. This was the last time that the Beatles performed together live as a band.

It was a cold, cloudy day in London when the Beatles ventured out onto the rooftop of their office building. Ringo, wearing his wife Maureen's red raincoat, positioned himself on the drum kit. John wore a brown fur jacket; George wore a black fur coat; Paul wore a black suit jacket; and Billy Preston wore a black leather jacket. Unlike the stage positions that John, Paul, and George had taken during their touring years and in most televised performances, it was John who took the center position instead of George. Paul, like he always had done, stood forward right of Ringo. George was off to the left, where John usually stood. To begin their impromptu concert, the Beatles played "Get Back."

The sound of music coming from the rooftop drew curious Londoners out of their offices. Some folks came out of windows and stood on nearby rooftops, while many more gathered on the street below. The Beatles ended "Get Back" and played "Don't Let Me Down." With dozens of people gathering on Savile Row, cars were having difficulty driving through the crowded street. Some local business owners called the police and complained about the noise and congestion. Unaware of what was going on down at street level, the Beatles continued to play and moved on to "I've Got a Feeling." While there were some complaints, there were also compliments from people on the street, who said that they loved hearing the Beatles' new songs. Then the Beatles played "One After 909."

One of the first songs that John and Paul wrote after the budding songwriters teamed up together, "One After 909" is a rock-and-roll song with lyrics about catching a train. Originally, the song was played with a straight four-four rock-and-roll rhythm. The Beatles made attempts to record "One After 909" in 1963, but they were not happy with the recording and abandoned the song. Since the "Get Back" sessions were about getting back to their rock-and-roll roots, it was entirely appropriate for the Beatles to revisit the song. In 1969, the Beatles played "One After 909" with a shuffle, swing beat. On the rooftop, John sang the lead vocals and played his Epiphone Casino guitar, Paul played bass and sang harmony, George played his bright-toned Fender Telecaster guitar, while Ringo shuffled away on his drums and Billy Preston played electric piano. During this song's film sequence, George plays his lead guitar riffs and solo enthusiastically, portraying a striking contrast to his unhappy mood during rehearsals. At the end of the song on the rooftop, John surprises everyone by singing a few lines from the classic Irish song "Danny Boy."

Meanwhile, the London police were not impressed with the Beatles' unannounced, disturbing-the-peace performance. A few bobbies entered 3 Savile Row and were greeted by Mal Evans, who took them up to the rooftop. The Beatles, with Billy Preston, played John's new song "Dig a Pony." The song was so new that John had not memorized the lyrics to the song, so a film crew member held a clipboard with a lyric sheet attached to it and kneeled in front of John. The lyrics are abstract, stream-of-consciousness Lennon. For example, John sings "do a road hog" and "roll a stoney." Unlike the album version, during the rooftop performance of "Dig a Pony," the song began with an abbreviated version of the chorus, with Paul singing "all I want is . . . ," and ended with "all I want is you." The album version begins with the four-bar bouncy guitar riff, which repeats before John comes in singing the lead vocals. As the Beatles dug a pony, Mal tried his best to persuade the police to let the Beatles continue to play and finish their planned set of songs. The Beatles launched into their closing reprise performance of "Get Back." The police instructed Mal to stop the Beatles' performance, so he turned off George's and John's amplifiers. Not willing to be shut down, a defiant George turned the amps back on. During the final last chorus, Paul ad-libbed lyrics about your mommy not wanting you to play on the rooftop and getting arrested by the police. The Beatles did not get arrested, but they had managed to get back together for one more live performance, which would be their last.

While George had quit the Beatles for about a week, John worked up the lead guitar solo in Paul's "Get Back." Musically, the song is made up of a simple rock-and-roll, three-chord progression. With this song, the Beatles did get back to their rock-and-roll roots. Evidently, the majority of the world's singles charts liked the Beatles' return to rock and roll. In the spring of 1969, "Get Back" was a number one hit single in eleven countries. Unlike the melodious riffing bass lines Paul played on so many Beatles recordings, he plays a simple, repetitive bass part in "Get Back." The lyrics "Jo-Jo" and "Tucson, Arizona," can be interpreted as a reference to Linda Eastman's first husband, Joseph Melville See, who was from Tucson. However, Paul had said in Miles's book, *Paul McCartney*, that the lyrics are not about anyone in particular. Instead, Paul claims that Jo-Jo is a fictitious character who is a man and a woman. Based on the lyrics "sweet Loretta Martin thought she was a woman, but she was another man," Loretta is the mixed-gender character in "Get Back." The song begins with a rhythmic build as Ringo drives the song, playing a steady drum pattern on his snare. Ringo's two cymbal crashes along with George's rhythm guitar striking out two chords introduce Paul singing the lead vocals. During the second chorus, John harmonizes with Paul, singing, "Get back." Billy Preston plays a dazzling syncopated electric piano solo. George's guitar playing and Ringo's cymbal crashes give the song dynamic rhythmic punches that contrast with the ongoing rhythm of the song and with John's lead guitar part.

The "Get Back" single, produced by George Martin, includes a suspended false ending after Billy Preston plays a descending piano riff toward the end of the song. Paul wails a high note, followed by Ringo playing drumbeats. The full band resumes playing the chorus, and the song finally fades out. The album version of "Get Back," produced by Phil Spector, has an entirely different beginning and ending. The song begins with the Beatles warming up and chatting. Paul says "Loretta" a few times and John sings an a cappella variation of the "Sweet Loretta" lyrics in the song. This introduction is cross faded with the beginning of the recorded single. At the end of the song, after the false ending, the band does not come back in playing the chorus. Instead, Spector spliced in sounds from the end of the "Get Back" rooftop performance, which includes Maureen Starr clapping and saying "yea," Paul thanking her with "Thanks, Mo," and John saying, "I'd like to say thank you on behalf of the group and ourselves and I hope we passed the audition."

Released in the United States in May 1970, watching *Let It Be* was a sobering experience. During the screening of the film, the audience was extremely quiet, taking in every word the Beatles had said. *Let It Be* revealed some of the animosity that was eating away at the group. When leaving the theater, no one was singing, rejoicing, or feeling uplifted, because the Beatles were finished.

The breakup of the Beatles was the result of numerous events and personal and business conflicts among the band. Brian Epstein's death, Yoko Ono's ongoing presence in the recording studio, Ringo feeling unappreciated and temporarily quitting, George's frustration with Paul and walking out during the "Get Back" sessions, and John forming another band were all contributing factors. Another incident that brought tensions to a head was when Paul released his first solo album, *McCartney*, in April 1970. John and George let Paul know that they had instructed Apple's parent company, EMI, to delay the release of the *McCartney* album to avoid it being released around the same time as the *Let It Be* album and movie. Paul ignored the instructions and released his album as planned on April 17 in the United Kingdom and on April 20 in the United States. On April 9, Paul sent advance copies of the album along with an interview to the London media. In the Q&A interview, Paul mentioned his break with the Beatles and that he had no future plans with the Beatles. The next day, the media announced that Paul had quit the Beatles and that the band had split up. John was furious, not because Paul had quit the band, but because John had announced to Paul at a band meeting on September 20, 1969, that he wanted a "divorce." For business reasons, John agreed not to go public with his leaving the band. It was John's band from the beginning. He started it, and he wanted to end it, not have Paul end the Beatles and use it as a publicity stunt to promote his *McCartney* album.

The disbanding of the Beatles was a tough pill to swallow. They had been a big part of millions of lives, and after many years of providing their worldwide fans with more than two hundred songs, inspiration, joy, and musical innovation, the Beatles ended their historic career.

The Beatles' movies document their evolution as songwriters, performers, and personalities. From fun-loving, witty mop-tops in *A Hard*

Day's Night and *Help!* to drug-induced psychedelic wizards in *Magical Mystery Tour* and *Yellow Submarine* to broken individual Beatles in *Let It Be*, the Beatles provided eye-popping visuals to their stunning musical achievements.

Suggested Listening: "A Hard Day's Night"; "Help!"; "You're Going to Lose That Girl"; "Magical Mystery Tour"; "Yellow Submarine"; "It's All Too Much"; "Let It Be"

8

BROADER HORIZONS
World Music Songs

With few exceptions, when it comes to world music and the Beatles, it's all about George Harrison and India. Indian music significantly changed George's life and influenced the Beatles' music.

It was in 1965, during the filming of the movie *Help!*, when George first heard Indian music. A group of Indian musicians in a restaurant scene played Beatles songs on Indian instruments. Because East Indians were part of the cast and played ongoing parts in *Help!*, it was appropriate for film composer Ken Thorne to score some of the scenes in the film using Indian instruments. Capitol Records' U.S. *Help!* album includes some of Thorne's Indian-flavored score, making it the first Beatles album to include exotic sounds. Also in 1965, David Crosby of the folk-rock band the Byrds told George about Indian sitarist Ravi Shankar. These two occurrences intrigued George, and he was inspired to explore Indian music and bought recordings by Ravi Shankar. A sitar virtuoso and international performer who played classical Indian music, by 1965 Ravi had recorded twelve albums that were released worldwide on the World Pacific and Angel record labels.

India had been a British colony for centuries, and not only trade but people flowed between the empire and its colony. Today, more than a million Indians live in England, especially in London. Indian restaurants are a common sight in England, as well as Indian craft shops that sell Indian instruments. Soon after George's exposure to Indian music, he purchased a sitar at the Indiacraft shop in London.

George was fascinated with the sitar and its bright, cascading sounds. When the Beatles were recording songs for the *Rubber Soul* album, George brought his sitar to the recording studio. John, with help from Paul, wrote a new song titled "Norwegian Wood (This Bird Has Flown)." Although John hadn't planned on using the sitar in the song, when George picked up the instrument and played the melody in the verse, the new sound struck the right chord with the Beatles. George also played a sitar solo, which doubled the acoustic guitar melody, and continued playing sitar throughout the song, giving "Norwegian Wood" an exotic, mystical quality. This light folk arrangement, with the featured Indian sitar, was an entirely new and different sound on a Beatles recording. Adding to the light nature of the song, Ringo played finger cymbals and Paul played a simple drone-like bass line. The cryptic lyrics describe an affair John was having at the time, and he sings the lead vocals with storytelling ease. During the bridge, Paul sings a high harmony part above John's lead vocals. A subtle harmonic shift happens on the first chord of the bridge when the song shifts from E major to E minor. This chord change is called a parallel modulation and creates a different mood in the bridge and gives "Norwegian Wood" rich harmonic diversity.

"Norwegian Wood" is unlike any of the songs the Beatles had previously recorded, mainly because of George and the sitar. Without the sitar, "Norwegian Wood" would still be an exquisite folk song. With the sitar, it became a groundbreaking world music pop-song sensation. This one song had enormous influence on other musicians and bands, including Brian Jones of the Rolling Stones. Brian learned how to play the sitar and featured it on the Rolling Stones 1966 hit song "Paint It Black." In 1967, the British rock band Traffic used the sitar prominently, played by Dave Mason, in the song "Paper Sun." With "Norwegian Wood," George had placed the sitar front and center as a new sound in pop music, but the sitar was just the beginning for George and his deep involvement with India and its music.

A year after the release of "Norwegian Wood," instead of having only one or none of his songs on previous Beatles albums, on the 1966 *Revolver* album there are three songs written by George. While the lead guitar solo played by Paul on George's "Taxman" does have distinct

Indian music characteristics, it's George's second song, "Love You To," which is significantly rooted in Indian classical music. Instead of George playing the sitar with the usual Beatles guitar, bass, and drum ensemble, with "Love You To" George recorded the song with Indian musicians from the Asian Music Circle, based in London. Paul does sing background vocals on the chorus with George's lead vocals, and Ringo plays the tambourine, but it's a remarkable departure to have an ensemble of outside Indian musicians play on a Beatles recording. The Indian ensemble consisted of the following instruments: sitar, tambura (also known as a tanpura), and tabla (small drums). The sitar is an instrument used for playing solos, known as *ragas* in Indian music. Having as many as twenty-one strings, the sitar has six or seven main strings and movable frets. The other strings are sympathetic resonating strings, which add to the overall sound of the instrument. The tambura, a tall, gourd-shaped instrument that looks similar to the sitar, usually has four strings and is used to accompany singers and instrumentalists. The strings of the tambura are typically tuned with the fourth string as the root of a chord—for example, G. The third and second strings are also tuned to G, but an octave above the fourth string. The first string is tuned to D, five notes above G, or to C, four notes above G. Ideally, the musician playing the tambura plays it with hardly any pulsed inflection when plucking the strings. This playing technique creates an uninterrupted, ongoing flow of sustained music, a harmonic foundation for singers and instrumentalists. The tabla is made of two hand drums. The smaller, high-pitched drum is tuned to match the root note of the tambura, while the bigger drum provides a lower, deeper, glissando-like whooping sound.

George's striking solo sitar introduction in "Love You To," played rubato (free of any set tempo), was an unprecedented musical move for the Beatles. It transports you to another world, a new Beatles world filled with intrigue and mysticism. The tabla, played by Anil Bhagwat, are the driving rhythmic force in the song. A tambura drones throughout "Love You To" and provides the tonal foundation for the sitar. In addition to George playing the sitar, another sitar is played by an Indian musician from the Asian Music Circle. Bhagwat's contribution was so significant that his name is listed on the back of the *Revolver* album cover next to the song title. After a complex sitar solo and last verse, the music accelerates and races away with a fade-out.

Some of the lyrics to "Love You To" are antiestablishment, reflecting the growing 1960s counterculture by speaking about the people who will "screw you in the ground." Other lyrics address love, such as "make love all day long" and "I'll make love to you." George also paraphrases the lyrics "life is very short" from "We Can Work It Out" when he sings, "A lifetime is so short." The *Revolver* album includes a good deal of experimentation and the use of backward recordings. With backward techniques in mind, the title "Love You To" includes the reverse lyrics ". . . to you." This could explain why the "To" isn't "Too." Hearing "Love You To" in 1966 was an extraordinary listening experience. It was also educational and expanded Western ears to music from an Eastern culture, clothed in a new George Harrison Beatles song.

John's mind-boggling song "Tomorrow Never Knows" begins with the droning sounds of a tambura. Played by George, the tambura lays down the tonal roots of the song. In addition to the tambura, George also plays the sitar. "Tomorrow Never Knows" has predominantly one chord, C, which gives it a singular harmonic center, similar to the way in which traditional Indian music is based on one key root note. However, a B flat chord is periodically superimposed with the C chord. Adding to the droning nature of the song, Paul plays one C note on his bass throughout the song, an octave lower than the tambura. John was inspired to write the spiritual lyrics after reading an adapted version of the *Tibetan Book of the Dead*. "Tomorrow Never Knows" is a unique synthesis of Indian, electronic, psychedelic, and rock music. With this song, the Beatles had created a new, sensational genre. You will discover more about "Tomorrow Never Knows" in the next chapter, "Recording Studio Wizardry: Psychedelic and Electronic Songs."

During the Beatles' break after their 1966 U.S. tour, George demonstrated his commitment to Indian music by traveling to India, where he studied sitar with Ravi Shankar. The six-week endeavor immersed George in traditional Indian classical music, yoga, and meditation. This was a complete cultural change for George compared with the hectic life of being a Beatle, and it was during this adventure that George found a new peaceful, spiritual path that enriched his life far beyond the physical comforts of the material world.

After the inclusion of an unprecedented three songs on *Revolver*, on the next Beatles album, *Sgt. Pepper's Lonely Hearts Club Band*, George contributed only one song: "Within You Without You." George began writing the song in early 1967 after having a conversation with artist and bass guitar player Klaus Voormann about metaphysics and spiritualism. George and the Beatles had met Klaus when they played in Hamburg, Germany, and in 1966 Klaus designed the cover of the *Revolver* album. After the Beatles disbanded, Klaus played bass on some of John's, George's, and Ringo's solo albums. The conversation with Klaus coincided with spiritual experiences that George had encountered while in India. After George played his semihollow Epiphone Casino electric guitar at the Beatles' last concert at Candlestick Park in San Francisco, he shifted his focus from the guitar to the sitar. Therefore, it's the sitar-centric "Within You Without You" and not a guitar song that appears on the *Sgt. Pepper's Lonely Hearts Club Band* album.

There's no Paul, John, or Ringo on this George song, only George and the Beatles' personal assistant Neil Aspinall, both playing the tambura. George also plays sitar and some acoustic guitar. Similar to the recording session of "Love You To," a group of Indian musicians from the Asian Music Circle play the tambura, tabla, dilrubas, and swarmandal. At the "Within You Without You" recording session at Abbey Road, for his Indian musician friends, George created a cozy environment, complete with carpets, walls adorned with Indian tapestries, burning incense, and low lighting. George's lead vocals melody is doubled on the dilruba, a bowed Indian string instrument. The dilruba is similar to the sitar, with movable frets and sympathetic strings, but it is smaller in size. The bowed notes played on the dilruba flow together smoothly and seamlessly. Gentle glissandi notes, played on a swarmandal, an Indian zither instrument, introduce the first and last verses. The verses in "Within You Without You" are in even time; however, the instrumental section is in five-four time, which is one of the time signatures used in Indian ragas. The droning tamburas and glissando of the dilruba, plus orchestral strings, create an overall hypnotic effect. With George Martin's added sliding string arrangement guided by George Harrison, "Within You Without You" is a stunning combination of Eastern and Western music and is one of the first of its kind to be released on a rock/pop album.

George felt the urge to express his innermost feelings with "Within You Without You." He had expanded his consciousness, with a little help from LSD, and this song was the perfect vehicle for his profound lyrics. Dealing with illusion, love, self-awareness, and inner peace,

George sings about love that could save the world and seeing beyond yourself and finding peace of mind. As if writing a script for an entire generation, these philosophical, Hindu-inspired lyrics resonated with hundreds of thousands of peace-loving, soul-searching hippies in 1967. At the very end of the song, there's laughter. It was George's idea to add some levity to the serious nature of the song and to tie "Within You Without You" to the conceptual nature of the *Sgt. Pepper's Lonely Hearts Club Band* album.

George's recordings of Indian music with the Beatles were so influential that in 1968, lectures about Indian music were offered to full-time students at the Hartford Conservatory of Music. As a voice major at the conservatory, I attended a lecture and held a sitar for the first time. During the 1970s, Indian music and world music courses were part of the curriculum at many learning institutions in the United States. In 1975, when I was studying music theory and composition at the California Institute of the Arts, I studied Indian music with Indian violinist Dr. L. Subramaniam. Dr. Subramaniam was, and still is, a masterful classical Indian music violinist. That summer of 1975, Dr. Subramaniam invited me to join him for his teachings at the Center for World Music in Berkeley, California. Honored, I eagerly accepted his invitation and attended numerous workshops and lectures at the center. Much to my delight, Dr. Subramaniam asked me to play the tambura at a concert he was giving in San Francisco. I was thrilled to be performing with such a highly gifted and respected violinist. Since I had already studied Indian music, I knew how to play the tambura. The performance took place at a church and was well attended. Dr. Subramaniam, along with a tabla player from the Center for World Music and myself playing the tambura, performed for more than an hour without any break. In order to play the tambura properly, I sat in a lotus position with my legs crossed and the tambura nestled between my legs. My job was to keep the tambura droning for every piece that was performed. Since all of the ragas that Dr. Subramaniam played had the same tonal center, I didn't have to change the tuning of the tambura. It was an enlightening experience to be playing with Dr. Subramaniam. At the end of the performance, Dr. Subramaniam and the tabla player stood up and exited the stage. I put down the tambura and was ready to stand up, but I couldn't. Because I had been sitting in the lotus position for such a long time, the normal circulation of blood flowing to my legs had been limited. I was numb from the waist down to my toes. Dr. Subramaniam helped me stand up as we both laughed. That was the end of my professional tambura-playing career.

Indian music sounds on the *Sgt. Pepper's Lonely Hearts Club Band* album went beyond "Within You Without You." "Lucy in the Sky with Diamonds" and "Getting Better" include the tambura despite the fact that these songs are more psychedelic than Indian. "Getting Better," which was mostly written by Paul, is a psychedelic song, but it does incorporate some Indian music characteristics. Rather than the song starting with a sustained horizontal droning sound, the same repetitive pitches are vertical, percussive, accented sounds played on electric guitars and keyboards. Both songs are covered in greater detail in the next chapter, "Recording Studio Wizardry: Psychedelic and Electronic Songs."

After the Beatles had shed their dayglow-colored Sgt. Pepper uniforms, they dressed in Indian-styled clothing. Colorful madras-print Nehru shirts and jackets, sandals, beads, and flower-print clothing were the hippest wardrobe styles in 1967. Clothing designers and manufacturers knew that whatever the Beatles wore would start a sudden craze. Sure enough, millions of teens began to buy and wear the same style of clothes that the Beatles wore—Indian-styled clothing.

George's very Indian "The Inner Light" was released on a Beatles single, as the B-side to the rocking "Lady Madonna" in March 1968. It was the first time that a song written entirely by George appeared on a Beatles single. The recording of the single happened just before the Beatles traveled to India to study meditation with the Maharishi. Historically, this time was the pinnacle of the Beatles' interest in meditation and Indian music, although unlike the three other Beatles, George's interest with Indian music and Hinduism stayed with him throughout his entire life.

While George was in Bombay, India, in January 1968, recording soundtrack music he had written for the movie *Wonderwall*, he also recorded all of the music to "The Inner Light." There are no Western instruments in the song, and none of the Beatles play any instruments in "The Inner Light." All of the music is played on Indian instruments by virtuoso Indian instrumentalists. For the first time on one of George's Indian songs, he doesn't play the sitar or tambura, nor do any of the Indian musicians. Instead of a tambura, the harmonium gives the song its droning sound. Rather than two tabla, the drums played on "The Inner Light" are the high-pitched pakhavaj and the tuned tabla tarang drums. The prominent instruments on the recording during the vibrant instrumental sections are the sarod, a non-fretted string instrument, and shehnai, a double-reed instrument that sounds similar to an oboe. The bansuri, a Southeast Asian bamboo flute, accompanies George's vocals during the verses. George added his lead vocals about meditation and self-knowledge to the Bombay recording when he returned to the Abbey Road studios. John's and Paul's vocals on "The Inner Light" are minimal, singing backing harmony only once toward the end of the song.

As you may have read in chapter 6, "A Lighter Side: Folk-Rock and Country-Rock Songs," "Across the Universe" was also recorded in February 1968, just before the Beatles traveled to India. At that time, the Beatles had embraced Indian music and were devoted to finding inner peace. Reflecting the prevalent Indian influence on the Beatles, on the original 1968 recordings and final releases in 1970 of "Across the Universe," George plays the tambura, and he also plays the sitar on the *Let It Be* album version of the song. The chorus, which begins with the mantra "jai guru deva om," is thoroughly Indian and when translated can be paraphrased as meaning "glory to the divine guru."

We're going to leave India and travel to France for the song "Michelle." The French-influenced song on the 1965 *Rubber Soul* album was written by Paul, who was inspired to write it after attending parties in Paris. To give the song a direct French connection, Paul sings some of the lyrics in the verse in French. A light, delicate song, Ringo's drumming is sparse, with just enough rhythmic beats to complement and support the acoustic rhythm guitars. The background *oohs* sung by John and George are soft and dreamy. With "Michelle," the Beatles take you to another foreign place in their diversified sonic landscape. You can read more about "Michelle" in chapter 4, "Playing America's Heart Strings: Love Songs."

The song "Girl," written by John, has similar instrumentation as "Michelle." Both songs were recorded around the same time when the Beatles compiled songs for their *Rubber Soul* album. John's lead vocals are tender as he tells a story about an imaginary girl. This girl is complex, causing you pleasure and pain, and even though you want to leave her, you can't. During the chorus, the sound of John inhaling is up front in the mix. He's sighing with desire for the girl, but the inhaling can also be attributed to the fact that the Beatles were smoking a lot of marijuana when they worked on *Rubber Soul*. The background voices sung by Paul and George during the bridge make a direct reference to a female body part. When producer George Martin asked if they were singing "tit, tit," the Beatles denied it and said they were singing "dit, dit." What gives "Girl" a world music sound is the Greek-influenced instrumental section that occurs before the last fade-out chorus. Inspired by Paul, who had visited Greece in September 1963, John, Paul, and George imitate Greek bouzouki instruments (although it does sound like a real bouzouki) with acoustic guitars and an acoustic twelve-string to deliver a Mediterranean-flavored, multilayered dance-like melody. Ringo joins in the dance, playing cymbal splashes on the second and fourth beats.

In July 1967, the Beatles were enchanted with the Greek islands and were planning on buying one. As Paul and George had said in *The Beatles Anthology* documentary, they thought an island would be a wonderful refuge from the rest of the world, someplace where they could live together and carry on with their creativity. While they were island shopping, they were also tripping on LSD. The Beatles found an island that met their fancy and instructed their business managers in London to purchase the island. But the whimsical idea was short-lived, and the purchase transaction was never completed. Even though the fun holiday adventure didn't result in a Beatles-owned island, the influence of Greece made an impact on the recording of "Girl."

Indian music and Eastern mysticism significantly influenced the Beatles. George's love of Indian music and meditation didn't stop when the Beatles ended. When George was a solo recording artist in 1971, Ravi Shankar asked George for help regarding refugees fleeing Bangladesh because of war and genocide. George's high regard and respect for Ravi is what inspired him to produce the *Concert for Bangladesh* at Madison Square Garden on August 1, 1971. George's all-star band at Madison Square Garden included Ringo Starr, Eric Clapton, Billy Preston, Klaus Voormann, Leon Russell, Jim Keltner, Apple recording artists Badfinger, and a special guest appearance by Bob Dylan. But before the all-stars performed, Ravi and his fellow Indian musicians played for forty thousand people, the combined audience for two shows. Ravi was hoping the concert would raise $25,000. Instead, it raised $250,000. To help promote the cause and increase awareness of the travesties happening in Bangladesh, George wrote and recorded the single "Bangladesh," released it a few days before the concert, and performed it as an encore at both concerts. Even though the song is about Bangladesh, the original home of Ravi Shankar, George didn't use any Indian instruments on the recording. Instead, George sang the lead vocals and played electric guitar and slide guitar, Ringo and Jim Keltner played drums, Klaus Voormann played bass, Billy Preston played organ, Leon Russell played piano, and Jim Horn played saxophones and arranged a horn ensemble. George's humanitarian soul is loud and clear when he sings the opening lyrics, asking everyone to help save some lives.

Thanks to the story line in *Help!* and David Crosby turning George on to Ravi Shankar, George led his Beatles bandmates into the world of Indian music and meditation. As a result, the Beatles released new songs containing sounds and dimensions unlike any other songs in their extensive catalog. Not only can you have a sensational sound experience, you can also travel with the Beatles as they evolve and synthesize world music into their musical vocabulary.

Suggested Listening: "Norwegian Wood"; "Michelle"; "Girl"; "Love You To"; "Within You Without You"; "The Inner Light"

9

RECORDING STUDIO WIZARDRY

Psychedelic and Electronic Songs

Starting with "Rain," "I'm Only Sleeping," and "Tomorrow Never Knows" and ending with "I Want You (She's So Heavy)," the Beatles created an amazing set of songs that far exceeded their rock-and-roll roots. In 1965 and 1966, John and Paul had discovered composers Karlheinz Stockhausen and Iannis Xenakis and their electronic music compositions. Stockhausen and Xenakis composed avant-garde music that had absolutely nothing to do with rock and roll or pop music. Their compositions consisted of electronic music, musique concrète—also known as sound collages—and contemporary orchestral music. Given John and Paul's curiosity and experimental tendencies, they were intrigued by Stockhausen's and Xenakis's compositions and were inspired to incorporate electronic music and sound collages into some of their songs. This was accomplished by using tape loops—a short piece of recording tape with music, voices, or sound effects on them which are looped/repeated. Using these electronic music techniques, the Beatles created a new genre and exposed their massive record-buying populace to a wave of unprecedented new songs.

As mentioned in chapter 2, the rock song "Rain" has backward vocals at the end of the song. Recorded in April 1966 when the Beatles were experimenting in the recording studio, the backward vocals happened by accident. Confirmed by engineer Geoff Emerick, John claimed that he had mistakenly played a recording of the song on his tape recorder after threading the tape with the end instead of rewinding it to the beginning. That explains how he heard his vocals backward and why his voice is backward at the end of the song. This accident opened the door for the Beatles to explore and develop backward recording techniques with songs on *Revolver, Sgt. Pepper's Lonely Hearts Club Band, Magical Mystery Tour, Yellow Submarine*, and the *White Album*.

"I'm Only Sleeping," on the U.S. *Yesterday and Today* album, is one of the first psychedelic Beatles songs to feature backward lead guitar parts. Backward guitars give the song a psychedelic character, and they gave audiences a new sound experience. The backward sounds are akin to an altered state of consciousness or a subconscious, dreamlike state of being, and it was easy for listeners to float away while listening to "I'm Only Sleeping." Six weeks following the *Yesterday and Today* album, in August 1966, the mind-blowing *Revolver* album was released.

This is what it was like to experience the Revolver *album for the first time. . . . Local AM radio stations have been playing selections from the new Beatles album, and you rush out to buy* Revolver. *You look at the album cover for a long time and see a black ink drawing of the Beatles' faces with superimposed images of the Beatles in varying sizes. At the very beginning of the album, you hear George's cool voice saying, "One, two, three, four, one, two . . ." After hearing "Taxman," you think someone mysteriously put a different album on the turntable. Sure, you recognize Paul's singing voice, but the song sounds like classical music. There are no guitars, basses, or drums on "Eleanor Rigby." How strange. How different. Then you hear the next song, and you think that maybe you're not listening to a Beatles album. Maybe you're listening to a foreign group of musicians playing strange instruments? You are relieved to hear George singing, albeit in a low voice, about life being short and a new life that can't be bought. "Love You To" intrigues you, and you have an entirely new Beatles experience. You are fascinated hearing the new songs, and then you listen to the last song, "Tomorrow Never Knows." What in the world are the Beatles doing? You think that you're high on drugs, but it's not drugs; you are high listening to this unprecedented Beatles song.*

The philosophical title of John's song "Tomorrow Never Knows" was a sign that Beatles fans would not know what to expect from the Beatles going forward. Certainly, no one other than the Beatles could have known that a song of this unprecedented magnitude, filled with an orgy of seemingly unrelated material, would be created in 1966. When you hear the tambura at the very beginning of the song, you're led to think it's another Indian-influenced George song. Without warning, Ringo plays a thundering repetitive drum pattern, a pattern he had never played before. Paul plays a continuous bass line, which locks in with Ringo's close-miked drum track. And what is that sound before John's opening lead vocals? Seagulls? Actually, it's recorded laughter played at a very fast speed. After the high-pitched laughter flies by, John asks you to turn off your mind and float downstream. How do you turn off your mind? By meditating and going within one's self. The esoteric lyrics "lay down all thoughts, surrender to the void" are soul searching and yearn for inner self-awareness. John wanted his vocals to sound unlike anything he had ever sung before and told George Martin that he wanted his voice to sound like a hundred chanting Tibetan monks. George Martin and engineer Geoff Emerick went to great lengths to try and accommodate John. Double-tracked recording techniques were applied to John's voice in the first three verses. During the last four verses, John's voice was recorded through a Leslie speaker cabinet, giving his voice a swirling effect. Even though he was initially pleased, John was not satisfied with his processed vocals. In the 1968 book *The Beatles*, written by Hunter Davies, John had said, "Often the backing I think of early on never comes off. With 'Tomorrow Never Knows,' I'd imagined in my head that in the background you would hear thousands of monks chanting. That was impractical of course and we did something different. It was a bit of a drag and I didn't really like it. I should have tried to get near my original idea, the monks singing. I realize now that was what it wanted." Fragmented orchestral sounds and high-pitched laughter are interspersed around John's vocals. Fast descending and ascending sitar-like arpeggios come racing into the soundscape, followed by a backward lead guitar solo played by Paul. The guitar solo sounds like the same lead guitar solo that Paul played on "Taxman"; however, on "Tomorrow Never Knows," it's slowed down, backwards, and fragmented. Abstractly, that guitar solo ties *Revolver*'s opening song, "Taxman," together with the last song, "Tomorrow Never Knows." After the guitar solo, immediately following John singing "that love is all . . . ," a high-pitched feedback occurs. More than likely it was accidental, and keeping it in the recording added to the electronic fabric of the song.

Influenced by Karlheinz Stockhausen, Paul asked John, George, and Ringo to create tape loops. The origin of the tape-loop sounds are a brief section from a symphony by Finnish composer Jean Sibelius, backward electric guitars sped up, backward and high-speed rapid sitar-like passages, and a laughing voice at double speed. With the working title "Mark 1," "Tomorrow Never Knows" is an outstanding Beatles creation that uses backward recording techniques, experimentation, electronic music, Indian music, rock music, and a pounding, unrelenting drum pattern. This new mixed-genre song is trance-like, filled with sensational electronic sounds that fly around John's hypnotic vocals. No one other than the Beatles could have created such a mind-expanding masterpiece in 1966. The title of the song is not in the lyrics, and the song isn't about tomorrow. "Tomorrow Never Knows" is timeless. It's about living in the moment; it's about now.

With the title "Tomorrow Never Knows," the Beatles were not kidding around. About five months after the release of the *Revolver* album, after months of group inactivity and rumors that the Beatles had broken up, "Strawberry Fields Forever" exploded onto the singles record charts.

With the February 1967 release of "Strawberry Fields Forever," the Beatles had transformed and reinvented themselves not only musically but also physically. I remember buying the new single and was astonished when I looked at the record sleeve. On one side of the sleeve is a photograph of the Beatles placed in an elaborate golden frame. This striking backlit photograph of the Beatles didn't look like the Beatles I had known for three years. None of the Beatles are smiling. They have serious expressions on their faces, and they have grown mustaches, plus George has whiskers on his chin. He wears a long Indian jacket and looks away from the camera. John is wearing wire-rimmed glasses for the first time. Paul, John, and Ringo look indifferent, almost sad. On the other side of the single sleeve are baby photos, some upside down and some sideways, that look like they were taken from a page in a scrapbook. The song titles are printed on the baby-photo side, but there's no "The Beatles" name on either side. The Beatles had always been clean shaven, so why are mustaches on their young faces? George grew a mustache before traveling to India, hoping to disguise himself and not be recognized. Paul had a motorcycle accident in December 1965 in which he chipped his tooth and split his lip. He waited almost a year before growing a mustache to cover up the scar on his lip. In the autumn of 1966, while George was in India, John was in Spain, acting in the movie *How I Won the War*, playing the part of a soldier named Musketeer Gripweed. Taking on the rugged look of a soldier, John had stubble on his face, and later that year he grew a mustache.

John had conceived the song "Strawberry Fields Forever" when he was in Spain and developed it on his return to England. He wants to take you to a place where nothing is real. What does John mean when he sings "nothing is real" and "living is easy with eyes closed"? These existential lyrics beg for an explanation. He goes on to say it's high or low, and I think I know, I mean yes, but disagree. It sounds like these are confusing strawberry fields. John had said in a 1980 *Playboy* interview that the song is about a place that he used to visit as a child. The abstract lyrics were his attempt of an introspective self-analysis. "No one is in my tree" is his way of saying that he was alone, by himself, and not like anyone else. Strawberry Fields is a very real place. It's the name of an orphanage in Liverpool that was run by the Salvation Army, close to where John lived with his aunt Mimi. When John was a young boy, he would play in the fields on the orphanage property and hear the Salvation Army's marching band.

Musically, "Strawberry Fields Forever" is a major departure from previous Beatles songs and recordings. Starting with flute-sounding tape loops played on a mellotron, the slow path to strawberry fields begins. The mellotron was prominently showcased by the Beatles, and this electronic keyboard ushered in a bevy of new sounds on a Beatles single. Ringo's style of drumming is new as he plays a wider variety of drum fills, along with the unusual sound of backward cymbals. There's also the use of four trumpets replicating a Salvation Army marching band, sweeping cellos, and the Indian zither-like swarmandal. John's voice guides you as he takes you down to strawberry fields, and the instrumentation, arrangement, and production of the song has you convinced that these fields are magical. Sliding guitars, a pulsating bass line, timpani drums, and prominent cellos take you away to John's dreamlike world. The song fades out, and when you think the song is over, surprisingly it fades back in, and you hear scrambled drumming along with a backward mellotron part and a blaring trumpet. What does John say at the very end of the song? "I buried Paul"? "Cranberry sauce"? "I'm very bored"? Listen to John's voice at the end of the fade-out and try to determine what he says.

To provide you with a historical perspective, here are some of the top-selling U.S. singles from January 1967: "I'm a Believer" by the Monkees; "Snoopy vs. the Red Baron" by the Royal Guardsman (the band's name is the same name as a VOX amplifier model); "Tell It Like It Is" by Aaron Neville; "Good Thing" by Paul Revere and the Raiders; "Standing in the Shadows of Love" by the Four Tops; "Sugar Town" by Nancy Sinatra; "Nashville Cats" by the Lovin' Spoonful; "Winchester Cathedral" by the New Vaudeville Band. These songs represent what pop songs sounded like prior to the release of "Strawberry Fields Forever." Even though the style of these hit songs varies from pop and rock to rhythm and blues and country rock, all of these songs are composed of elements from the standard song formation—verse, bridge, and chorus—and had common chord progressions. The songs were recorded with the basic guitar, keyboard, bass, and drum ensemble and are relatively simple compared to the complexity of "Strawberry Fields Forever." Listen to any of the songs listed above and then listen to "Strawberry Fields Forever" and you will hear how radically different the new Beatles single was at the time when it was released. "Strawberry Fields Forever" completely changed the recording industry standard and raised the creative bar to new heights.

No longer touring but still basking in the fame and fortune that Beatlemania had given them, the Beatles could indulge in spending lots of time in the recording studio and being inventive. "Strawberry Fields Forever" was the result of using the recording studio as the place where the Beatles unleashed their creativity. Songs on the *Sgt. Pepper's Lonely Hearts Club Band* album were created in that same innovative environment.

"Lucy in the Sky with Diamonds" takes you on a psychedelic ride through looking-glass ties, marmalade skies, and marshmallow pies. But when you look for Lucy with kaleidoscope eyes, she's gone, up to the sky, draped in diamonds. The song, written by John and with a few lyrics from Paul, begins with verses in three-four time then goes into a four-four-time chorus. After the chorus, it seamlessly returns to three-four-time verses. "Lucy in the Sky with Diamonds" begins with a celestial-sounding organ played by Paul. The melody that Paul plays on the organ is harmonically complicated yet perfectly matches and supports

John's lead vocals. The pre-chorus instrumentation moves up just a notch to a new key. Bridging the pre-chorus to the chorus, Ringo pounds out three beats. During the verses, George plays the tambura, and on the choruses he plays lead guitar through a Leslie speaker. Getting even higher and closer to the "sky," John and Paul sing the song's title as the music peaks. The inspiration and song's title came from a pastel painting that John's son Julian had created. Julian had a crush on his nursery school friend Lucy. Four-year-old Julian told John that the painting was Lucy, in the sky with diamonds. The psychedelic lyrics filled with drug-drenched images and the initials in the song's title led some people to believe that "Lucy in the Sky with Diamonds" was a song about LSD.

Paul's song "Getting Better" bursts with positive energy, juxtaposed with John's "it can't get no worse" lyrics. The first two verses address anger and cruel teachers; the third verse is about beating a woman. Unfortunately, these lyrics were autobiographical for John, who had a violent side and used to lash out and hit some of the women in his life. Positive Paul washes away all that negativity with "it's getting better, all the time." Paul's brilliant bass playing is syncopated, dancing around the punchy, consistent staccato downbeats from the guitars and keyboards. George Martin joins in on a virginal, a small keyboard instrument similar to the harpsichord but with only one string per key. He also adds to the percussive sound by hitting the strings of a pianet with mallets. Paul's lead vocals are surrounded by John and George singing background vocals. On the lyrics in the chorus, "better, better, better," the arching background vocals get higher as "better" is repeated. The title of the song came about when Jimmie Nicol was drumming with the Beatles in 1964, filling in for Ringo, who was having his tonsils removed. After the Beatles played a concert, Paul asked Jimmie, "How's it going?" Jimmie responded by saying, "It's getting better." The song is a prime example of how Paul's and John's lyric writing contrasted and complemented each other, one expressing anger and violence and the other hope of better times.

In January 1967, when the Beatles were in Kent, England, filming a promotional video for their "Strawberry Fields Forever" and "Penny Lane" single, John stopped in a local antique shop and bought an old circus poster. The nineteenth-century poster was the inspiration for John's song "Being for the Benefit of Mr. Kite!" Most of the lyrics to the song were taken from the poster, though John changed the name of the horse from Zanthus to Henry. Paul claims to have written the song with John; however, John had suggested that he wrote the entire song. In Hunter Davies's book *The Beatles*, John said, "I had all the words staring me in the face . . . from this old poster I'd bought. I hardly made up a word just connecting the lists together. I was just going through the motions because we needed a new song for *Sgt. Pepper* at that moment." In a 2013 *Rolling Stone* interview, Paul said, "I have great memories of writing it with John. I read occasionally, people say, 'Oh, John wrote that one.' I say, 'Wait a minute, what was that afternoon I spent with him, then, looking at that poster?'" It's fascinating what the Beatles created based on the words from the poster. To give "Being for the Benefit of Mr. Kite!" a circus-sounding atmosphere, John asked George Martin to create carnival sounds. Martin played the organ, piano, harmonium, and glockenspiel and created the magical electronic collage in the instrumental section. He gathered a collection of carnival, organ, and calliope tape recordings and instructed Geoff Emerick to cut the tapes into pieces and arbitrarily splice them together. The result is dizzying and sensational. "Being for the Benefit of Mr. Kite!" begins with a burst of harmonicas played by John, George, and Ringo, followed by Ringo's drumroll introducing the first verse. John sings the lead vocals and harmonizes with himself when he sings "challenge the world," "Henry the horse," and "Mr. Kite is topping the bill." Ringo's drumming in the song is minimal, so it doesn't obscure the sonic collage sounds. During the verses, Ringo hits his hi-hat on the second and fourth beats and he kicks his bass drum on the first and third beats, playing along with Paul's bass line. Then he replaces his hi-hat hits with tom-toms for the chorus. The song is in four-four time, but after John sings "waltz," the middle instrumental section is in three-four time so Henry the horse can dance a waltz. Ringo switches to hitting his hi-hat on the second and third beats for the waltz section, and George Martin plays the swirling keyboard instruments in three-four time. Getting back to the four-four-time verse, a pounding rhythm and cymbal crash announces the last verse. Mr. Kite was probably a rich man, but not as rich as the Beatles.

Who keeps money in a big brown bag? Who is the rich man? In the summer of 1967, the Beatles were rich men, and Brian Epstein was a rich man, too. As their manager, Brian traveled on tours with the Beatles. Back in those wild touring days, Brian collected the Beatles' performing fees, and invariably, Brian was paid cash in brown paper bags. Getting paid in cash was a way to avoid having to pay taxes on the unreported earned money. Brian's management fee was on the high side, as much as 25 percent, compared with average fess that ranged from 10 to 15 percent. Not only was Brian receiving money from the Beatles, but he was also earning money from the other performing/recording artists he managed. Those artists included Billy J. Kramer and the Dakotas, Gerry and the Pacemakers, the Cyrkle, Sounds Incorporated, and Cilla Black. The Beatles reveled in their riches, but they also liked to poke fun at Brian for having made so much money off them. "Baby You're a Rich Man," the B-side to the "All You Need Is Love" single, is actually two different songs combined together in a perfect juxtaposition. John wrote the verse section using the working title "One of the Beautiful People." Paul wrote the "Baby You're a Rich Man" chorus. "Beautiful People" was a 1967 summer of love phrase used to describe people who were "hip" and turned on to drugs. Riches were often the antithesis of the hippie drug culture, but the Beatles managed to benefit from the best of both worlds. The song begins with pianos played by John and Paul, and Ringo sets the rhythm by playing drums, tambourine, and maracas. Paul comes in with a melodious bass line, followed by John playing the clavioline, an electronic keyboard instrument. During the verses, the clavioline sounds like a drippy oboe. Ringo's drum fills in the second and third verses are exceptional sweeps across his snare and tom-tom drums. George's electric guitar chug-a-chug part sounds muted and processed. When listening to the ending chorus, you will hear a non-Beatle voice. Mick Jagger of the Rolling Stones chimed in, singing the song's title and "too." At the end of the chorus, before it fades out, you will hear something rude. John sang "a rich fag Jew," mixed in with Paul and George singing "a rich man, too." Brian, being a homosexual Jew, could not have been pleased with John's personal jab. But Brian knew that John often made off-the-cuff remarks and probably knew not to take him too seriously.

In one of the most innovative Beatles songs, John said he was the walrus, and in the song "Glass Onion," John said "the walrus is Paul," referring to Paul wearing a walrus costume on the cover of the *Magical Mystery Tour* album. In any event, these walruses are otherworldly. The lyrics in John's song "I Am the Walrus" are unlike any other lyrics

in the Beatles' catalog of songs. John had received a letter from a stu-
dent in Liverpool who was analyzing Beatles lyrics in an English class.
Intrigued, John was inspired to write a song with the most confusing
lyrics possible. Highly abstract to the degree of sounding absurd, some
of the lyrics in the verses are "sitting on a cornflake," "kicking Edgar
Allan Poe," "custard dripping from a dead dog's eye," and "pornographic priestess." Some of the lyrics are based on a nursery rhyme that John
was familiar with when he was a child. John's walrus was inspired by the
poem "The Walrus and the Carpenter," written by Lewis Carroll, from
the book *Through the Looking-Glass*. John wrote some of the lyrics
while on acid trips. The piercing tone of John's vocals are intensely
bright with a cutting edge. The repetitive two-note melody in the verses
is based on John hearing a European siren wailing outside his home in
England. When John sings "policemen sitting pretty little policemen,"
the lyrics are appropriately matched with the two-note siren melody.
This two-note melody is a variation of John singing "nobody was really
sure if he was from the house of Lords" in "A Day in the Life." The
chords in "I Am the Walrus" are based on the seven notes in the musical alphabet, A, B, C, D, E, F, and G, and John chose to use all major
chords. John sang the orchestral parts to George Martin to guide
George as he wrote the string, brass, and woodwind arrangement. The
song begins with an electric piano played by John and tambourine
played by Paul, followed by low-register violins and cellos. Then Ringo
plays an explosive drum rhythm that introduces John's haunting lead
vocals. During the verses, cellos mimic the vocal melody. After John
sings "I am the egg man" and "they are the egg men," background
voices sing a glissando *whoo*. Although John said that he is the egg man,
Eric Burdon, who was the lead singer of the British rock band the
Animals, claims to be the real egg man. Eric was known to break eggs
on the bodies of naked women before having sex with them, and John
had witnessed such a "happening." After the lyrics "see how they run,"
the cellos play a series of rapid, syncopated descending notes. Then
John sings a sustained, high-pitched "crying" backed by even higher
background voices. Cellos play the song's opening two-note siren melody, followed by another ascending "crying" with sweeping *whoo*s. After
the "yellow matter custard" lyrics, French horns play a countermelody
to John's vocals. Immediately following the nonsensical lyrics "goo goo
g'joob," the song is rudely interrupted with a blast of scrambled radio

noises and voices. Isolated strings play a melody that introduces a new section of the song. John sings "sitting in an English garden" with a different melody from the rest of the song, and then the arrangement quickly returns to the "I am the egg man" chorus. After the lyrics "the joker laughs at you," sixteen vocalists from the Mike Sammes Singers chime in with, "ho, ho, ho, hee, hee, hee, ha, ha, ha." Ray Thomas and Mike Pinder from the Moody Blues also sing some of the background vocals. John sings a series of *j'oob*s, and then the song begins a long end chorus, with ascending strings climbing to their upper register. Mixed in with the ending arrangement are spoken excerpts from Shakespeare's play *King Lear*. It just so happened that John had turned on a radio and heard *King Lear* being broadcast on a BBC program and wanted to include some of it in "I Am the Walrus." It's during the long ending and fade-out of the song where you can hear lines from the play interspersed with the music and chorus. The addition of the *King Lear* lines contribute to making "I Am the Walrus" an experimental, psychedelic song. During the long fade-out, the background voices are so obscured that their actual content is open for interpretation. Layered multiple voices sing a variety of phrases, making it difficult to hear exactly what they are saying. "Oomph, oomph, stick it up your jumper," "everybody's got one," and "everybody smokes pot" are possibilities. While John was singing about the walrus and eggs, Paul was interested in honey pies.

"Wild Honey Pie," one of the songs on the *White Album*, has Paul playing all of the instruments and singing the multitracked vocals. Less than a minute long, this peculiar experimental song was created on the spot. A series of chords descends and return to the first chord, and Paul screeches "Honey Pie." This same pattern repeats, and at the very end of the song, Paul says, "I love you, honey pie." As Paul had stated in the book *Paul McCartney: Many Years from Now*, the song "was a reference to the other song I had written called 'Honey Pie.'" The Beatles weren't sure if they wanted to include "Wild Honey Pie" on the album, but since Pattie Harrison liked it a lot, the song found its place as a filler between "Ob-La-Di, Ob-La-Da" and "The Continuing Story of Bungalow Bill." "Wild Honey Pie" is a strange-sounding little ditty, psychedelic and funny.

"Wild Honey Pie" is a strange song, but compared to "Revolution 9" it's not *that* strange. First of all, "Revolution 9" is not a song; it's an electronic piece of music created in the style of musique concrète. A song has lyrics set to a melody and sung with a relatively short musical composition. Song elements are usually composed of melodic rhymed-lyric verses, sometimes with added harmony, and a wide variety of rhythms played on a number of different musical instruments. "Revolution 9" does not possess these elements, and more than likely you will not find it in any Beatles songbooks. Instead, it is a wild collage of mixed sounds composed of spoken words by John, George, and Yoko Ono; moaning; laughter; orchestral excerpts from classical music compositions; a choir of high-pitched singing voices; audience noises; instrumental fragments; a speeding car; gunfire; breaking glass; cheers from a soccer game; and extensive backward recording techniques. The majority of these sounds were on tape loops that were faded in and out during the mixing process. Hearing "Revolution 9" for the first time in late 1968 was a mind-boggling experience. Here, again, the Beatles had introduced something completely unlike their previous recordings. Ranked the fifth-worst song in *Rolling Stone* magazine's "Readers' Poll: The Worst Songs of the Sixties," many Beatles fans at the time couldn't bear to listen to this orgy of sounds. For them, it was far too radical and didn't conform to a customary song's structure. "Revolution 9" is John's creation, along with Yoko's and George's input. Paul did not want "Revolution 9" to be on the *White Album*, and he and Ringo did not participate in the recording. The piece was influenced by Yoko Ono and her avant-garde conceptual artwork, plus musique concrète compositions by Karlheinz Stockhausen.

"Revolution 9" begins with a repetitive voice that says "number nine," bouncing from left to right speakers with a faint piano playing in the background. John liked the sound of the "number nine" voice and brought it in and out of the mix at various times throughout the piece. It just so happens that the number 9 has a lot of relevance to John's life. His birthday is October 9, 1940; as a young boy, John lived at 9 Newcastle Road in the Wavertree section of Liverpool; Brian Epstein heard the Beatles for the first time at the Cavern Club in Liverpool on November 9, 1961; the Beatles performed on *The Ed Sullivan Show* for the first time on February 9, 1964; and John met Yoko at the Indica Gallery in London on November 9, 1966, where he first encountered her conceptual artwork. During the "Revolution 9" soundscape, backward and fast-rushing music flies by with cymbal crashes, a baby's voice, and opera excerpts. The overall stereo panning travels from speaker to speaker and engulfs the listener. Like most people, you will probably be somewhat shocked when you listen to "Revolution 9." John's tape-loop creations peaked with "Revolution 9," and going forward he no longer used this electronic music technique with any of his songs.

In the cellar of the house where I lived with my father during the summer of 1968, there was a reel-to-reel, two-track tape recorder I used to record my band the Pandemoniums when we rehearsed. I had a collection of old hubcaps, bells, some tools, and there was an old radio on a Formica table. There was also a washing machine, a vacuum cleaner, and a sink and toilet in the nearby bathroom. One evening, on track one I recorded a bunch of sounds composed of hitting the hubcaps, ringing the bells, switching on the radio and twisting the dial, turning the vacuum cleaner and washing machine on and off, and flushing the toilet and running water in the sink. While not listening to what I had recorded on track one, on track two I recited lyrics that I had not set to music, made noises with my voice processed through a Fender Echoplex, and made sliding electric guitar sounds by running the strings up and down a microphone stand. When I played the tape, I was fascinated with hearing the arbitrary mix of the two tracks together. While I was recording a musique concrète composition, the Beatles were working on "Revolution 9." Months later when I heard "Revolution 9," I thought that the Beatles and I had a psychic connection, having created similar pieces.

"Revolution 9" is entirely different from previous Beatles recordings, and the *White Album* cover is an extreme, radical departure from the two previous Beatles album covers. The album covers for *Magical Mystery Tour* and *Sgt. Pepper's Lonely Hearts Club Band* are loaded with dynamic, vivid colors, the Beatles dressed in animal costumes, and dozens of faces and flowers. While it's logical to think that the *White Album*'s cover design was John and Yoko's idea, it was actually Paul who wanted to come up with something entirely different. Pop artist Richard Hamilton designed the blank white album cover with the name "The Beatles" in raised print in the lower-right corner and numbers stamped nearby. Replicating numbers assigned to limited editions of artwork, the stamped numbers on the cover gave the *White Album* an art collector's prestigious status. The "limited edition" concept is clever but funny given the fact that approximately five million copies of the album were made. Inside the double album were four detached photos of the Beatles. John, Paul, George, and Ringo do not look happy, and Paul hadn't shaved for a number of days. The four separate photos depict the Beatles as individuals, unlike earlier photos when they were together as a group. The individual photos also parallel the fact that many of the songs on the *White Album* are not recorded by all four Beatles. The splintering signs of the band were visible, but no one really noticed the Beatles coming apart.

John had a fascination with tape loops and backward recording techniques, but it was George whose interest with electronic music led him to buy a synthesizer. When George was in Los Angeles in November 1968, he met with Bernie Krause, who was an expert with the synthesizer. George was producing Jackie Lomax's album, and Bernie played the synthesizer on some of the album's songs. Intrigued with the instrument, George asked Bernie to demonstrate the varied sounds the instrument could make. George recorded Bernie's demonstration and purchased a Moog synthesizer. In England, George experimented with the synthesizer, and in May 1969 he released a solo album titled *Electronic Sound* on Zapple Records, a division of the Beatles' Apple Records company. Unfortunately, the album was not well received and was buried with scathing reviews. To add insult to injury, "No Time or Space" on the entire second side of the album, was an edited version of Bernie's recorded demonstration, of which George claimed to be the composer. On the original recording, George did give an "assisted by Bernie Krause" credit on "No Time or Space." But George's preoccupation with electronic music occurred before his solo *Electronic Sound* album.

George's first electronic song had been "Only a Northern Song" on the *Yellow Submarine* album. George, John, and Paul created a bed of sound made up of forward and backward tape loops. The instrumental sections are filled with studio effects, discordant trumpet blasts played by Paul, spoken voices, and an ever-present Hammond organ played by George. The ending section of the song is akin to the kind of sound collage that John would later develop in "Revolution 9." George sings, "It's only a northern song," but as an electronic, psychedelic sonic creation, it's much more than just another northern song.

"It's All Too Much" was written by George, who sings lead vocals and plays an organ. The song is loaded with guitar feedback played by

George and John, and Ringo's drumming is unusually busy. George, John, and Paul overdubbed heavy handclaps on the second and fourth beats throughout the long six-minute, twenty-eight-second recording. Written and recorded in 1967, a few months before the summer of love, the song embodies the spirit of that ideological summer with the lyrics "love that's shining all around." When you listen very carefully, toward the end of the song, George sings "you are too much, John," and "we are dead." Apparently at that time, John was too much for George. At the very end of the song, John's and Paul's background vocals sing "tuba" and "Cuba" instead of "too much." Recorded at a time when George and John were taking LSD, the music and lyrics of "It's All Too Much" captured the psychedelic drug culture prevalent in the flower-power hippie movement that was happening in 1967. The song was considered for inclusion in the *Magical Mystery Tour* movie but was held back and put in the *Yellow Submarine* movie and its accompanying soundtrack album. Adding fanfare to the song, George Martin wrote an arrangement consisting of four trumpets and a bass clarinet and recorded it as an overdub. In retrospect, George Harrison had said in the October 1999 issue of *Mojo Magazine* that he didn't like those instruments added to his song. The trumpets and clarinet were too much for Harrison.

Soon after the Beatles returned to England from their transcendental meditation experience in India with the Maharishi, George wrote "Long, Long, Long." One might think that having spent six weeks in India, George would have written another Indian song using a sitar, tabla, and tambura, but George actually refrained from using Indian instruments on future Beatles songs. However, the recurring acoustic guitar part he plays on "Long, Long, Long" does sound like a sitar. George's lead vocals in the verses are soft and tender and at times almost a whisper. Ringo plays only a few brilliant drum fills in the verses and then plays a steady beat and more drum fills during the bridge section. At the end of the bridge, George's vocals dramatically peak on the words *oh, oh*. Lyrically, the song tells of great longing for someone or something. In the last verse, George "can see you" and "be you." "Long, Long, Long" can be interpreted as George expressing love for his wife Pattie or about George finally finding spiritual love. The peculiar psychedelic ending of the song is the happenstance result of a wine bottle rattling on a Leslie speaker cabinet while Paul played the Hammond organ. Making the ending of "Long, Long, Long" even stranger, George wails like a cat in heat, Ringo plays a fast drumroll, George makes bright string noises on his guitar, and Ringo ends the song with a thud. As was the case with the *White Album*, the *Abbey Road* album has several songs that do not feature all of the Beatles, as they were functioning more like four individuals rather than a group. Therefore, John didn't contribute anything on "Long, Long, Long" or on George's other song, "Savoy Truffle."

"I Want You (She's So Heavy)" is a long, complex, blues, heavy-rock, electronic music song written by John. The seven-minute, forty-four-second song is a direct statement from John declaring how much he emphatically wants Yoko. Repeatedly. Three years prior to the Beatles recording "I Want You (She's So Heavy)," Bob Dylan had recorded and released a single titled "I Want You." Both Bob Dylan's and John's song contain the lyrics "I want you so bad," but the melody and musical elements of John's song are radically different from Bob Dylan's folk tune. While the lyrics are minimal and repetitive, the music evolves beyond a more common three-chord blues progression. The last song on side one of the *Abbey Road* album, "I Want You (She's So Heavy)" begins with explosive electric guitars playing an abbreviated musical chorus in three-four time. The introduction ends with an altered A major chord, and the first chord in the verse is an A minor chord, illustrating another parallel modulation used by the Beatles. The many verses, played in four-four time, begin, and John sings "I want you," followed by three beats on drums, guitar, and bass. Then John sings "I want you so bad," followed by four beats played by the band. John plays the same vocal melody on his guitar as he imitates his singing voice with the guitar on all of the verses. The combined vocal/guitar effect is sensual. John wants Yoko so bad it's driving him mad. After he sings "driving me," a transitional musical bridge occurs, with Paul playing a solo bass line. There's more "I want you, I want you so bad," but this time John's voice intensifies. The transitional bridges returns, and then the "heavy" part of the song kicks in. John sings "she's so," and after the guitar chorus riff and organ are played, he screams "heavy." Back in the 1960s, *heavy* was a popular word used to describe something deep or intense. Without a doubt, John found Yoko to be "heavy." Unlike the first chord in the verses, the "heavy" section of the song begins with a D minor chord played in three-four time. Harmonically, the song has two different tonal/key centers and different time signatures. We return to the verse chord progression, where John plays a bluesy lead guitar solo right up to the musical bridge, and this time Paul plays a rhythmic variation of his bass solo. Another "she's so heavy" chorus takes place, with a brilliant organ part played by Beatle buddy Billy Preston. One more verse happens with an added conga part, and Paul plays a rapid descending bass run. After John sings "driving me mad," leading into the bridge, he rips his vocal chords screaming an emotional, primal "Yeah!" John wants Yoko, and she is driving him mad. The final massive "heavy" musical chorus begins.

A wall of omnipresent electric guitars play a two-part riff in the ending chorus. Multilayered, repetitive arpeggio guitars play simultaneously with a thick recurring, melodic low-string guitar riff overdubbed several times played by John and George. Paul doubles the low guitar riff on his bass. As the end chorus builds, Ringo's drumming is jazzy, the screeching background voices are haunting, and Paul's soaring bass runs are remarkable. What makes "I Want You (She's So Heavy)" an electronic song are the sound effects added to the long musical ending. Gradually, the sound of white noise, produced from the Moog synthesizer, takes over the song, growing louder and more aggressive with each musical repetition. Adding to the swirling noise is a howling wind machine played by Ringo. The combined synthesizer noise with the wind machine lifts the song off the ground and propels you off your feet and into a cosmic space. As the song intensifies with no ending in sight, suddenly you are stunned with an abrupt, cliff-hanging silence. When John was working on the final mix of the song, he told the engineer to cut the tape exactly where the song comes to a screeching halt. It is a shocking ending that no one could have anticipated.

While recording the *Abbey Road* album, the Beatles were acutely aware that their individuality was much stronger than their desire to continue working together as a group. Knowing that *Abbey Road* would be their last album, the Beatles temporarily put aside their differences, focused on their gifted musicianship, and created an outstanding album. The photo on the album cover is simple: The Beatles are walking across Abbey Road on a crosswalk, called a zebra crossing in England. Dressed in a white suit, a full-bearded John with flowing long hair leads the crossing, followed by Ringo with a beard in a black suit, clean-shaven Paul in a navy-blue suit, and a long-haired, bearded George dressed in a denim shirt and jeans. This *Abbey Road* cover formation is unlike the historical sequence of how the band came together. John started with the Quarrymen; Paul then joined the Quarrymen, followed by George; and Ringo joined the Beatles. During the 1960s, it was commonplace to refer to the Beatles as John, Paul, George, and Ringo, yet the Beatles appear in a different order on this album cover. In 1969, their images were so well known worldwide that their name didn't need to be printed on the cover. Their name does appear on the back cover, along with a tile sign identifying the thoroughfare known as Abbey Road. Appropriately enough, the *s* in the Beatles' name is cracked, perhaps symbolizing that when *Abbey Road* was released in 1969, the Beatles had cracked—they were unofficially no longer a band.

In the span of three years, from 1966 to 1969, the Beatles had created an unprecedented collection of psychedelic electronic songs that have stood the test of time. When they were originally released, Beatles fans and critics alike were awestruck. Today, when listeners hear these songs for the first time, it must be a mind-expanding listening experience.

Suggested Listening: "Rain"; "I'm Only Sleeping"; "Tomorrow Never Knows"; "Strawberry Fields Forever"; "Baby You're a Rich Man"; "I Am the Walrus"; "Revolution 9"; "I Want You (She's So Heavy)"

10

ORCHESTRAL DIMENSIONS
Strings, Woodwinds, and Brass Songs

With George Martin, a classically trained musician who played the oboe and keyboards, as the Beatles' primary record producer and Phil Spector, who produced the *Let It Be* album, the Beatles had the resources to add orchestral instruments and saxophones to several of their songs. Starting with "Yesterday" and ending with "The Long and Winding Road," the Beatles added an air of sophistication to these songs and blended together different musical genres.

As Paul had said in *The Beatles Anthology*, one morning he woke up with a melody in his head. Paul thought it was something he had heard before and that the tune belonged to an existing song. He asked a number of people in the music business if they recognized it, but no one did. So Paul claimed it as his song. Initially, he didn't have any lyrics to go along with the melody and came up with the working title "Scrambled Eggs." In 1965, for a rock/pop group to use a string quartet on a single was completely out of the ordinary. Plus there are no drums, no electric guitars, and no bass guitar. No other Beatles sing or play any instruments on "Yesterday," so it really is a solo Beatle recording. This was Paul's first taste of performing as a solo artist, and his solo artistry would blossom and become prevalent on some of his songs on the *White Album*. John, George, and Ringo were not keen on releasing "Yesterday" as a Beatles single, believing that the song did not represent the group. After all, it's only Paul singing and strumming an acoustic guitar, backed by a string quartet arrangement written by George Martin. Paul sings of troubles that are far away, and he thinks that they are here to stay, so he resorts to believing in the better times of yesterday. "Yesterday" is a nostalgic song that looks back instead of looking forward. It's a song about losing a love and blaming oneself for saying something wrong, something hurtful. All that's left is a longing for a time before the hurt, when loved ones were happy together. After the first verse, the string quartet comes in and enhances the melancholy mood of the song. Paul needs a place to hide and finds it by going back to "Yesterday." Taken by surprise with this unusual Beatles record, the young public quickly fell in love with and embraced the new sophisticated song and made it a number one hit in the United States. Indirectly, "Yesterday" exposed many Beatles fans to the sounds of a string quartet for the first time, as well as to a new musical genre: classical pop.

A year after "Yesterday" soared up the record charts, the Beatles released "Eleanor Rigby" as a single. Instead of a string quartet, "Eleanor Rigby" is backed with a double string quartet, also known as a string octet arranged by George Martin. This time, Paul doesn't play an acoustic guitar, and John and George sing harmony on the chorus with Paul. Like "Yesterday," no electric guitars, bass, or drums are on "Eleanor Rigby"—the only instruments being used are the strings. Interestingly, the Beatles chose to pair both "Yesterday" and "Eleanor Rigby" with songs sung by Ringo on the B-side to the singles, providing a sharp contrast. The country-twanged "Act Naturally" is on the "Yesterday" single, and the lighthearted, fun "Yellow Submarine" is on the "Eleanor Rigby" single. This unusual paring exemplifies the Beatles' diversity as writers and recording artists, as well as their unpredictably.

The lyrics to "Eleanor Rigby" are sad and portray loneliness. While the song is about "all the lonely people," the main characters are the fictional Eleanor and Father McKenzie. The short two-minute, eight-second song begins with the "lonely people" chorus. Then Paul sings with a somber emotional tone and introduces Eleanor, who keeps her face in a jar. What? Abstract lyrics for sure, but by this time most listeners accepted the Beatles as being artistic and poetic. In the second verse, Paul introduces Father McKenzie, who writes a sermon that no one will hear. Paul tells us in the last verse that Eleanor dies and Father McKenzie buries her. Sadly, no one came to the grave. Paul wrote

"Eleanor Rigby," with some help with the lyrics from John, George, Ringo, and John's childhood friend Pete Shotton. Pete was one of the original members of John's first band, the Quarrymen, and remained a close friend of John's. Prior to Paul writing the song, his girlfriend Jane Asher turned Paul on to the Italian baroque composer Antonio Vivaldi, who was known for his brilliant string arrangements. Paul chose to have a string backing on "Eleanor Rigby." The string players play their instruments with a bouncy staccato flair, which parallels the stark, explicit lyrics. Remarkably, this sad, classical-sounding song became a number one hit in August 1966. The success of "Yesterday" and "Eleanor Rigby" reveals that as the Beatles continued to evolve as songwriters and recording artists, their audience was willing to grow along with them and welcome the new, innovative songs.

The tone of Paul's lead vocals in his song "For No One" is quite similar to the way he sings "Eleanor Rigby." The lyrics in both songs are sad, and there are tearful eyes in "For No One." Written by Paul about his failing relationship with Jane Asher, he wastes no time singing about a dying love. Straightaway, his mind aches because she no longer needs him. Her love has vanished, a love that should have lasted years. Fittingly, the working title for this song was "Why Did It Die?" This short two-minute song doesn't have a chorus but is composed of verses and bridges. "For No One" moves to another key in the bridge when Paul sings "and in her eyes." Adding to the lamenting emotion of the song, a French horn plays a solo where normally a guitar or keyboard solo would occur. Not including the French horn, the performance on "For No One" is almost solo Paul, supplemented only by Ringo on drums and percussion. John and George do not partake in the recording. Paul plays the piano and bass guitar and also plays the clavichord keyboard, which dates back to the late Medieval and Renaissance periods. The single strings inside the clavichord are lightly struck by depressing its keys, and when mixed in with the piano part, the combined sound is percussive. By adding the clavichord and the French horn to "For No One," Paul and George Martin had created a new sonic experience for the listener. This unique song appropriately fits in with the other new songs on the groundbreaking *Revolver* album, and it stands on its own as a classical/pop ballad. Harmonically, the heartbreaking "For No One" is unresolved. The song ends with a questioning, suspenseful chord, echoing a lack of closure often felt when a romance fades.

A striking contrast to the sad sentiment of "For No One," "Got to Get You into My Life" is a bright, upbeat, happy song. It's a song about finally finding someone you love. Right? Wrong. As Paul had said in the book *Paul McCartney: Many Years from Now*, "Got to Get You into My Life" is about marijuana. Paul, and all of the Beatles, smoked a lot of pot in 1965, 1966, 1967, and so on. Without knowing about Paul's covert way of writing a song about his love for smoking pot, it's completely natural to think that "Got to Get You into My Life" is an exciting love song about someone. However, the lyrics "I need you, every day of my life" and "you were meant to be near me" are not about a person, they're about a cannabis plant. Blaring trumpets and saxophones announce the beginning of the song and accompany Paul throughout "Got to Get You into My Life." George plays an electric guitar riff in the musical interlude toward the end of the song. In addition to Ringo drumming, he constantly hits a tambourine, and John contributes to the song by playing electric rhythm guitar and the organ. The use of brass instruments in "Got to Get You into My Life" was a precursor to Paul using a high-register trumpet the following year in a new song.

"Penny Lane" was more commercial than the progressive "Strawberry Fields Forever." Both songs were released as a double-sided single in February 1967. Paul wrote the song about his and John's familiar surroundings around the street named Penny Lane in Liverpool. A piano-dominant song, Paul, John, and George Martin all play pianos, but what sets "Penny Lane" apart from other Beatles songs is the piccolo trumpet. Paul had seen a BBC televised broadcast of Johann Sebastian Bach's *Brandenburg Concerto* No. 2, which features the piccolo trumpet. This unique instrument can play musical notes an octave higher than the typical trumpet. By using the piccolo trumpet in "Penny Lane," once again the Beatles had showcased an instrument never heard in a pop song. Additionally, George Martin wrote an arrangement of backing instruments that included flutes, oboes, an English horn, flugelhorn, piccolos, and trumpets.

Like many songs written by Paul, including "Can't Buy Me Love," "For No One," "Eleanor Rigby," and "Hello, Goodbye," "Penny Lane" does not have a musical introduction. Instead, vocals start at the very beginning of the song. Immediately, Paul sings about the local shops and suburban activities that take place on Penny Lane. There's the barber, the banker, the fireman who keeps his fire engine clean, and a pretty nurse who sells poppies. During the verses and choruses, Ringo hardly plays any cymbals. His drumming is predominately snare hits on the second and fourth beats, and he also rattles a fire-engine bell. Paul's active bass playing is dominant and melodious. John and George harmonize with Paul on the choruses. "Penny Lane" ends with the sound of rushing cymbals and high-pitched feedback. The song was a number one hit sensation, but along with "Strawberry Fields Forever," these two songs caused a problem for rock-and-roll bands at the time. With very few exceptions, no bands that played the Top 40 hits of the day had a mellotron, violins, cellos, or a piccolo trumpet. So when playing at local venues, the bands—including my band, the Pandemoniums— were stumped and couldn't play "Penny Lane" and "Strawberry Fields Forever," as requested by the long-haired and mini-skirted audience.

Prior to the Beatles releasing "Penny Lane" and "Strawberry Fields Forever" and some of the progressive songs on *Revolver*, the Pandemoniums and hundreds of other bands played many of the Beatles songs that were suitable for guitars, bass, and drums. The songs on the albums released in 1964 and 1965 were perfect for the basic rock-and-roll band instruments. Audiences loved hearing "She's a Woman," "I Feel Fine," "Ticket to Ride," and countless others. In 1967, when the Beatles became a recording studio band and continued to evolve and create more complex songs, the majority of bands could no longer play the Beatles' current hit songs. Even the Beatles themselves couldn't play these songs live, and they didn't have to because they had stopped touring.

"Eleanor Rigby" is a classical pop song embraced with a striking double string quartet, but with "She's Leaving Home," Paul delved even deeper into classical music elements. Augmenting a double string quartet, an additional cello, an upright double bass, plus a harp were added. Uncharacteristically for Paul, "She's Leaving Home" is a rare song he wrote in three-four time. Anxious to get the song recorded, Paul worked with another arranger, Mike Leander, because George Martin was unavailable. Martin did make a few changes to Leander's score prior to recording. A bittersweet song about a teenage girl leaving home and paining her distraught parents, similar to "Eleanor Rigby," "She's Leaving Home" is one of the few songs that does not include any of the Beatles playing instruments. Paul sings the lead vocals and John sings harmony during the choruses, but George and Ringo are not on the recording. The song begins with a lyrical harp passage that introduces Paul's vocals. The song's structure is a series of verses and cho-ruses. On the chorus when Paul sings "She . . . is leaving . . . home," John sings harmony beneath Paul's high vocal pitches. "Everything money could buy" and "What did we do that was wrong?" sings John. "She's Leaving Home" is an exquisitely beautiful song and a classical pop masterpiece.

With the exception of "She's Leaving Home," most of the songs on the *Sgt. Pepper's Lonely Hearts Club Band* album are progressive and psychedelic pop. However, Paul's song on that album, "When I'm Sixty-Four," could be called regressive. The style of this song harks back to dance hall songs from the 1940s. Paul had written "When I'm Sixty-Four" long before the Beatles recorded it in December 1966. Paul's father, Jim, a dance hall musician who played the trumpet and piano, turned sixty-four on July 7, 1966, so the timing was right to make the song a reality. "When I'm Sixty-Four" showcases clarinets arranged by George Martin. The song begins with a trio of clarinets, playing the melody in the verses and accompanying Paul's lead vocals throughout the song. Paul plays a punchy bass line along with Ringo playing his drums with brushes. Ringo also plays some dazzling, rapid rhythms on the cymbals and he rings the chimes. Instead of George, John plays lead guitar. John and George sing background vocals during the bridge. "When I'm Sixty-Four" ends the same way it begins, with three clari-nets. Uncharacteristic of the other songs on *Sgt. Pepper's Lonely Hearts Club Band*, "When I'm Sixty-Four" adds variety to the turned-on marching band album.

"Good Morning Good Morning" wakes you up with a crowing roost-er. John was inspired to write the song after seeing a Kellogg's Corn Flakes television commercial. After the rooster, the song begins with a chorus of voices greeting you with "good morning." The rhythmic meter of the song is unusual for a rock song, with the chorus and bridge in four-four time and the verses in a combination five-four and three-four time. Ringo navigates the time changes and provides a rhythmic cohe-siveness by playing persistent beats, snare drum fills, and cymbal crashes. With "Good Morning Good Morning," it was John's turn to use brass instruments in a song. Three saxophone players from the group Sounds Incorporated, as well as two trombonists and a French horn player, were brought into Abbey Road Studios. This brass ensemble provides a rich, growling accompaniment to "Good Morning Good

Morning." If the rooster hadn't woken you up, then Paul's screaming lead guitar solo will. The song ends with the chorus of voices singing "good morning, good morning, good," only to get drowned out by racing horses and barking dogs on a hunt. When it comes to sound effects, "Yellow Submarine" is loaded with them. But "Good Morning Good Morning" was the first Beatles song to include animal sounds.

Let's travel back to the time when flower-print clothing was popular and the Beatles had just released their Sgt. Pepper's Lonely Hearts Club Band *album. . . . It's a perfectly warm, late spring evening. Your girlfriend sits next to you as you drive your father's car away from the populated city. The car heads toward the nearby countryside. You know of a secluded country road where you can be alone with the girl who says that "Penny Lane" is in her ears and in her eyes. And you believe her. Parked beneath a large maple tree, you listen to the local AM radio station play hit songs that are on the Top 20 charts. You hear "Groovin'" by the Young Rascals, "Friday on My Mind" by the Easybeats, and "On a Carousel" by the Hollies. You roll down the driver's side window and hear crickets chirping along to the songs. Then suddenly, the sound of a dreamy acoustic guitar and a singing voice demands your attention. Captivated, you listen intently as magic unfolds before your awestruck ears. A song about sad news, a man blowing his mind in a car, and the English army winning the war intrigue your young mind. Then an amazing groundswell sound of an orchestra sliding up to the stratosphere interrupts the song. The orchestra suddenly stops, and another song about falling out of bed pops in. As if by magic, the beginning section of the song returns, and the voice sings about four thousand holes and wants to turn you on. The orgasmic ascending orchestra returns and peaks on the instruments' highest notes, followed by a slamming chorus of piano chords. You have never heard anything like it before and are dumbfounded by such an outrageous piece of music. The DJ announces that what you heard was "A Day in the Life" from the Beatles' new album,* Sgt. Pepper's Lonely Hearts Club Band.

How do two musically unrelated songs fit together and become a masterpiece? Put John and Paul together in the recording studio in 1967. John had developed a song about current events that he had read about in newspapers, and Paul had a song about starting one's day. And how do these different songs blend so well together? By having record producer George Martin bridge the songs with a forty-piece orchestra playing a gigantic discordant glissando. Martin instructed the musicians to start the section by playing their lowest note on their instruments and gradually slide up to their highest note. To increase the dissonance and intensity, he recorded the orchestra's surging crescendo a number of times and mixed them together. This improvised avant-garde technique was unusual for the classical orchestral instrumentalists, and the result was ear shattering. As the closing song on the *Sgt. Pepper's Lonely Hearts Club Band* album, "A Day in the Life" is sequenced *after* Pepper's Band ends the show. Therefore, "A Day in the Life" is not included in the Pepper's Band repertoire. During the introduction, Paul adds piano and bass to John's acoustic guitar. In the first verse about sad news, Ringo doesn't play his drums, but George keeps a steady beat playing maracas. In the second verse about someone dying in a car crash, Ringo enters the song playing perfectly placed drum fills around John's lead vocals. At the end of the third verse, when John says that he'd love to turn you on, the dynamic orchestra climbs its way up to the top notes with a cliff-hanging ending. A ringing alarm clock sets up Paul, and he sings his song about waking up, rushing out of the house, getting on a bus, having a smoke, and slipping off into a dream. The word *dream* is pivotal as it leads the listener back to the orchestra and John's *ah*s bathed in reverb. This musical bridge connects with John's part of the song and the last verse about filling holes in Albert Hall. John wants to turn you on one more time, and the orchestra returns and rises to a screeching halt. After a slight pause, a crashing piano chord is played on three different pianos by John, Paul, Ringo, and Mal Evans, along with George Martin playing a harmonium. This thunderous chord is sustained for more that forty seconds before fading away. A breathtaking ending to a brilliant, one-of-a-kind song, the Beatles did turn on millions of listeners who bought the *Sgt. Pepper's Lonely Hearts Club Band* album.

When it came to adding orchestral instruments to Beatles songs, George Martin was extremely important and essential. Sometimes John and Paul had orchestral instruments in mind but didn't have the technical skills to arrange the music they were hearing in their heads. George Martin's classical training gave him the ability to structure the Beatles' orchestral desires and write the arrangements for the classical musicians who frequented Abbey Road Studios for the Beatles' recording sessions. Such is the case with "All You Need Is Love." It's unusual that the song begins with a brass ensemble playing not an English anthem but, of all things, the French national anthem, "La Marseillaise." This was a radical departure from what other rock and pop bands were recording in 1967. American listeners were fascinated and surprised when they heard "La Marseillaise," and most of them didn't know what it was. John plays the harpsichord, a keyboard instrument that was popular during the seventeenth- and eighteenth-century baroque and early classical music periods. Rich, deep cellos precede John's opening lead vocals, and a swinging brass section answers John when he sings "all you need is love" during the choruses. A dancing piccolo trumpet, saxophone, and strings play in the extended chorus, arranged and conducted by George Martin. During the ending chorus, strings play a section of "Greensleeves" as the song begins to fade out. Adding to the use of orchestral instruments in "All You Need Is Love," Paul not only plays an electric bass but also an upright double bass, playing pizzicato by plucking the strings, and George Harrison bowed some violin, an instrument he had never played before. Tapping back to the first instrument he learned how to play, John overdubbed a banjo part. "All You Need Is Love" is a great example of the Beatles evolving as songwriters in the recording studio and incorporating orchestral instruments into their songs, with significant help and contributions from George Martin.

Paul's "Ob-La-Di, Ob-La-Da" is happy-go-lucky song on the Beatles' double *White Album*. Given the fun nature of the recording, with laughter here and there, spoken words, and vocal effects supplied by all four Beatles, you wouldn't know or have guessed that the Beatles were quarrelling with each other during the recording sessions. The disagreements reached such an intense level that John stormed out of the studio. Upon returning, John banged out the piano introduction, which Paul actually liked. After the song begins with the bright piano, handclaps lead in Paul's vocals. His *da . . . , da, da, da* bass line is bouncy and lyrical. John plays upbeats on the piano, contrasting with Ringo's downbeat drumming and Paul's bass lines, which gives the song a reggae quality. As reported in a *New York Times* article, Paul had said that the "Desmond" in this storytelling song is a reference to Desmond Dekker, a Jamaican reggae musician who was riding a wave of success in England at the time. In the book *Paul McCartney: Many Years from Now*, Paul said the lyrics in the chorus were taken word for word from Jimmy

Scott-Emuakpor, a Nigerian conga player with whom Paul was familiar. Jimmy used to say, "Ob-la-di, ob-la-da, life goes on, brah." When Paul told Jimmy he was going to use those words, Jimmy wanted to be paid. Eventually, Paul sent Jimmy a check for a nondisclosed amount. John and George sing spirited vocals with Paul on the choruses. The instruments played by the Beatles are standard: piano, acoustic guitar, bass, drums, and percussion. The horn arrangement that George Martin wrote provides a syncopated countermelody to Paul's vocal in the bridge sections and the vocals in the third and fourth choruses. The horns make you want to get up and dance to the uplifting "Ob-La-Di, Ob-La-Da." John and George sing twelve high-pitched *la*s on the second chorus. It's such a clever harmony part, I wish they did it more than once. If you want some fun, then listen to "Ob-La-Di, Ob-La-Da."

Continuing on with some songs from the *White Album*, we encounter the piano-centric song "Martha My Dear," written by Paul. As was the case with many songs on the *White Album*, this is a solo-Beatle recording. "Martha My Dear" features Paul playing all of the instruments except for the added strings and brass instruments arranged by George Martin. Paul had a sheepdog named Martha, thus the title of the song. Additionally, in a BBC Radio interview, Paul said that the song is probably about Jane Asher. The song begins with Paul playing a bouncy, spirited syncopated piano part. Violins, violas, and cellos accompany his lead vocals in the first verse and continue playing throughout the song, with the exception of the brass solo in the middle. The bridge, which lifts the song to a higher key, happens quickly and includes the added trumpets, French horn, flugelhorn, trombone, and tuba. Paul brings in his electric guitar, bass, and drums in the "take a good look around" section of the bridge, which drives the song into the bright brass ensemble solo based on the melody in the verses. The bridge reoccurs, followed by a quick musical transition that brings "Martha My Dear" back down to its original key. The song ends with a verse that is a lyrical variation of the first verse. With a dynamic, toe-tapping song like this, we'll never forget you, Martha.

Going from Paul's sheepdog to lyrics about pigs, the *White Album* also includes "Piggies," written by George. Adding to the eclectic nature of the album, "Piggies" is a classical pop song that uses a harpsichord and a double string quartet along with the sound of grunting pigs. In this satirical song, George used the words *piggies* and *piggy* to portray the greedy, elitist establishment. The classical tone is immediately established at the beginning of the song with a harpsichord introduction, followed by George singing the lead vocals and playing acoustic guitar and Ringo playing the tambourine along with Paul's solid bass notes. Straightaway, George engages you by asking, "Have you seen the little piggies?" After the word *worse*, the first sounds of grunting pigs occur. Strings accompany George in the second verse, where he says that bigger piggies have clean shirts. The sound of George's voice changes to a bright nasal tone in the bridge when he sings, "There's something lacking" and "What they need's a damn good whacking!" The middle classical instrumental section takes place and features the harpsichord and string section. For the last verse, George, John, and Paul belt out operatic-styled vocals, and the grunting pigs return. In what sounds like an afterthought, George says, "One more time," and the strings play the two final chords to "Piggies," followed by more piggy grunts. The harpsichord is played by Chris Thomas, a classically trained musician who produced "Piggies." George Martin was away on holiday when the basic tracks were recorded. Upon Martin's return, he wrote the string arrangement and added it to the song.

Another antiestablishment song, John sings about people who want a revolution on the single "Revolution" and "Revolution 1" on the *White Album*. There are three different versions of "Revolution," and appropriately titled "Revolution 1" was recorded before the raucous single version; "Revolution 9" was recorded after "Revolution 1" and before the single. The lyrics address the social unrest and protests against the Vietnam War that were happening in the late 1960s, but the word *revolution* also pertains to a circular motion, which is akin to the name of the Beatles' album *Revolver*. After all, long before the advent of cassette tapes, compact discs, and downloading digital files, discs were the only available format, whether singles or albums, that revolved on turntables.

Contrary to the lyrics, the slow tempo and John's mellow lead vocals of "Revolution 1" don't sound like a revolution at all. The sound of John's soft-toned vocals was achieved by him lying on the floor while singing. After a loud lead guitar introduction, the music shuffles along, with John playing an acoustic guitar, Paul playing a bass line that parallels John's guitar part, and Ringo playing a simple groove rhythm. George's and John's lead guitars puncture the mellow atmosphere, especially during the choruses. The structure of the song is the same as the "Revolution" single: verse, bridge, chorus. Paul's bass line descends in the bridge when John sings, "When you talk about destruction." John sings conflicting lyrics in the first bridge when he says "count me out . . . in." At the time, he wasn't sure if he was "in" or "out" with the social revolution. In a 1970 *Rolling Stone* magazine interview, John said, "I wanted to talk, I wanted to say my piece about revolution. On one version, I said 'Count me in' about violence, in or out, because I wasn't sure. But the (single) version we put out said 'Count me out,' because I don't fancy a violent revolution happening all over. I don't want to die, but I begin to think what else can happen, you know, it seems inevitable." On the album version, trumpets and trombones come in with brass accents on the bridge and continue playing on the choruses and remaining verses. Paul and George sing, "Don't you know it's gonna be" and retro doo-wop-styled "ohm-shoo-bee-doo-wop" background vocals during the choruses. In the second and third verses, Paul and George sing beautiful harmonies with John's lead vocals, along with some doo-wop lyrics. The trombones play a feel-good, bouncy rhythm in the second and third verses, and trumpets augment the trombones in the choruses. John's vocals get somewhat wilder during the end fade-out chorus. In addition to Paul's and George's vocals in the doo-wop section, there's a third voice. Francie Schwartz, who was living with Paul in 1968, sings along with Paul and George. Francie had come to London that year to pitch an antiestablishment film idea she had for the Beatles' newly formed Apple company. Paul was attracted to her, and he invited Francie to move in with him. He also secured her a job at Apple working with Derek Taylor, the Beatles' press officer. The relationship between Paul and Francie fell apart after Jane Asher surprised Paul with a visit. Jane found Paul in bed with Francie. That was the definitive end of the crumbling relationship Paul had with Jane, and his relationship with Francie soon faded away.

Francie Schwartz and I would meet several years later when I was seeking a personal assistant and ran an ad in the local newspaper. While reviewing résumés, one name leaped off the page—Francie Schwartz. We met for coffee, and I soon discovered that she really was Paul's 1968 girlfriend. She had written a book about her time with Paul and the Beatles titled *Body Count*. As she told me about her time with Paul, even though she was more than qualified, I realized that I couldn't hire her. My interest in the Beatles and her history with Paul would prevent me from focusing on my work.

While Francie is real, "Honey Pie" is based on a fictitious character. Paul wrote the song about a working girl in northern England who had become a movie star in Hollywood. On the *White Album*, "Honey Pie" recalls the style of dance hall songs from the 1920s. Paul introduces the song rubato style—void of any strict time and rhythm. With scratchy sounds heard when playing an old record, Paul sings a nasal-pitched vocal style reminiscent of the crooning singer Rudy Vallee and says, "Now she's hit the big time." On the first verse, a snappy four-four time is established. The saxophones and clarinets give "Honey Pie" a 1920s dance band sound. Saxophones and clarinets were popular instruments with 1920s dance bands such as Paul Whiteman and His Orchestra. John and Paul play rhythm guitars on "Honey Pie," and together with Ringo's brushed snare drum, they almost sound like a banjo, another instrument played in dance bands. Surprisingly, John didn't play banjo on the song. The sound and laid-back style of the lead guitar parts, played by John and Paul, perfectly complement the dance band sound. George plays a six-string bass and firmly plants most notes on the first and third beats, which lock in with Ringo's bass drum. Keeping in character with 1920s dance bands, Ringo plays his drums with brushes. During the instrumental solo, Paul sings a high falsetto vibrato voice, sounding like Tiny Tim, who was a popular novelty singer in 1968 with the hit song "Tiptoe Through the Tulips."

Following "Honey Pie," "Savoy Truffle" also depicts the wide range of styles and eclectic mix of songs on the *White Album*. Written and sung by George, "Savoy Truffle" features three tenor and three baritone saxophones. George wrote the song about his friend Eric Clapton and his love for chocolates, including truffles found in boxes of Mackintosh's Good News chocolates. Some of the lyrics are taken from the names of the assortment of chocolates in the Good News box, including "creem tangerine," "ginger sling," "montelimart," and "coffee dessert." This is another song on the *White Album* that John does not participate in. Chris Thomas plays the electric piano and organ on "Savoy Truffle" and also arranged the saxophones. When the saxophones were initially added to the recording, George wasn't happy with them and thought they sounded "too clean." He asked Chris to make them sound distorted, thus the saxophones sound heavy and gritty. After a few quick beats from Ringo, the song begins with a syncopated electric piano part. The tone of George's electric guitar is piercing, especially in the second chorus and the middle solo with the bright, blaring saxophones. During the "have them all pulled out" chorus, which refers to a warning about the possible fate of Eric Clapton's teeth, Paul sings a high harmony part with George's lead vocals. Ringo plays busy drum fills during the bridge, and overall the sound of his drums is rather thumpy with a lot of bottom end, which makes for a strong contrast with the ultra-bright saxophones. We move on from George's sweet chocolates to John's sweet lullaby.

"Good Night" is a prime example of how diverse John was as a songwriter. Going directly from the avant-garde, improvisational "Revolution 9" to "Good Night" provides the listener with a striking contrast of styles between John's two compositions. A beautiful, lush song with an orchestra accompanying Ringo's lead vocals, John wrote "Good Night" as a lullaby for his five-year-old son Julian. There are no guitars or drums on "Good Night," and no performances by John, Paul, or George. George Martin wrote and conducted the twenty-seven-piece orchestra and played the ethereal celesta keyboard, and the Mike Sammes Singers sang the background vocals. Ringo delivers perhaps his best vocal performance with a tender and sensitive interpretation of the lyrics. "Good Night" is a heartwarming song that sends you off to a peaceful place where you can hopefully experience sweet dreams.

Taking in the totality of the diverse variety of songs on the *White Album*, beginning with "Back in the U.S.S.R." and ending with "Good Night," the listener can easily get knocked-out, excited, and inspired by the Beatles' progressive creative output. From musical genres that include rock and roll, folk, hard rock, classical pop, musique concrète, dance band, and the blues, the *White Album* is a true testament of the Beatles' ability to write and record music that far surpasses any one genre. The Beatles cannot be stereotyped to one sound, style, or category.

"Golden Slumbers," written by Paul, is the sixth song in the medley on side two of *Abbey Road*. Paul delivers emotionally charged lead vocals, which begins as a lullaby with lyrics inspired by a poem written by Thomas Dekker, an Elizabethan dramatist. The opening lyrics address how there once was a way to get back home. Those words tie in with the overall lyric theme to "Get Back," specifically getting back to where you once belonged. It sounds like Paul wants to relive the harmonious, fun-loving days of the Beatles, but he knows that won't happen. His voice is heart-wrenching when he sings the title "Golden Slumbers" and "smiles awake you when you rise." George Martin's rich, thirty-piece orchestral arrangement underscores the dramatic nature of the song. There are no guitars on "Golden Slumbers" and no John, as he was recovering in a hospital from a car accident in Scotland. George Harrison plays the bass while Paul plays the piano, and Ringo plays the drums and the overdubbed timpani. The emotional sounds of "Golden Slumbers" segue into "Carry That Weight," the next song in the medley.

Ringo provides the transition into "Carry That Weight" with a quick drum pattern, a variation of what he played as the transition from "Sun King" into "Mean Mr. Mustard." "Carry That Weight" begins as a boisterous song, with all four Beatles singing the title, then flows into the orchestra majestically playing a melody from "You Never Give Me Your Money," followed by George's electric guitar passage. Then Paul and George sing a verse to "You Never Give Me Your Money" with different lyrics, and after four beats of the orchestra and full band, we return to the "Carry That Weight" chorus. John's only participation on the song is his singing on the chorus. What is the "weight" that the Beatles are singing about? Despite their differences at the time of recording the *Abbey Road* album, they were cognizant of the fact that *together* they had created an outstanding body of music, and that no matter what they did as individual artists, it would not measure up to what they had achieved as the Beatles. They would carry the weight of that reality for a long time. In the 1988 documentary film *Imagine: John Lennon*, John said "Carry That Weight" was Paul "singing about all of us." George's arpeggio electric guitar part, similar to the one he played at the end of "You Never Give Me Your Money," transitions to the final song in the medley, "The End," but this time the orchestra accompanies the electric guitar.

"The End" showcases each Beatle's musical prowess. The song begins with vibrant electric guitars playing uplifting riffs as Ringo lays down the rhythmic foundation with his tom-toms and crash cymbals. After Ringo pounds out eight beats on his drums, Paul screams, "Oh yeah, all right!" For the first time on a Beatles album, Ringo performs a drum solo. He keeps steady beats going on his bass drum and plays syncopated on and off beats on his tom-toms and snare drums, spread across the stereo spectrum. Then John, Paul, and George join in with their guitars and sing "love you" along with Ringo. Now it's time for Paul, George, and John to shine, playing a sequence of lead guitar solos. Paul plays the first one, followed by George and then John. They each play a solo in that order three times, and John ends this section with his low, distorted, growling guitar, immediately followed by a solo piano playing a steady C major chord. George's lyrical, sweet lead guitar, harmonizing *ahs*, and sweeping strings end the song. The closing lyrics, sung by Paul, say, "And in the end, the love you take is equal to the love you make." These poetic words are the bottom line in the last recorded song with all four Beatles. Fittingly, "The End" was the end of the Beatles. Millions of fans throughout the world never wanted the Beatles to end, and they had no idea how significant "The End" really was.

As covered in chapter 7, "Acting Naturally: Movie Songs," unlike the majority of Beatles recordings produced by George Martin, the *Let It Be* album and "The Long and Winding Road" single were produced by Phil Spector. Phil added a lush, thirty-five-piece orchestra with a harp (arranged by Richard Hewson) and a fourteen-part female choir (arranged by John Barham) to Paul's "The Long and Winding Road." Phil did this without Paul's knowledge and without his approval. Upon hearing Phil's production, Paul was furious, and in a letter to Allen Klein, the Beatles' business manager, he demanded that the harp be eliminated and the orchestra and choir minimized. Paul's instructions were ignored, and the song was released. Paul claimed that the release of Phil Spector's production of "The Long and Winding Road" was one of the reasons why Paul had quit the Beatles. Surprisingly, when Paul has performed "The Long and Winding Road" with his touring bands, he has used a modified synthesized version of Phil's lush orchestral arrangement.

The Beatles' career was filled with surprises and unexpected turns. The nontraditional rock-and-roll instruments added to some of their songs contributed to the evolution of the Beatles. From a listener's perspective, the strings and brass instruments on Beatles songs created intrigue, sophistication, and an ongoing appeal with their recordings. While they used new sounds and instruments, they knew not to overdo it. If they had used the piccolo trumpet on additional songs beyond "Penny Lane" and "All You Need Is Love," the distinctive sound of the trumpet would lose its impact. Instead, the Beatles moved on and used different instruments, and in doing so their songs and the sound of the band continued to evolve.

Suggested Listening: "Yesterday"; "Eleanor Rigby"; "For No One"; "A Day in the Life"; "Penny Lane"; Piggies"; "The Long and Winding Road"

11

GIFTED EXTRAS

Guest Musicians Revealed

While most of the Beatles' songs were recorded with only John, Paul, George, and Ringo, occasionally guest musicians joined them in the recording studio. When that happened, with few exceptions, these musicians were uncredited. Because the Beatles themselves could not play some of the wide range of instruments they wanted to include in some of their songs, guest musicians were invited to Abbey Road Studios. George Martin had access to the best musicians in London, and he hired them to play on several Beatles recordings.

The first "guest" musician was their record producer, George Martin, who played keyboards on numerous Beatles songs. Paul, John, or George could have played the piano, organ, or electric keyboards that George Martin played, but he was already in the studio and, being a classically trained musician, he was certainly technically proficient enough to play those instruments. On their early recordings, it saved time to have Martin play instead of having one of the Beatles take the time to do a keyboard overdub. In his capacity as a keyboard player and integral creative producer, George Martin can be called the fifth Beatle.

Drummer Andy White was hired by George Martin to play with the Beatles when they recorded "Love Me Do," and "P.S. I Love You" on September 11, 1962. As covered in chapter 4, "Playing America's Heart Strings: Love Songs," Ringo had recently joined the Beatles, but

George Martin was not impressed with Ringo's drumming. Thus, Martin brought in studio drummer Andy White. Earlier in his career, Andy had formed a jazz band and toured northeast America, backing up Chuck Berry, the Platters, and Bill Haley and His Comets. Andy's rock-and-roll experiences sidelined Ringo at the recording session. Ringo certainly felt uncomfortable and awkward, but Andy's position with the Beatles was temporary. As history has shown, Ringo played the drums on the Beatles' recordings except for the songs on which Paul, and to a lesser extent John and George, played the drums. Given the formative working relationship with George Martin, John, Paul, and George Harrison didn't object to Andy recording with them. But without a doubt, John, Paul, and George wanted Ringo as their drummer.

In 1965, three years after the Andy White recording session, the Beatles recorded "You've Got to Hide Your Love Away," and it was time for another guest musician to record with the band. John wanted a flute solo in the song, and because none of the Beatles could play the flute, George Martin arranged to have John Scott, a London classical composer, jazz musician, and conductor, come to the recording session. As a conductor, Scott worked with the London Symphony Orchestra and the Munich Symphony Orchestra, and as a soloist he recorded with Henry Mancini and film composer John Barry. Rather than having a solo in the middle of the song, which would have been the typical placement, the flute solo occurs at the end of the song. Scott recorded a tenor flute part over the chords played in the verse. Then he overdubbed an alto flute, playing the same notes an octave higher. John Scott was not credited for his performance, so listeners didn't know who played the flute solo. If they had seen the movie *Help!*, they would have been led to believe that the indoor gardener in the "You've Got to Hide Your Love Away" scene played the flute.

In 1966, the Beatles took a radical departure from their rock and pop songs and recorded George's Indian-instrument-dominant "Love You To." For the first time on a Beatles recording, a guest musician was credited for his contribution. Tabla player Anil Bhagwat's name was printed on the back cover of the *Revolver* album, next to the song title. Bhagwat and the other guest musicians on Beatles recordings were hired with the understanding that they would not be credited (with the exception of Billy Preston). However, George made an exception and gave him credit. More detailed information on "Love You To" can be found in chapter 8, "Broader Horizons: World Music Songs."

Paul's "For No One" on *Revolver* is a sophisticated song, especially with the addition of the French horn. Paul was fond of the instrument and asked George Martin to bring in a French horn player. Martin hired Alan Civil, a classical musician who played the French horn with the prestigious Royal Philharmonic Orchestra and the BBC Symphony Orchestra, to play the horn solo in "For No One." George Martin explained the instrument's range to Paul, stating that E is the highest note. Paul wanted an F, and Alan was reluctant to play that note because it was too high for the French horn. Upon Paul's insistence, Alan played one of the highest notes in the extreme upper register of the horn's range. In his book, *Here, There and Everywhere*, Geoff Emerick wrote about Alan being under a lot of pressure because it was hard to hit the high note. Geoff said, "We felt that Alan, being the best horn player in London, could actually hit it, even though most horn players couldn't. He was breaking out into a sweat, telling everyone it shouldn't be done. But eventually he gave it a go, and pulled it off." In addition to the full solo, Alan also played a condensed version of his solo as a countermelody to Paul's lead vocals during the song's last verse.

As mentioned in the previous chapter, the piccolo trumpet is the featured instrument in "Penny Lane." It was played by David Mason, who had studied at the Royal College of Music and became a member of the Royal Opera House Orchestra and the Royal Philharmonic Orchestra. Paul wanted a piccolo trumpet on "Penny Lane," and George Martin invited David to play the part. In his book *All You Need Is Ears*, Martin explained why the recording session was challenging. He said the piccolo trumpet is difficult to play in tune, and no music had been prepared. Martin had met professional musicians who said, "If the Beatles were real musicians, they'd know what they wanted us to play before we came into the studio." Fortunately, David Mason wasn't one of them, and George Martin thought David was intrigued to be playing on a Beatles record. George Martin went on to say, "Paul would think up the notes he wanted, and I would write them down for David. The result was unique, something that had never been done in rock music before." Geoff wrote that David was a true professional and played the part perfectly the first time through, including the demanding solo. Geoff said, "It was, quite simply, the performance of his life. And everyone knew it, except obviously Paul." Paul wanted David to play the part again, but George Martin intervened, saying, "Good God, you can't possibly ask the man to do it again. It's fantastic." Paul was embarrassed and angered by George Martin's remark, but he relented and the session ended.

Another example of George Martin hiring outside musicians to play on a Beatles recording is Paul's song "She's Leaving Home." In addition to the string players, Martin hired Sheila Bromberg to play the harp, the featured instrument that starts the song and continues throughout. This recording session on March 17, 1967, marked the first time a female musician performed on a Beatles record. Sheila recalled in a 2011 BBC interview that Paul wasn't pleased with the way the harp sounded, so several takes were recorded. Still, Paul was hearing something different in his head but was having difficulty expressing how he wanted the harp to sound. As it turned out a few days later during the mixing session, George Martin took what Sheila had played initially and processed her part with some delay effects. That was the harp sound Paul had in mind.

As I mentioned in the "Never Too Much: More Rock-and-Roll Originals" chapter, there are four saxophones on "Lady Madonna," and the tenor saxophone solo was played by jazz musician Ronnie Scott. Ronnie was a musician who worked on the Cunard ship *Queen Mary* in the late 1940s and sailed to New York City, where he heard emerging jazz musicians. In London, in addition to being a studio player, he also owned the Ronnie Scott's Jazz Club. Tenor saxophonist Bill Povey and baritone sax players Bill Jackman and Harry Klein rounded out the saxophone quartet on "Lady Madonna." Harry recalled the "Lady Madonna" recording session in Mark Lewisohn's book *The Complete Beatles Recording Sessions*. Harry said that when they arrived at the studio, no music had been written, so they played a few riffs. Eventually, Paul heard something he liked, and the quartet went on to record the riff about one hundred times. When Ronnie heard the released recording, he was not pleased. His solo was mixed in the background, obscured by John, Paul, and George singing "bah, bah, bah, bah." However, the ensemble of four saxophones with Ronnie leading the quartet is loud and clear in the musical passages at the end of the choruses.

In 1968, when John's electric guitar was screaming with "Revolution" and Paul's electric guitar was blistering with "Helter Skelter,"

George's guitar was weeping. George's lyric commentary on the state of world affairs may not be uplifting, but the music is. The inspiration for "While My Guitar Gently Weeps" came from the Chinese *I-Ching: The Book of Changes*, which George arbitrarily opened and saw the words *gently weeps*. When the Beatles were recording George's song, John and Paul showed little interest in it. George played a variety of lead guitar solos, which included a backward electric guitar part, but he was not satisfied. He thought of his friend Eric Clapton and asked him to come to Abbey Road and play the solo. Initially, Eric was reluctant to play on a Beatles record because at that time no other major recording artist had done so. But with George's persuasion, Eric agreed. To mask Eric's sound, the engineer Chris Thomas processed the solo to sound more like a Beatles lead guitar. In doing so, everyone outside of the Beatles' innermost circle thought it was George who played the solo. In a 1977 *Crawdaddy* magazine interview, George said that Eric was nervous, but Eric's presence at the recording session helped to negate John and Paul's lack of interest in the song.

"While My Guitar Gently Weeps" is a dynamic song, with a slow build that peaks with Eric's lead guitar solo. Even the ending fade-out is powerful, with Eric cranking out bending notes and George wailing, almost crying, "Yeah, yeah, yeah." While *yeah*s were common lyrics in earlier Beatles songs, their use in this weeping song aren't cheerful at all. The song begins with Paul playing the piano and thick, full bass notes, George strumming his acoustic guitar, and Ringo making a swishing sound when hitting his hi-hat between the second and third beats. Eric announces the first verse with his opening lead guitar riff. This arrangement is the musical background for George's lead vocals in the first verse. A more stabbing lead guitar introduces the second verse, with Paul singing a harmony part above George's vocals but not on the lyrics to the song's title. Vocally, the bridge contains some of George's highest singing with an arcing melody as he says he doesn't know how someone controlled and bought and sold you. This may have been a covert comment from George about how the Beatles had been commercialized and turned into a sales product. George overdubbed an organ on the bridges where Paul's bass line, tightly locked in with Ringo's bass drum, dances around George's vocals. In the third verse, George and Paul sing about the world turning, while George's guitar gently weeps. Eric's weeping guitar solo begins on the last chord of the verse. It bends, wails, and climbs to the highest note in the solo and lands on the beginning of the bridge. George brings the organ back in during the solo, playing long, sustained notes, and the organ continues on the bridge. Adding some variety to the bridge, Ringo overdubbed a tambourine part, hitting it on the fourth beats in the first section and then switching to hitting it on the second beats. On the last verse, George and Paul sing about love that is sleeping, all the while George's guitar gently weeps. The organ returns again for the ending section. When George and Paul sing their highest note on "weeps," Eric comes back in strong. He plays a variation of his guitar solo during the long fade-out. Eric also plays the same high note that he played at the end of his lead guitar solo. Mixed in with Eric's guitar is George crying "oh, oh, oh." John's contribution to the song is minimal; he plays an electric guitar part that is barely audible. The sound of Paul's bass guitar is different from most of his previous recordings. Instead of using his Hofner or Rickenbacker bass, Paul used a Fender Jazz Bass guitar. The way it was produced, the chunky bass sound is deep and has a cutting top end as well. And the leaping notes that Paul plays during the instrumental ending creates a low contrasting melody. Eric's lead guitar part perfectly matches George's voice and the weeping nature of the song.

On the same album as "While My Guitar Gently Weeps," the country-rock song "Don't Pass Me By" is the first song in the Beatles' catalog that is written entirely by Ringo. Putting aside his song to accommodate John's and Paul's songs, Ringo had "Don't Pass Me By" in his head for about six years before the Beatles recorded it on the *White Album*. Ringo is very busy in this song, singing the sole vocal track and playing the drums, maracas, congas, sleigh bells, a cowbell, and a tack piano. Paul also plays piano, plus a grand piano and bass guitar, but George and John are not on the recording. The sound of the pianos is unusual. They were recorded while being played through a Leslie speaker cabinet, and as a result the pianos mixed together sound like a calliope organ. What gives "Don't Pass Me By" a country sound is the violin, played by jazz and blues musician Jack Fallon. A popular London studio musician, Jack had worked with several jazz musicians, including Ronnie Scott. Once Ringo sings the first verse, Jack plays the violin, or I should probably say the fiddle, throughout the entire song. The song begins with Ringo playing a solo drum introduction. Ringo's drums are fat and full and blend in nicely with the piano tracks. Jack accompanies

Ringo's vocals and plays riff passages between the verses and choruses. The addition of the fiddle puts the song in a country-rock category and distinguishes it from other songs in the Beatles' catalog. While there are many Beatles songs with violins, no other song has a violin part played with such a country flair.

The guest musician who was the most visible and publicly known to record with the Beatles was Billy Preston. Billy played electric piano and organ on several Beatles recordings in 1969, performing on "Get Back," "Don't Let Me Down," "Something," "I Want You (She's So Heavy)," "Dig a Pony," "Dig It," "Let It Be," "I've Got a Feeling," "One After 909," and "The Long and Winding Road." Not including George Martin, Billy was the only musician who worked and recorded with the Beatles on many recordings. He made such a big impression that John wanted him to join the band. Paul didn't like the idea, but Billy continued to record with the Beatles as a guest artist. The relationship between the Beatles and Billy started in 1962 when the young fifteen-year-old was playing organ with Little Richard's band. They met when the Beatles were the opening act for Little Richard at the Star Club in Hamburg, Germany. George, being the youngest Beatle, bonded with Billy. Seven years later when George walked out and temporarily quit the Beatles in January 1969, George saw Billy at a Ray Charles concert in London. That's when George asked Billy to attend the "Get Back" sessions. While the Beatles did print Billy's name on the "Get Back" and "Don't Let Me Down" single, they chose not to include his name on the "Let It Be" and "The Long and Winding Road" singles or on the *Abbey Road* and *Let It Be* albums. George's friendship with Billy continued beyond the Beatles, and the two musicians would perform together again. In August 1971, when George staged his *Concert for Bangladesh* at Madison Square Garden in New York City, Billy was part of George's all-star band. George died on November 29, 2001, and a year later at a memorial concert titled *A Concert for George*, Billy was part of the superstar band that Eric Clapton directed. Billy sang a heartfelt rendition of George's song "Isn't It a Pity."

Not including "What's the New Mary Jane" (which wasn't released until 1996 on *Anthology 3*, long after the Beatles broke up), "You Know My Name (Look Up the Number)" is the most satirical, zany song in the Beatles' song catalog. The B-side of the 1970 "Let It Be" single, the Beatles recorded the song in May and June of 1967, and John and Paul finished it in April 1969. John came up with the title after seeing a logo with similar words on a telephone book, and the lyrics are minimal, including only a few more words than the title. John envisioned the song as a comedic parody of a lounge singer's act, so it's no surprise that the song is somewhat of a spoof. After John introduces Paul as Denis O'Dell (who was the associate producer of the film A *Hard Day's Night*), Paul sings the lounge singer bit at a fictitious nightclub called Slaggers. Beginning with a rhythm section and handclaps, Paul plays piano and bass, John and George play guitars, and John and Paul belt out the lyrics. It segues into the lounge singer section, which has a Latin rhythm, with Ringo playing drums, timbales, and bongos, and John playing the maracas. The Beatles added clapping, sound effects, and chatter to the lounge bit to replicate a nightclub environment, while Paul sings tongue-in-cheek with lots of vibrato in his lower register. The next section has John singing/speaking in his upper vocal range with background sound effects. During the last section of the song, John mumbles a bunch of gibberish in a low voice. A tenor sax solo chimes in before the song ends with John and Paul singing, "That's gonna be, that's all." Then someone burps and John mumbles more gibberish, possibly saying "America" at the very end. Despite the fact that John and Paul were not getting along in 1969 when they recorded their vocal tracks, they rose above their differences, exhibited a sense of humor, and had fun with the song. The guest musician playing the alto sax solo for this song is Brian Jones, multi-instrumentalist and founding member of the Rolling Stones. Brian was friends with the Beatles, especially with George. In *The Beatles Anthology*, George said Brian would visit him often and they would exchange musical ideas. "We share similar positions in the most prominent bands in the universe; me with John and Paul, and him with Mick and Keith," said George. Brian recorded his sax solo on "You Know My Name (Look Up the Number)" during the 1967 recording session, at a time when the Rolling Stones and the Beatles were spending time with each other both socially and in the recording studio. Brian, Mick Jagger, and Keith Richards were at Abbey Road Studios when the Beatles performed the world broadcast of "All You Need Is Love." Mick sang on "Baby You're a Rich Man," and John and Paul sang background vocals on the Rolling Stones song "We Love You."

The guest musicians added their expertise to these songs and made them complete. Even though some of their names are not well known, their performances and solos are, making them indelibly cast forever in these Beatles songs.

Suggested Listening: "P.S. I Love You"; "She's Leaving Home"; "While My Guitar Gently Weeps"; "Don't Let Me Down"; "You Know My Name (Look Up the Number)"

THE END

The four Beatles ended their recording career with "The End" on *Abbey Road*, but it wasn't the end. Today, there are dozens of radio shows worldwide that play Beatles songs every week. Hundreds of books have been written about the Beatles, and many colleges offer courses on the Beatles and their music. Even years after the Beatles disbanded, films about them have been produced. Paul McCartney and Ringo Starr continue to perform throughout the world and sing Beatles songs to thousands of die-hard fans.

The Beatles started their career playing cover songs by some of their favorite recording artists. While the Beatles were together and even after they went their separate ways, hundreds of recording artists have covered Beatles songs. "Yesterday" alone has been recorded by thousands of artists, as well as dozens of other songs, including "Michelle," "Hey Jude," and "Something," which have been covered hundreds of times. This illustrates the everlasting influence the Beatles have had on singers and musical groups across the globe and how their music continues to live today and will continue tomorrow. Their music has no boundaries and connects with people of every demographic, race, color, and faith. It's the quality of the Beatles' songs that makes them timeless, and the songs will play on indefinitely.

I hope you enjoyed reading this book and that you learned many things about the Beatles, the time when they were together—in the recording studio, on their tours, making movies—and their eclectic collection of songs. There will be no final word on the Beatles, because the Beatles will never end.

SELECTED READING

Davies, Hunter. *The Beatles*. New York: Dell, 1968.

Emerick, Geoff, and Howard Massey. *Here, There and Everywhere: My Life Recording the Music of the Beatles*. New York: Gotham Books, 2007.

George Harrison interview. *Crawdaddy*, February 1977.

Harrison, George, John Lennon, Paul McCartney, and Ringo Starr. *The Beatles Anthology*. Milwaukee, WI: Chronicle Books, 2000.

John Lennon interview. *Playboy*, January 1981.

John Lennon interview. *Rolling Stone*, December 1970 and January 1971.

Lewisohn, Mark. *The Complete Beatles Recording Sessions: The Official Story of the Abbey Road Years, 1962–1970*. London: Hamlyn, 1988.

Lindsay-Hogg, Michael. *Luck and Circumstance: A Coming of Age in Hollywood, New York, and Points Beyond*. New York: Alfred A. Knopf, 2011.

Martin, George, with Jeremy Hornsby. *All You Need Is Ears: The Inside Personal Story of the Genius Who Created the Beatles*. New York: St. Martin's Press, 1979.

Miles, Barry. *Paul McCartney: Many Years from Now*. New York: Henry Holt, 1997.

Schwartz, Francie. *Body Count*. San Francisco: Straight Arrow Books, 1972.

Sheff, David. *All We Are Saying: The Last Major Interview with John Lennon and Yoko Ono*. New York: St. Martin's Griffin, 2000.

INDEX

ABOUT THE AUTHOR

Brooke Halpin is a classically trained musician, award-winning composer, published author, and painter. He had the great fortune of meeting John Lennon and Yoko Ono at John's thirty-first birthday party and on separate occasions met Paul McCartney and Ringo Starr. He produces and hosts the weekly syndicated radio show *Come Together with the Beatles*, which airs on www.kbu.fm and www.wrockradio.com. Brooke has written *The Everything Piano and Keyboards Book*, the quiz book *Do You Really Know The Beatles?*, and *A Magical Mystery Time*, a novel based on a true story. As a composer, Brooke wrote the music to the Academy Award–winning film *Molly's Pilgrim*, the PBS special *More Than Broken Glass: Memories of Kristallnacht*, and Rudolf Nureyev's ballet *Cristoforo* for the Hungarian National Ballet Company. A recipient of a MacDowell Arts Colony fellowship, Brooke is a graduate of the California Institute of the Arts and the Hartford Conservatory of Music.